Touching God

Anthem Nineteenth-Century Series

Anthem Nineteenth-Century Series incorporates a broad range of titles within the fields of literature and culture, comprising an excellent collection of interdisciplinary academic texts. The series aims to promote the most challenging and original work being undertaken in the field, and encourages an approach that fosters connections between areas including history, science, religion and literary theory. Our titles have earned an excellent reputation for the originality and rigour of their scholarship, and our commitment to high quality production.

Series Editor

Robert Douglas-Fairhurst, Oxford University, UK

Editorial Board

Seamus Perry, Oxford University, UK
Archie Burnett, Boston University, USA
Michael O'Neill, Durham University, UK
Dinah Birch, University of Liverpool, UK
Clare Pettitt, King's College London, UK
Linda K. Hughes, Texas Christian University, USA
Jo McDonagh, King's College London, UK
Simon J. James, Durham University, UK
Kirstie Blair, University of Glasgow, UK
Adrian Poole, University of Cambridge, UK
Jan-Melissa Schramm, University of Cambridge, UK
Heather Glen, University of Cambridge, UK
Angela Leighton, University of Cambridge, UK
Christopher Decker, University of Nevada, USA

Touching God

Hopkins and Love

Duc Dau

ANTHEM PRESS
LONDON · NEW YORK · DELHI

Anthem Press
An imprint of Wimbledon Publishing Company
www.anthempress.com

This edition first published in UK and USA 2013
by ANTHEM PRESS
75–76 Blackfriars Road, London SE1 8HA, UK
or PO Box 9779, London SW19 7ZG, UK
and
244 Madison Ave. #116, New York, NY 10016, USA

First published in hardback by Anthem Press in 2012

Copyright © Duc Dau 2013

The author asserts the moral right to be identified as the author of this work.

Cover photograph of Auguste Rodin, 'The Cathedral Hands', Musée Rodin;
photo © Susan Sherratt 2009

All rights reserved. Without limiting the rights under copyright reserved above,
no part of this publication may be reproduced, stored or introduced into
a retrieval system, or transmitted, in any form or by any means
(electronic, mechanical, photocopying, recording or otherwise),
without the prior written permission of both the copyright
owner and the above publisher of this book.

British Library Cataloguing-in-Publication Data
A catalogue record for this book is available from the British Library.

Library of Congress Cataloging-in-Publication Data
The Library of Congress has cataloged the hardcover edition as follows:
Dau, Duc.
 Touching God : Hopkins and love / Duc Dau.
   p. cm.
 Includes bibliographical references and index.
 ISBN 978-0-85728-443-3 (hardback : alk. paper)
 1. Hopkins, Gerard Manley, 1844–1889–Criticism and interpretation.
 2. Love in literature. I. Title.
 PR4803.H44Z6164 2012
 821'.8–dc23
        2012004989

ISBN-13: 978 1 78308 048 9 (Pbk)
ISBN-10: 1 78308 048 5 (Pbk)

This title is also available as an ebook.

CONTENTS

Acknowledgements   vii
Abbreviations   ix

Introduction	Love and Touch	1
Chapter One	Confluence and Reflection	17
Chapter Two	Virgin Marriage and the Song of Songs	35
Chapter Three	Conception, Pregnancy, Birth	67
Chapter Four	Caressing, Conversing, Kissing	83
Chapter Five	Homecoming	101

Notes   115
Bibliography   133
Index   141

ACKNOWLEDGEMENTS

Many hands have touched this project, which began over a decade ago at the University of Western Australia. Daniel Brown and Kieran Dolin guided me through much of it with their patience and perspicacity. Tony Hughes-d'Aeth shared ideas and his life with me. Judy Johnston always lent a sympathetic ear. For discussions, suggestions and assistance of one kind or another, I thank Andrew Lynch, Bob White, Steve Chinna, Anne Scott, Ian Saunders, Bill Taylor, Michael Levine, Hilary Fraser, my colleagues at 73 Fairway, and Gail Jones. Philippa Martyr read the entire manuscript at a later stage and offered thoughtful suggestions and encouragement. Of the friends I made at the University of Western Australia, I am especially grateful to Darren Jorgensen, Megan Kingdon, Natalia Lizama, Olivia Mair, Caitlin McGuinness and Lavinia Vaz.

Scholars elsewhere have left their mark on this book. I thank James Finn Cotter, Lesley Higgins and Jude Nixon, whose readings of an earlier version helped sharpen the manuscript, enabling it to take its present shape. I am indebted to Fred Roden for being a wonderful, wise, generous friend and mentor. Email conversations with Deborah Lutz assisted in amorphous but, no doubt, significant ways. I would be remiss if I did not mention Kirstie Blair, Emma Mason, Margaret Harris and Jock MacLeod for their support of my work.

I could not have completed this project without the support of my family and friends. I thank my parents, Thap and Kim, my siblings, An and Jimmy, and brother-in-law Michael. Of the friends who provide me with perspective on the things that matter, I wish to single out Fiona Rutkay and Matthew Fenwick, for understanding the impulse to write; Fiona Whittaker, Julian Figg and Juliana Koh, for friendships that eased my move to Perth and sustain me to this day; Zoë Hyde, for technical expertise and conversations on topics innumerable and delightfully strange; Katie Crocker, for being Katie and for happily eating my first attempt at gourmet vegan cooking; Sarah Rutherford, whose memory I will always cherish; Nandi Chinna, for the gift of poetry; and 'the crew', for emotional support and hours of laughter. Last – but of course by no means least – I thank Tennille Crooks for her love during the final stages of the project.

Several libraries were generous in making materials available to me. I am grateful to the community of Campion Hall, Oxford, for allowing me access to the Hopkins Archives; I especially thank Master Gerard Hughes and Graham Pugin for their hospitality. I am appreciative to Penelope Bulloch and Alan Tadielo of Balliol College Library for their kind assistance with the Jowett Papers. I am also indebted to Colin Harris of the Bodleian Library, and to James Hodkinson and Mihaela Repina of the Farm St Library, London. The librarians of the University of Western Australia's Reid Library and Scholars' Centre also deserve a special mention.

I would like to thank Tej Sood and Janka Romero of Anthem Press for their professionalism and faith in the project. The editorial team deserves a grateful mention for its assistance. Many thanks to the two anonymous readers chosen by the press; it was a privilege to see my work through your eyes. I am indebted to Jasmina Brankovich and Lisette Kaleveld for their copy editorial interventions.

A shortened version of Chapter Four was published as 'The Caress of God's Breath in Gerard Manley Hopkins', *Sydney Studies in English* 31 (2005): 39–60; portions of Chapter Two appeared in 'Perfect Chastity: Celibacy and Virgin Marriage in Tractarian Poetry', *Victorian Poetry* 44 (2006): 77–92; and a portion of Chapter Three appears in 'Reassessing Gilbert and Gubar: Women, Creativity, Hopkins', *Australasian Journal of Victorian Studies* 16 (forthcoming). I am grateful to the editors of these journals for permission to reprint the sections here.

Part of this project was funded by an Australian Postgraduate Award and a University of Western Australia Winthrop Scholarship.

ABBREVIATIONS

Bridges *The Letters of Gerard Manley Hopkins to Robert Bridges.* Edited by Claude Colleer Abbott. 2nd ed. London: Oxford University Press, 1955.

Dixon *The Correspondence of Gerard Manley Hopkins and Richard Watson Dixon.* Edited by Claude Colleer Abbott. 2nd ed. London: Oxford University Press, 1955.

Further Letters *Further Letters of Gerard Manley Hopkins Including his Correspondence with Coventry Patmore.* Edited by Claude Colleer Abbott. 2nd ed. London: Oxford University Press, 1956.

Journals *The Journals and Papers of Gerard Manley Hopkins.* Edited by Humphrey House and Graham Storey. 2nd ed. London: Oxford University Press, 1959.

Oxford Essays *Oxford Essays and Notes.* Edited by Lesley Higgins. Vol. 4, *The Collected Works of Gerard Manley Hopkins.* Oxford: Oxford University Press, 2006.

Sermons *The Sermons and Devotional Writings of Gerard Manley Hopkins.* Edited by Christopher Devlin. London: Oxford University Press, 1959.

Introduction

LOVE AND TOUCH

Touching God argues for the importance of love in the work of the Victorian poet, Gerard Manley Hopkins (1844–1889). In this book I look upon the Jesuit as a poet of romantic love, as one who wrote love poems to God. Celibacy did not hinder Hopkins' capacity in this regard. Taking his lead, I consider sexual intercourse as merely one among several expressions of passion, not as the ultimate act of intimacy. Indeed, at a time when the majority of English Protestants regarded religious celibacy with deep suspicion, celibacy afforded Hopkins the opportunity to speak of his love freely. Far from denying the corporeal, he articulated in his writings a love that is still familiar to readers today. Depictions of the body and its acts of tenderness – notably touching – played a central role in his writings on love. He appealed to many recognisably romantic and sexual tropes, such as touching hands, melting and merging subjects, beating hearts, magnetic attraction, mutual gazes, kisses, embraces, fecundity and homecoming. These and other images direct readers to a love that unifies and a touch that soothes as much as it electrifies. As *Touching God* demonstrates, awareness of the spiritual eroticism in Hopkins' work is vital to a fuller understanding of his poetry.

Scholars in recent years have looked at the cultural, literary, intellectual, scientific and religious milieus in which Hopkins lived.[1] *Touching God* draws on, but also departs from, these well-known studies by insisting on the centrality of love in his poetry. I look at love by directing a spotlight on several of the key theological, philosophical and literary writings known to Hopkins. In this study of ideas, the bulk of my engagement is with the poet's intellectual heritage. Because of this, I draw on biographical and ecclesiastical information only when they account for Hopkins' particular interest in a particular aspect of love. Hopkins often understood and articulated erotic love through images of reciprocal touch. Therefore I direct my gaze to three aspects of his writings: intellection, emotionality and tactility.

A study of love in Hopkins' writings cannot overlook the wealth of scholarship exploring his same-sex desires. Over the years, a number of scholars have looked in detail at his attraction to men.[2] Hopkins' biographers,

Norman White, Robert Bernard Martin and, in particular, Paddy Kitchen, have meticulously documented and studied the poet's infatuation with some of his male friends and peers, including the cousins Robert Bridges and Digby Mackworth Dolben.[3] Kitchen's biography was the first to discuss Hopkins' undergraduate confessional notes, which documented the poet's extreme scrutiny of his 'sins', including his same-sex attraction to fellow undergraduates, strangers and choristers, among others, as well as his occasional attraction to women. Norman Mackenzie has since published these notes in *The Early Poetic Manuscripts and Note-books of Gerard Manley Hopkins in Facsimile*.[4]

Julia F. Saville's groundbreaking *A Queer Chivalry: The Homoerotic Asceticism of Gerard Manley Hopkins* is the first and, to my knowledge, only major book devoted exclusively to Hopkins' same-sex desires. Building on the work of Alan Sinfield and other queer theorists, Saville uses the term 'queer' to register moments of homoeroticism and to 'resist [Hopkins'] more reductive (if perhaps forceful) appropriation as either gay or homosexual'.[5] Saville uses Lacanian theories of sublimation and courtly love to understand Hopkins' poetics of homoerotic asceticism. She argues that Hopkins' poetic career was 'a continuous process of negotiating desire through self-discipline, self-denial, and even at times self-hatred'.[6] Saville adds, 'Hopkins developed his own queer brand of chivalry, addressed adoringly to a beloved of his own sex but in a mode associated with the rigorous self-restraint on which a Victorian sense of manliness was predicated'.[7] Thus, in the sensuous sonnet, 'The Windhover', Hopkins carefully unleashes one kind of desire ('the yearning after the ecstasy of sublime flight, representable in terms of visual spectacle and visual indulgence') only to restrain it with another ('the curtailed desire for the modest satisfaction derived from humble service, in which the gaze is harnessed for the execution of the menial task at hand').[8] My study touches on, and indeed complements, elements of Saville's important study. Nonetheless, *Touching God* employs, as it will be clear, a different methodology and a more theologically encompassing approach in exploring Hopkins' religious (homo) eroticism.

The vast majority of critics who recognise the erotic sensuality of Hopkins' verse and other writings have, unsurprisingly, focused on his fascination with male bodies. As I have argued elsewhere,[9] existing studies of the body in Hopkins' writings pay attention to one or more of the following: voyeurism and homoerotic desire, asceticism and renunciation, guilt and sin, torture and suffering, popular Christian and Catholic thought, muscularity and masculinity, and class.[10] I will refer to a number of these critics later in the book, but for the time being I will mention a couple. In his fine study, 'Hopkins's "Bellbright Bodies": The Dialectics of Desire in His Writings', Dennis Sobolev argues that Hopkins' 'Christ, our Hero' sermon (*Sermons*, 34–8) weaves in and out of various spiritual and erotic discourses. In the sermon, Hopkins describes Christ's physical beauty thus:

> In his body he was most beautiful… [H]e was moderately tall, well built and tender in frame, his features straight and beautiful, his hair inclining to auburn, parted in the midst, curling and clustering about the ears and neck as the leaves of a filbert, so they speak, upon the nut… But he could not have pleased by growth of body unless the body was strong, healthy, and beautiful that grew… I leave it to you, brethren, then to picture him, in whom the fulness [sic] of the godhead dwelt bodily, in his bearing how majestic, how strong and yet how lovely and lissome in his limbs, in his look how earnest, grave but kind. (35–6)[11]

Sobolev contends that, while the sermon proceeds from the carnal to the spiritual realm, Hopkins' homoerotic discourse finds something akin to a queer-friendly space in the Catholic adoration of the saviour's body. After all, the words of the sermon were delivered to a congregation, not scribbled away privately in shame:

> [T]here is something deeply unconventional in both Hopkins's intense feeling for male physicality and his almost obsessive celebration of Christ's body. It seems that at this particular point of the sermon Hopkins's Catholic discourse is interwoven with another one: the discourse of the male body and male beauty, which is an inseparable part of the discourse of homoeroticism. Or, to put it another way, in Hopkins's sermon the homoerotic discourse seems to find a space for its half-hidden existence and oblique articulation within the traditional discourse of Catholicism.[12]

Hopkins' admiration for the 'strong' and 'lovely' male body is witnessed in other, more secular, examples. Joseph Bristow locates Hopkins' later poems of working-class male bodies within similarly homoerotic and homosocial contexts. Bristow aligns Hopkins with other admirers of muscular male bodies, such as E. M. Forster and John Addington Symonds, and argues that Hopkins' descriptions of bodies such as that of the titular figure of 'Harry Ploughman' display his 'persistent fantasy of their unassailable virility'.[13] The poet's fascination with virile male forms has led to comparisons with the American poet, Walt Whitman.[14] Such comparisons are due also in part to Hopkins' assertion of a similar, though unspecified, quality between himself and Whitman (*Bridges*, 155).[15] Poet Philip Dacey has capitalised on the link between the two poets in his volume *Gerard Manley Hopkins Meets Walt Whitman in Heaven and Other Poems*, which contains some explicitly homoerotic poems.[16]

Studies of Hopkins' same-sex desires have shed valuable light on his poetry, and I encourage readers to consult these sources. The acknowledgement of his same-sex desires forms a backdrop to *Touching God*, even as the book differs from most queer readings of Hopkins by emphasising the priority he accords to his relationship with Christ, the prime object of his desires and, in his own words, 'the one with whom I am in love' (*Bridges*, 66).[17] Studies of Hopkins' desires have likely focused on the unrequited nature of his feelings towards men, his concurrent anxieties over these attractions and his subsequent self-restraint or self-punishment. However, just as the body 'is never simply one thing in Hopkins's texts',[18] desire is never simply one thing in his writings. With this in mind, I look at the desire he actively cultivated, celebrated and, just as importantly, believed was requited: his longing for Christ. For Hopkins, consummation with Christ takes place at the intersection of celibacy and desire, at the interpenetration of spirituality and sexuality. As we will see, one of the models for this kind of love is St Augustine.[19] If we are to understand Hopkins' desire, in both his life and his texts, we will need to look in detail at his use of the word 'love'.

Eros and *Amor*

The word 'love' appears 125 times in Hopkins' surviving sermons.[20] Given this, it is surprising that Hopkins scholarship has not explored in detail the uses and significance of the word in his thought and poetry. As long as this oversight remains, the most vital aspect of his relationship with Christ will continue to be undervalued.[21] Hopkins' conversion provides a good starting point for exploring the nature of love in this relationship. His decision to convert to Roman Catholicism in 1866 (*Journals*, 146) was arguably momentous, proving fundamental to his subsequent theology, poetry and relationship with Christ. Shortly after his conversion, he tells his mother that the Catholic Church 'only wants to be known in order to be loved' (*Further Letters*, 93).[22] In a letter to his friend E. H. Coleridge, he declares that transubstantiation, the presence of Christ in the Eucharist, is that which makes Catholicism '*loveable*' (17).[23] Later, he would write that the exiled Catholic nuns who drowned aboard the wrecked ocean liner, the *Deutschland*, were 'Loathed for a love men knew in them' ('The Wreck of the Deutschland', stanza 21).[24]

It is obvious, then, that Hopkins' conversion was an experience of newfound love. His leap of faith was, above all, a leap of love. After all, one cannot half believe in God. 'Both sexuality and spirituality', says David M. Carr, 'require an openness to being deeply affected by someone outside oneself, whether one's lover or God. Both involve the whole self'.[25] Religious belief entails an openness to something beyond oneself, an immersion into the unknown, and commitment; only then can faith be experienced in its completeness. The same can be said of love. Hopkins' conversion, made in defiance of parental and societal expectations, was one of his most romantic acts.

I have been discussing the importance of love in Hopkins' writings. But what do I mean by that word? The love I focus on is that which for Hopkins surpasses even the greatest of filial affections. In Greek it is called *eros*, in Latin *amor*. Hence, rather than looking to the love most associated with Christianity, *agape* (in Greek) or *caritas* (in Latin), I concentrate on *eros* and *amor*. Not that the two loves are incompatible. Unlike Anders Nygren, I do not draw a sharp distinction between *eros* and *agape*.[26] *Eros* has been used by a number of early Christian writers to name an acceptable and, indeed, the highest love for God. What's more, the term is capable of signifying a non-appetitive love more akin to *agape* than Nygren had cared to admit.[27] As we shall see, *eros* and *agape* either overlap or complement one another in Hopkins' writings; the difference between them is not one of kind but of degree. *Eros* holds a special significance that has hitherto been uncharted in Hopkins scholarship. Paraphrasing from Thomas à Kempis' *The Imitation of Christ*, he uses the word *amator* (lover), a variation on *amor*, in a sermon: '*nobilis amator non tam* etc' (*Sermons*, 20).[28] The phrase, from the chapter 'On the Proof of a True Lover', is written from the point of view of Christ, who declares, 'A wise lover values not so much the gift of the lover, as the love of the giver... A noble lover is not content with a gift, but desires Myself above all gifts'.[29] The *amator* values love and desires – feels *amor* for – Christ above all others.

The use of erotic language (the language of *eros*) has existed throughout centuries of Christian discourse. Christian writers, particularly those of an ascetic or mystical bent, did not shy away from drawing on the word *amor* to signal their desire for God. St Bernard of Clairvaux, the medieval abbot, uses the word unreservedly in his seminal collection of sermons, *On the Song of Songs*. The 1840s heralded a reawakening of interest in Bernard's writings, evident in the rising number of English translations from that time onwards.[30] This revival was spurred on by the High Church Anglican group known as the Oxford Movement or the Tractarians. Hopkins, a Tractarian in his early undergraduate days at Balliol College, Oxford, was familiar with Bernard's writings.[31] Bernard proclaims in one of his sermons on the biblical text, the Song of Songs,

> I love because I love: I love that I may love... Love is the only one of the motions of the soul, of its senses and affections, in which the creature can respond to its Creator, even if not as an equal, and repay his favor in some similar way.[32]

The word translated as 'love' is *amor*, while 'I love' is *amo*. Bernard argues that *amor* is a person's most fitting response to God. Only human *amor* can, to the highest degree of satisfaction, respond to divine *Amor*: 'the love of a bridegroom – or rather of the Bridegroom who is love – asks only the exchange of love and trust. Let the Beloved love in return. How can the bride – and the bride of Love – do other than love? How can Love not be loved?'[33]

The Song of Songs is commonly regarded as depicting the marriage of God with Israel or the Church. From another viewpoint, it appears to align the mystical quest with human erotic experience. Its two protagonists delight in one another, they long to be together and search for each other when they are apart. Unlike the forbidden fruit of Eden, the sweet fruit of the Song of Songs is what reunites us with God. In her discussion of the Song of Songs and Jewish mysticism, Sara Srivi makes the following assertion:

> This 'reaching out [for one another]' which lies at the root of our *instinctive* erotic experiences, and of which the *Song of Songs* gives such a poignant, heartfelt expression, also lies at the very roots of our *spiritual* quest. And this is the reason why the spiritual quest has never been solely about moral conduct or theological principles or even practical precepts; but also, and perhaps primarily, about a *concrete* experience of the erotic yearning of the soul.[34]

St John of the Cross, the Counter-Reformation mystic, expresses this 'erotic yearning of the soul' – and its consummation with Christ – in his mystical verse. In his exposition of the poem commonly known as 'The Dark Night of the Soul', which draws directly on imagery from the Song of Songs, he says, 'it is love alone that unites and joins the soul with God'.[35] The Song of Songs furnished John of the Cross, Bernard of Clairvaux and, later, Hopkins with a means of comprehending and describing the erotic impulse for the divine other. As Saville puts it, the Song of Songs 'makes available a means for articulating sensual, corporeal pleasure in the name of spiritual grace'.[36] And vice versa. Hopkins almost certainly never had a sexual experience with another person, but, as we shall see in Chapter Two, much of his knowledge of *eros* originated either directly or indirectly from the Song of Songs.

Christian interpretation of the Song of Songs is indebted to Origen's third century commentary on the text. At Balliol College, where Hopkins would go on to achieve First Class Honours in *Literae Humaniores*, he read the work of Origen and admitted to possessing 'a real feeling' for the Platonist theologian (*Further Letters*, 17).[37] Origen's Greek commentary on the biblical book uses the word *eros*, while the Latin translation by Rufinus employs *amor*. Origen appeals to the language of Plato's *Symposium* in making the following claim:

> [T]he soul is moved by heavenly love and longing when, having clearly beheld the beauty and the fairness of the Word of God, it falls deeply in love with His loveliness and receives from the Word Himself a certain dart and wound of love [*vulnus amoris*].[38]

The dart refers to the arrow of Cupid or Eros, the god of love, who is mentioned in the same paragraph. In essence, Origen is saying that God is *Eros*.[39] In spite of this, he believes the Bible substitutes 'a more respectable word', such as 'charity' or 'affection', in place of 'desire' or 'passion'. This substitution, he argues, is 'for the sake of the weaker [readers]'.[40] He notes that in rare instances, the Bible 'calls the passion of love by its own name, and invites and urges souls to it… [I]n the book that is called the Wisdom of Solomon it is written of Wisdom herself: *I became a passionate lover* (amator) *of her beauty*'.[41] Origen concludes,

> So it makes no difference whether we speak of having a passion for God, or of loving Him; and I do not think one could be blamed if one called God Passionate Love (*Amorem*), just as John calls Him Charity (*Caritatem*). Indeed I remember that one of the saints, by name Ignatius, said of Christ: 'My Love (*Amor*) is crucified,' and I do not consider him worthy of censure on this account.[42]

Similarly, in his *City of God*, Augustine defends the use of *amor* to describe a person's love for the deity.[43] While Augustine acknowledges that in the Bible the love for God and neighbour 'is more commonly called "charity" (*caritas*)',

> it appears in the same sacred writings under the appellation 'love' (*amor*). For instance, when the Apostle is giving instructions about the choice of a man to rule God's people, he says that such a man should be a lover (*amator*) of the good.[44] And when the Lord himself had asked the apostle Peter, 'Are you more fond (*diligis*) of me than those?' Peter replied 'Lord, you know that I love (*amo*) you'[45]… [W]hen Jesus asked for the third time, he himself said, 'Do you love me?' instead of, 'Are you fond of me?' And then the evangelist goes on, 'Peter was grieved because the Lord said to him, for the third time: "Do you love me?"' Whereas in fact it was not the third time; the Lord said, 'Do you love me?' only once, but he had twice asked, 'Are you fond of me?' From this we infer that when the Lord asked, 'Are you fond of me?' he meant precisely the same as when he asked, 'Do you love me?' Peter, in contrast, did not change the word he used to express the same meaning, when he replied the third time, 'Lord, you know everything. You know that I love you'.[46]

Augustine says that 'quite a number of people' distinguish between 'charity' and 'love', holding the first 'in a good sense' and the second 'in a bad sense'. Nevertheless, he argues, 'the Scriptures of our religion, whose authority we rank above all other writings, do not distinguish between "love" and "fondness" or "charity". For I have shown that "love" also is used in a good sense'.[47]

Hopkins positions himself within this Christian tradition, which acknowledges that the most fervent emotion for Christ may indeed be known as *caritas*, but is more fittingly understood as *amor*. In a sermon delivered in the same year, he alludes to both charity and *amor* when describing the love for Christ: 'Love for Christ is enthusiasm for a leader, a hero, love for a bosom friend, love for a lover' (*Sermons*, 48).[48] In this context, the word 'love' incorporates feelings of varying intensity, culminating in the 'love for a lover'. Hopkins regards this final love, this *amor*, as the foundation upon which stands his marriage with Christ; he declares in his 'Christ, Our Hero' sermon, delivered a month earlier, that Christ 'is the truelove and the bridegroom of men's souls' (35). It is Christ who teaches the believer to love (*amare*): 'Doce me amare', says Hopkins in a Latin hymn ('*Ad Matrem Virginem*', line 22). Thus, while *amor* is not the only love, it is the best love. For instance, 'Love of God', says Hopkins, 'means the preferring his will to ours: it is the love of a subject for his ruler. By this we shall be saved, *but this is but a cold sort of love*... Now when we love God he first loved us, first loved us as a ruler [of] his subjects before we loved him as subjects [would] their ruler' (*Sermons*, 48).[49] In contrast, 'we love Christ with *a fonder love than that* / he with a fonder love than that first loved us' (48; emphasis added). This 'fonder love' can only be *amor*, 'love for a lover'.

Reciprocal Touch

In 1868, Hopkins entered the Society of Jesus, founded by St Ignatius of Loyola. In the *Spiritual Exercises*, Ignatius argues that love (*amor*) is given 'in mutual interchange':

> In the first place two things are to be noted here. The first is that love ought to show itself in deeds more than in words. The second, that love consists in mutual interchange on either side, that is, in the lover giving and communicating to the beloved that which he has, or of that which he has or can give, and so in turn the beloved to the lover. So that if one has knowledge he gives it to him who has it not, and likewise if he has honours or riches; and the other in turn does the same. (*Sermons*, 192–3)[50]

Love is reciprocal and complementary; it hinges on a process of mutual giving. In his interpretation of this text, Hopkins says, 'all God gives us or does for us He gives and does *in love* and therefore that all we do towards God we should do in love' (194).⁵¹ Hopkins believes this kind of exchange governs our ideal relationships with others. Take, for example, 'Felix Randal', a poem about a priest and a dying parishioner:

> This séeing the síck endéars them tó us, us tóo it endéars.
> My tongue had taught thee comfort, touch had quenched thy tears,
> Thy tears that touched my heart, child, Félix, poor Felix Randal... (Lines 9–11)

The priest offers 'tongue' and 'touch' to comfort the suffering Felix Randal. In turn, the man's struggle 'touch[es]' the priest's 'heart'. The poem does not use the word 'love', but it bears witness to love's capacity to affect the life of another. The alliance of alliteration and chiastic structure within line 9 and between lines 10 and 11 reproduces a love that is given, received and returned in symmetry. The second chiasmus leads to the double mention of tears and touch: touch that quenches tears and tears that touch the heart.

Ignatius' notion of love's 'mutual interchange' is consonant with a theory of relationships proposed by contemporary French feminist, Luce Irigaray, in her work titled *To Be Two*. Within the scheme of Irigaray's ideal relationship between the sexes, two people perform what she calls the caress:

> The caress is an awakening to you, to me, to us... The caress is an awakening to intersubjectivity, to a touching between us which is neither passive nor active; it is an awakening of gestures, of perceptions which are at the same time acts, intentions, emotions. This does not mean that they are ambiguous, but rather, that they are attentive to the person who touches and the one who is touched, to the two subjects who touch each other.⁵²

Irigaray holds that the caress, an 'awakening' to intersubjectivity, forms and is formed by the touch between two subjects. Compare this idea with Maurice Merleau-Ponty's illustration of the handshake in *The Visible and the Invisible*: 'The handshake...is reversible; I can feel myself touched as well and at the same time as touching'.⁵³ Touch is both an act and being acted upon; one touches and is at the same time touched. The handshake shows us that touching is reciprocal, 'reversible'. This reversibility forms a circle of action, a kind of embrace: 'There is a circle of the touched and the touching, the touched takes hold of the touching', says Merleau-Ponty.⁵⁴ In a rather erotic description, he declares that reversibility is 'the finger of the glove that is turned inside out':

> There are two caverns, two opennesses, two stages where something will take place – and which both belong to the same world, to the stage of Being[.] There is not the For Itself and For the Other[.] They are each the other side of the other.⁵⁵

In the circle of the touched and the touching, there is no hierarchy; I am open to the other, just as the other is open to me. Reversibility is a mutual openness that enables me to know and be known by the other.

The eroticism that is, as it were, touched on by Merleau-Ponty is brought to the fore in Irigaray's theory of the caress. For Irigaray, touching calls forth the touch of the other; it calls on the other to participate in a relationship of common love, attentiveness and concern. The caress at once draws on and expresses our regard for the otherness of the other. When two beings caress, they declare their love and respect for each other's alterity. 'We need to love much to be capable of such a dialectic', says Irigaray. 'One must love enough to generate and not wound: love the other as a whole… Respect him as a font derived from his own alterity'.[56] Indeed, fusion would obliterate the very otherness that distinguishes us from, and allows us to touch, the other:

> Consuming [the other] does not produce one's existence. Instead, difference can protect this existence: I am if you are, to be together with you allows me to become. The two, this two, is the bit more which is indispensable if I am to be. Closing myself up in consumption, in possession, in production, does not make me one. What makes me one, and perhaps even unique, is the fact that you are and I am not you.[57]

The caress enables the caresser and the caressed 'to become', to become one and yet remain two: 'Distanced by our difference', Irigaray says, 'but present to each other'.[58] This touch fills an obligation in the act of loving, which is, to be ourselves and to be 'present' with the other.

Irigaray employs the idiom of heterosexual romantic love to argue for equality between the sexes. I take up this language to explore the romantic relationship between the self and Christ. Irigaray's ideas afford a useful tool for channelling, arranging and discussing concepts of touch and love in Hopkins' work. Religion has been 'of central significance' in the three phases of Irigaray's writings.[59] And indeed, in her special introduction to the edited collection, *Religion in French Feminist Thought: Critical Perspectives*, Irigaray describes the reciprocal relationship between the self and the other in spiritual terms. In a section entitled 'The religious is that which binds', she declares,

> Any relation that does not correspond to establishing a link between the one and the other does not seem to obey the exigencies of the religious.
> The most religious rapport between us is that in which the bond is reciprocal in the present, and which conserves life and promotes becoming for each other.[60]

For Irigaray, 'becoming' means 'human becoming' and 'human flourishing', the pursuit of which 'seems the spiritual task most adapted to our age'.[61] This flourishing is what makes humans 'divine': 'we generally fail to recognise that becoming divine corresponds to becoming perfectly human. Split between the one and the other, we have lost the path of the one and of the other'.[62] Becoming divine involves entering into a relationship with the other. Thus, in another section, entitled 'To come back to oneself and open oneself to the other', Irigaray argues,

> It would be desirable that personal becoming accompany the becoming of the other. It is not for all that a question of falling back into a simply collective becoming. Becoming is rather to be sought actively in the relation with every other, while also preserving equilibrium between the active and the passive. Being able to give cannot exclude being able to receive. Progressing thanks to the concern that we have for the other presupposes that in our development we also take into account what the other brings to us. Such behaviour undoes genealogical, hierarchical rigidities: we are no longer parent or child, but in a reciprocal relation with the other.[63]

Irigaray's call for reciprocity finds resonance in Ignatius' concept of 'mutual interchange' and Merleau-Ponty's understanding of reversibility.

Touching and Loving

Touching God incorporates the intersecting thoughts of Ignatius, Irigaray and Merleau-Ponty to explore the relationship between the self and the other, between the lover and the beloved. Love will by and large be the focus of attention; at other times touch will take precedence. The rest of the time the book will discuss love and touch together. Always, when it talks about one, it will also gesture towards the other. Love and touch are for Hopkins the two sides of each other, just as the inside of a glove is inseparable from its outside; without one there is not the other. For Hopkins, Christ is the other whom we caress and by whom we are caressed. In this very contact is union, and it requires the two to remain two. Revd Benjamin Jowett, Hopkins' lecturer at Balliol College, illustrates this point:

> [H]ow far can one touch itself and the others? As existing in others, it touches the others; and as existing in itself, touches only itself… Two objects are required to make one contact; three objects make two contacts; and all the objects in the world, if placed in a series, would have as many contacts as there are objects, less one. But if only one exists, and not two, there is no contact.[64]

Susan Stewart has written, 'Of all the senses, touch is most linked to emotion and feeling'.[65] Thus, in one of his best-known erotic addresses to God, Augustine employs the language of the senses and concludes with touch:

> You called and cried out loud and shattered my deafness. You were radiant and resplendent, you put to flight my blindness. You were fragrant, and I drew in my breath and now pant after you. I tasted you, and I feel but hunger and thirst for you. You touched me, and I am set on fire to attain the peace which is yours.[66]

We long to touch the ones we love. In contemplating the nature of, and the need for, touch, Hopkins, like Augustine, accesses a means of understanding his love for God. This sense in particular seems to offer an 'authentic' experience of love and other experiences. 'Touch, regarded [in the nineteenth century] as the least regulated of senses, was frequently appropriated for the purpose of exploring presumably authentic and unmediated human experience', argue Colette Colligan and Margaret Linley.[67] 'The haptic dimension of the human sensorium allowed for a suspension of perception, a releasing and blending of the senses rather than a concerted modern drive to focus them'.[68] We witness this 'releasing and blending of the senses' in Hopkins' poem 'I wake and feel the fell of dark, not day':

> I wake and feel the fell of dark, not day.
> What hours, O what black hours we have spent
> This night! what sights you, heart, saw, ways you went!
> And more must, in yet longer light's delay. (Lines 1–4)

Touch is so important to Hopkins that other senses can be understood in relation to it. How does one 'feel' the impact of the torturous dark? Darkness is experienced as a blow, a 'fell', as much to the sense of touch as to that of sight. The word 'fell' is also, of course, a pun on 'The Fall'. Hence, in his desolation, the speaker equates his distance from God with humanity's fall from the light – and the sight – of grace. Feeling only 'the fell of dark', he has no sense of the caress of God.

Love touches. It is a *feeling*; we 'feel' it. We feel it within and in relation to the other, in the space between us and at the moment of contact. For Hopkins, love forms an inescapable impression, whether hard-hitting or soothing, on our physical, mental and spiritual being; 'Thou art lightning and love, I found it, a winter and warm', he says to the divine other in 'The Wreck of the Deutschland' (stanza 9). Such love is 'past télling of tóngue' (stanza 9). While Christ's love is fundamental to Hopkins' existence, he finds it difficult to describe without appealing to the language of the senses. In this instance, the language is more than figurative. Thus, God is not simply *like* 'lightning and love,…a winter and warm'; he *is* these things ('Thou art'). Jason Rudy notes that Hopkins seeks to bring together 'different modes of touching' (poetic, physiological and spiritual) and that lightning, a violent form of electricity, acts as a figure for 'poetic touching' in 'The Wreck of the Deutschland'.[69] God's touch is literally electrifying: it shocks, astonishes, terrifies, overwhelms – words describing also the effects of passion. Stemming from the heavens and bridging material and immaterial worlds, this lightning is Eros' arrow in the heart and the blinding light at Paul's conversion (which is referenced in stanza 10).[70] Conversion, the meeting of the human with the divine, is accompanied by an intense emotional and physical response: 'I did say yes / O at líghtning and láshed ród; /…/ Thy terror, O Christ, O God' ('The Wreck of the Deutschland', stanza 2). By associating the rod of self-flagellation with God's lightning and the 'yes' of conversion, Hopkins suggests its possible purpose as a device for reliving the 'terror' and the passion (that is, the suffering) of conversion. And yet, humans would be unable to survive the continual shocks of lightning and rod.

How else might God and humans touch? As Hopkins suggests, God seeps into the skin, either as a coldness that makes us shiver or as a heat keeping us warm. His touch, whether violent in intensity or soothing in the extreme, provokes the gamut of sensations. In another, less literal, example, the connection between love and touch resonates as a figure of speech linking intimacy with communication. Do we not dread the possibility that the one we love will not want to 'keep in touch'? Hopkins' fear of 'losing touch' with Christ is clearly evident in the metaphor of the 'dead letter' in his poem 'I wake and feel the fell of dark, not day': 'And my lament / Is cries countless, cries like dead letters sent / To dearest him that lives alas! away!' (lines 6–8). By witnessing its presence and his fear of its absence, we understand the importance of touch to Hopkins' language of 'feeling, love in particular'.[71]

Hopkins was a lover of nature, observing over countless hours its movements to glean its theological significance. In Chapter One, I locate representations of divine love, touch and union within Hopkins' preoccupation with water circulation and visual reflection. Hopkins observes that water returns to the air through evaporation, just as water from a fountain returns to its source. Likewise, as humans we continually return to the source of our being: the divine other. In 'The Wreck of the Deutschland', the central poem discussed in this chapter, Hopkins dramatises this return through the exemplary image of 'turning', or conversion. Conversion, the first act of loving God, enables us to acknowledge the touch of the other and touch the other in return. Hopkins' meditations on reflections on water draw a link between water, light and reflection. Influenced by Greek and Christian authors alike, Hopkins regards love as the driving force behind the desire, in Paul's words, to see God, not through a dim mirror but 'face to face'. The mirror is for Hopkins a fitting trope of love, reflecting as it does the nature of the relationship between the lover and beloved.

In Chapter Two, I explore celibacy and its association with the supreme cultural symbol of union: marriage. I argue that Hopkins' idealisation of virginity reflects both his adopted Catholic beliefs and his Tractarian roots. Inspired by Michel Foucault, I argue that virginity is a choice and a legitimate sexual and spiritual way of being. In Hopkins' opinion, the dedication of his virginity in celibate marriage to Christ is an expression of his *amor* and absolute fidelity. I pay particular attention to the Song of Songs and its appropriation in the poetry of Coventry Patmore, Alfred Tennyson and Digby Mackworth Dolben to understand its use in the formation and affirmation of Hopkins' belief in virgin marriage and his expression of same-sex desires.

Chapter Three focuses on love as mutual openness and exchange by exploring the individual's pneumatic (or spiritual) conception of Christ. It is the first of two chapters exploring the importance of breath exchange in Hopkins' writings. To his mind, humans attain both perfection and perfect union with God when they open themselves to his presence. Conception provides Hopkins with one of the best examples for rendering this receptiveness. Keeping in mind the reciprocity of love, Hopkins imagines the believer as one who receives the Word through the Spirit and gives birth to the Word through utterance.

Chapter Four extends the discussion of breath exchange. Here I explore a model of intimate exchange that Hopkins deploys to great effect: the circulation of breath, which enables each participant to touch the heart of the other. Conversation is founded on the openness of each person to the voice of the other. Unlike a monologue, a conversation demonstrates one's engagement with another being and requires the complementary acts of speaking, listening and sympathy. While poetry may indeed be an act of love, uttering as it does the poet's feelings for and to God, the most intimate and complete exchange of breath is given by the kiss on the mouth. This act is both implied and directly referred to in Hopkins' poems. The kiss provides him with one of the supreme instances of the intertwining of *amor* and touch.

In Chapter Five, I conclude with the theme of homecoming. Returning home enables one to rediscover what one had lost in leaving it. For Hopkins, union is reunion, and redemption is humanity's return to Eden. In his later years, he was an Englishman teaching in Ireland and looking back nostalgically on his homeland. Reacting additionally to the pollution in the English cities to which he had been posted as a priest, Hopkins envisions his spiritual home – Eden – as a pristine, spring garden freshly blooming, its inhabitants correspondingly virginal or 'revirginalised'. And at the very heart of Eden is Christ, the one for whom Hopkins most yearns.

Finally, in a study of love, touch and union, I believe it is only appropriate to gravitate towards theories of union and equality. It is not within the scope of *Touching God* to interrogate Hopkins' ideas of union with God. When I refer to Hopkins, and indeed God, as being both receptive and active, I refer to Irigaray's feminist language of touch, Merleau-Ponty's notion of reversibility and Ignatius of Loyola's concept of mutual love. Two beings become open to the gift of each other through the reciprocity of touch, and this is what I hold to in my study. I believe that the theories herein illustrate the equality between the two who love, irrespective of their gender. I associate this equality with *amor*, and it is *amor* that Hopkins idealises in the relationship between himself and the divine other.

Chapter One

CONFLUENCE AND REFLECTION

Unity in Nature

Before talking about Hopkins I wish to briefly return to Merleau-Ponty's concept of reversibility, which offers an approach to understanding humanity's being with nature and, by extension, God. Galen A. Johnson argues that Merleau-Ponty 'was committed until the end to the primacy of bodily perception as the starting point for ontology'.[1] Nowhere is this more evident than in *The Visible and the Invisible*, published posthumously in 1964. In this work, particularly in the chapter, 'The Intertwining – the Chiasm', Merleau-Ponty informs us that perception encompasses not simply touching and seeing, but also seeing as touching.[2] Perception is essentially contact between the self and the other. As Jones puts it, perception is contact with differentiation, and contact is possible because of reversibility.[3] In the words of Merleau-Ponty, 'there is a reversibility of the seeing and the visible… [T]he visible takes hold of the look which has unveiled it and which forms a part of it'.[4] In other words, the things I see also see me:

> [T]he vision [the seer] exercises, he also undergoes from the things, such that, as many painters have said, I feel myself looked at by the things, my activity is equally passivity…so that the seer and the visible reciprocate one another and we no longer know which sees and which is seen.[5]

Reversibility is possible because we are located within the world we perceive and inhabit. In short, 'my body sees only because it is a part of the visible in which it opens forth'.[6]

   Drawing on these thoughts, I argue that perception can provoke a physical sensation, along with a cognitive and emotional response, that can transform us intellectually, emotionally, spiritually. Perception is not only an act that we perform; it also happens to us: 'my activity is equally passivity'. As Hopkins says in his ecological poem 'Ribblesdale', 'what is Earth's eye, tongue, or heart else, where / Else, but in dear and dogged man?' (lines 9–10). Yes, 'where / Else' do we perceive the flesh of the earth but elsewhere – in the intertwining of the visible and the invisible. 'Sensible experience for Hopkins', James Finn

Cotter informs us, 'leads to knowledge and to love'.[7] In the intertwining the 'eye' can indeed lead – where else? – but to the 'heart'. Hopkins had a lifelong and deeply held interest in nature, the arts and aesthetics; he originally wanted to be a painter (*Further Letters*, 231). His journals, like many of his poems, are filled with detailed perceptions and descriptions of the land, water flow and clouds.

These intersecting interests encouraged him to look at the world as if it were a painting or a work of art. For instance, a number of Hopkins' remarkable descriptions of nature in his poetry and journals originate from John Henry Parker's *Introduction to the Study of Gothic Architecture* and the two-volume *A Glossary of Terms used in Grecian, Roman, Italian and Gothic Architecture*.[8] Like Merleau-Ponty, who tells us that, 'as many painters have said, I feel myself looked at by the things', Hopkins remarks in a journal entry, 'What you look hard at seems to look hard at you' (*Journals*, 204).[9] Hopkins concludes the entry with the assertion, 'Unless you refresh the mind from time to time you cannot always remember or believe how deep the inscape in things is' (205). 'Inscape' is a Hopkins coinage that appears to suggest, in the simplest terms, something like an 'inner landscape'. Hopkins uses it in relation to the landscape, art and sound. While it has an obvious aesthetic element and is sustained by the visible (or the auditory), it moves well beyond the visible: it is 'deep…in things'. The inscape will not be seen in its proper light unless the viewer is open to perceiving it:

> Stepped into a barn of ours, a great shadowy barn, where the hay had been stacked on either side, and looking at the great rudely arched timberframes – principals(?) [sic] and tie-beams, which make them look like bold big *A*s with the cross-bar high up – I thought how sadly beauty of inscape was unknown and buried away from simple people and yet how near at hand it was if they had eyes to see it and it could be called out everywhere again. (221)[10]

If we look hard enough at a thing, it will look back at us; we will see its 'buried' inscape and arrive at a new insight. Hopkins says elsewhere, 'I saw the inscape though freshly, as if my eyes were still growing' (228).[11] The awareness of inscape makes way for the reversibility of the seeing and the being seen, of the self and the other. 'Binsey Poplars', another ecological poem, describes and laments the felling of poplars along the banks of the Thames, close to the village of Binsey. Referring to the delicate state of nature, the poet proclaims his love:

> Since Country is so tender
> To touch, her being so slénder,

That, like this sleek and seeing ball
But a prick will make no eye at all… (Lines 9–15)

Nature is 'so tender / To touch' that anything more violent than a caress would 'únsélve / The sweet especial rural scene' (lines 21–2) and destroy the scene's inscape.[12] If 'scene' is a pun on the word 'seen', and if 'a prick will make no eye at all', then a lost 'scene' would lose its capacity to look back at us. In our very blindness to the 'scene' of the other, we will have destroyed her 'eye[s]' and lost 'a mutual enfolding'.[13]

Interactions between elements within nature also mirror the intertwining of nature with humans. Hopkins commonly uses descriptions of water and seascapes to demonstrate how natural elements intermingle with, and alter, each other. In his undergraduate essay, 'How far may a common tendency be traced in all pre-Socratic philosophy?', Hopkins argues that, to the mind of Thales, moisture is both 'the principle of all things' and 'a network or skeleton tying all things together' (*Oxford Essays*, 205, 206).[14] Although Hopkins argues that Thales' ontology was flawed, he nevertheless values its argument: 'Although these various systems [of Thales and Empedocles] broke up on examination[,] the advance they made by the suggestion of a unity in nature cannot be over-valued' (205). The possibility of 'a unity in nature' implies a 'principle' akin to the microcosmic structure of a gothic cathedral with which Hopkins was so familiar through his reading of Parker.

In Hopkins' ontology, this binding principle is what he calls 'instress'. 'Instress', J. Hillis Miller explains, 'weaves nature together and makes it one, as the strands in a rope or web are one, or as the threads in a piece of cloth are unified'.[15] Hopkins says in his notes on Parmenides, 'all things are upheld by instress and are meaningless without it' (*Oxford Essays*, 127).[16] As we have seen, his criticism of Thales does not prevent him from describing moisture as 'a network or skeleton tying all things together'. The sea, he says, consists of 'a webby space of foamy water' (*Journals*, 177);[17] it has 'little walking wavelets edged with fine eyebrow crispings, and later nothing but a netting or chain-work on the surface' (184).[18] Watersprigs from a waterfall form a sequence of droplets in the air that 'are strung of single drops, the end one like a tassel or heavier bead, the biggest' (233).[19] Likewise, clouds, which are visible examples of moisture in the air, are 'ropy, the coiled folds being taken back across…from bottom to top westwards' (138),[20] and 'roped like a heavy cable being slowly paid and by its weight settling into gross coils' (212).[21] In another depiction of clouds, he invokes his own description of Thales' system of moisture: 'Clouds growing in beauty at the end of the day. In the afternoon a white rack of two parallel spines, vertebrated as so often' (138).[22] Hopkins' perception of water and moisture as a system of webs, links and coils – indeed, as a skeleton – points to nature's intertwining, design and unity.

We again witness Hopkins' perception of nature's unity in an observation of waves rebounding off a sea wall. He writes about the sea:

> The laps of running foam striking the sea-wall double on themselves and return in nearly the same order and shape in which they came. This is mechanical reflection and is the same as optical. (*Journals*, 252)[23]

By referring to optics and 'mechanical reflection', he is clearly extrapolating from the basic law of specular reflection, which holds that the angle at which a ray is incident to a surface must equal the angle at which it is reflected from it. Similarly, he appeals to the wave theory of light when associating the waves hitting the sea wall with the light waves bouncing off a reflective surface. These waves return to the direction from which they came and as a result seem to 'double on themselves' by overlapping with the oncoming waves. While this observation does not at first seem to have a theological significance, it nonetheless provides Hopkins with a visible example of a divine pattern. Immediately after the observation he concludes enigmatically, 'indeed all nature is mechanical, but then it is not seen that mechanics contain that which is beyond mechanics' (252). The key indicator of a pattern is recurrence or repetition. Thus, the repetitive and ordered movement of waves off sea walls forms a pattern signifying that 'all nature is mechanical'. The act of a wave hitting the sea wall appears to return the wave and its movement to itself, and this act is repeated, mirrored.

What do waves and walls have to do with love and God? Hopkins' assertion that 'mechanics contain that which is beyond mechanics' refers, like inscape itself, to what is beyond, but nonetheless also present in, the very visible. It alludes to the workings of God, described as 'máster of the tídes' and 'the wáll' in Hopkins' most famous (aquatic) poem, 'The Wreck of the Deutschland' (stanza 32). The interaction between the sea wall and the waves exemplifies the central concerns of this book: the touch between the self and the other and the mutual interchange of love. Just as the water's movement is given back to itself when it touches the wall, so does the beloved, like a mirror, receive and return the love that he or she has received. A wave cannot 'double upon' itself unless it touches something other than itself. For Hopkins, God is the wall, the other who returns his love.

The return of a wave to itself, like the returning of love to the lover, is analogous to the process of union, separation and reunion, of Eden, Fall and Redemption. This trajectory forms the plot of the romance as redemption story, which the final chapter explores. Similarly, Hopkins' undergraduate poem, 'The earth and heaven, so little known', observes a world in flux, transforming and returning to its source:

> There is a vapour stands in the wind;
> It shapes itself in taper skeins:
> You look again and cannot find,
> Save in the body of the rains.
>
> And these are spent and ended quite;
> The sky is blue, and the winds pull
> Their clouds with breathing edges white
> Beyond the world; the streams are full. (Lines 17–24)

Fallen rain touches the earth, evaporates and ascends as 'vapour'. It is found again 'in the body of the rains', that is, in clouds. The full-bodied clouds will eventually disperse and become rain to fill the streams.

Hopkins uses his observation of water circulation to depict humanity's separation from, and reunion with, God. In one of his religious notes, he compares the soul to boiling water in a pot, saying, 'the water must always be getting hotter, never cooler, while the pot is on fire' (*Sermons*, 208).[24] He decries the state of becoming 'cooler', whereby the soul lapses into spiritual 'tepidity' (207) and 'lukewarmness' (208). Disordered in this case, it is no longer driven by mechanics. Hopkins declares, 'while we strive, though we commit faults, we are not lukewarm; when we give up struggling and let ourselves drift, then tepidity begins' (208). In his view, we must continually 'strive' to reach God. It would be worse for the soul to 'drift' midway on its journey than for it to be perpetually cool.

Hopkins reiterates that we should be hot towards God. 'Fervour…is properly the being on the boil, the shewing the stir of life, of a life not shared by all other things, and the being to pass, by evaporation, into a wholly spiritual condition', he says (*Sermons*, 208). With this image, Hopkins calls for personal transformation into an advanced or symbolically higher state of existence. As we move towards God, we should resemble the upward movement of vapour. Hopkins' association of 'being on the boil' with 'the stir of life' is based on the untranslatable pun concerning the Greek words *zeō* ('to boil, to be hot') and *zōē* ('life'); Aristotle makes use of it in *De Anima* when he says, 'those who say that the soul is…hot will say that it is also for this reason that life is so called'.[25] When we display 'the stir of life' we exhibit what is most indicative of our love for God: vigour and motion, not the signs of cool and tranquil water. As Hopkins argues elsewhere, 'God gave things a forward and perpetual motion' (*Sermons*, 198–9).[26] The fervour of love should impel us towards God.

The water cycle is contingent on a constant and circular motion. The same may be argued of love. 'The barley drink disintegrates if it is not constantly stirred', says the Presocratic philosopher Heraclitus.[27] While Heraclitus' image is characteristically mysterious, it suggests the notion of endurance through vigilant motion. Like the barley drink, love must exhibit 'the stir of life' if it is to escape stagnation and disintegration. 'Love is a great reality, and if it returns to its beginning and goes back to its origin, seeking its source again, it will always draw afresh from it, and thereby flow freely', says Bernard of Clairvaux.[28] Digby Mackworth Dolben argues a similar point in an untitled poem that Hopkins copied just before entering the Society of Jesus:

> Strange, all-absorbing Love, who gatherest
> Unto Thy glowing all my pleasant dew,
> Then delicately my garden waterest,
> Drawing the old, to pour it back anew. (Lines 1–4)[29]

The sun is synonymous with an 'all-absorbing' element called Love, that is, God. The dew is drawn to Love's heat and invariably falls to earth as rain in a cycle of ascent and descent. This circulation makes possible the continual watering of the soul's 'garden', perhaps a reference to the sexually charged garden of the Song of Songs.[30] The dew represents another life-giving element, love, which Love gathers, absorbs and tenderly (or 'delicately') returns to revive the giver-recipient.

In 'Trees by their yield', Hopkins links the dissolution of love to the soul's barrenness and dryness:

> Trees by their yield
> Are known; but I –
> My sap is sealed,
> My root is dry.
> If life within
> I none can shew
> (Except for sin),
> Nor fruit above, –
> It must be so –
> I do not love. (Lines 1–10)

Elsewhere, 'Time's eunuch' calls on the Lord to 'send my roots rain' ('Thou art indeed just, Lord', line 14). It seems, then, that only God can renew the flagging soul and 'refresh' the one who loves not. Hopkins writes in an unpublished sermon, 'the Holy Ghost is such a Paraclete… He is called, as his hymn ['*Veni Creator*'] says, the living fountain, for what does he do but make a motion through the soul, cheer it, refresh it, and turn its barrenness into thriving growth'.[31]

Touching and Melting

> Thee, God, I come from, to thee go,
> All dáy long I like fountain flow
> From thy hand out, swayed about
> Mote-like in thy mighty glow.
> ('Thee, God, I come from, to thee go', lines 1–4)

The hand is the body part most associated with touch. With the evocative image of touching hands, Hopkins is able to represent, either individually or at once, redemption, creation and the mutual interchange of love. In 'Thee, God, I come from, to thee go', the fountain's circular flow represents humanity's separation from, and return to, God. The speaker's declaration that he is 'like fountain flow / From [God's] hand out' implies the 'hand' that moulded him is the very thing he will grasp upon his return. The act of gripping is also found in the imperative, 'Grásp Gód', in 'The Wreck of the Deutschland' (stanza 32). This phrase complements the description of touching hands in stanza 1: 'Óver agáin I féel thy finger and find thée'. The speaker 'féel[s]' the touch of God's 'finger' in an emphatic and mutual gesture of welcome and reception. By announcing that he 'féel[s]' God's finger 'Óver agáin', he argues for the possibility of reunion.

God's finger represents both his love and the means by which he communicates it. Hopkins juxtaposes Ignatius' 'Contemplation for Obtaining Love', from the *Spiritual Exercises*, with '*Veni Creator*' to argue that God's finger is the Holy Spirit who is 'the bond and mutual love' between God, Christ and humanity:

> [T]he Holy Ghost is called Love ('Fons vivus, ignis, *caritas*' [living fountain, fire, love]); shewn 'in operibus', the works of God's finger ('Digitus paternae dexterae' [The Finger of God's right hand]); consisting 'in communicatione' etc, and the Holy Ghost as he is the bond and mutual love of Father and Son, so of God and man… (*Sermons*, 195)[32]

God acts and communicates through his finger, the Spirit who is known as Love. We can see, then, how God and humans might touch in 'mutual love'.

Hopkins, following Augustine, maintains that the most intimate touch is God's presence within us. In his *Confessions*, Augustine argues that touch forms the basis of attachment between beings and things[33] and that God's touch best fulfils our need for loving contact with another: 'Soft endearments are intended to arouse love. But there are no caresses tenderer than your charity [or love]'.[34] Similarly, Hopkins holds that no other being has the capacity to enter our hearts and affect us to the extent of which God is capable: 'God's finger touch[es] the very vein of personality, which nothing else can reach' (*Sermons*, 158).[35] He repeats this argument elsewhere when he cites Augustine:

> Neither do I deny that God is so deeply present to everything ('Tu autem, O bone omnipotens, eras superior summo meo et interior intimo meo') that it would be impossible for him but for his infinity not to be identified with them or, from the other side, impossible but for his infinity so to be present to them…so intimately present to things. (128)[36]

Hopkins' Latin is a paraphrase of the well-known declaration from Book Three of the *Confessions*: 'But you were more inward than my most inward part and higher than the highest element within me'.[37] Augustine encountered the divine other in the most secret places of his soul. As Gary Brent Madison puts it, 'what Augustine discovered by going "inside," into his innermost self, was nothing other than Otherness itself'.[38] To illustrate the extent to which God touches the individual, Hopkins says, 'God rests in man…as the hand in the glove' (*Sermons*, 195).[39] But that is not all: his presence is as the finger of the glove turned inside out. God's presence is such that it is only possible to distinguish between his being and that which he inhabits because he is infinite and all else is finite. He is at once the other within us and, in the words of theologian Gerard Loughlin, 'the other side of our skin; the inside of our outside'.[40]

The first awareness of God's touch occurs at the moment of conversion. The experience leads us, first, to become aware of God's presence and, second, to respond by touching his 'finger'. By making way for receptiveness, conversion enables the reciprocity of touch. If God is infinite, it follows that he is present also in the unbeliever. It is through conversion that we come to know – and feel – God's presence, as we turn to him, recognise his touch, and reciprocate. Indeed, the act of turning is implicit in the very word. According to the *Oxford English Dictionary*, 'conversion' originates from the Latin word *convertere*, which means, 'to turn about, turn in character or nature, transform, translate, etc., f. *con-* together, altogether + *vertere* to turn'. Conversion heralds a state of being together with God, whereas the time before conversion is marked by the solitude of self-imposed exile. God's presence, while known, can still be resisted, shunned, turned away from. In the memorable words of Augustine, 'You were with me, and I was not with you'.[41] 'Once I turned from thee and hid', announces Hopkins in 'Thee, God, I come from, to thee go' (line 9).

Like the prodigal son returning home from a life astray, however, Hopkins seeks to (re)turn to the 'Father': 'Bad I am, but yet thy child. / Father, be thou reconciled' (lines 13–14).[42] Conversion reconciles us to God and opens us to his plenitude. Hence, in 'The Wreck of the Deutschland', a poem that charts, among other things, the process of conversion, Hopkins implores Christ to 'Gush! – flush the man, the being with it, sour or sweet / Brim, in a flásh, fúll!' (stanza 8). Hopkins experiences the living fountain flooding the whole of him, so much so that, like a vessel filled and flushed with water, he is touched and filled to the 'Brim'.

'The Wreck of the Deutschland' continues the link between faith, love and water flow, wherein the 'heart' of the converted is not simply 'flushed' but also 'melt[ed]' (stanza 6). The believer's 'hard' heart (stanza 7) melts when it comes into contact with God's 'fire in him' (stanza 10). Impressions of heat and melting are conventional descriptions of the sensations of love. Hopkins refers to this convention in an early poem 'A Voice from the World', in which the speaker declares to his beloved, 'This ice, this lead, this steel, this stone, / This heart is warm to you alone' (lines 141–2). The saints went further and spoke of the burning sensation of longing. John of the Cross speaks of 'en amores inflamada' ('burning with love's long hungers').[43] Augustine says, 'My God, how I burned, how I burned with longing to leave earthly things and fly back to you'.[44] And also, 'O love, you ever burn and are never extinguished. O charity, my God, set me on fire. You command continence; grant what you command, and command what you will'.[45] The literary origins of these descriptions go back at least as far as ancient Greece. Hopkins was well versed in Greek poetry, including the writings of Pindar and Sappho, both of whom Anne Carson cites when she notes that Eros, the god of love, is described in Greek poetry as 'the melter of limbs'.[46] Similarly, for Hopkins, God's 'softening touch'[47] allows the formerly 'hard' and unreceptive individual to 'warm' towards him. The penetration of God's warmth into the heart of the newly converted is akin to spring's sudden thawing of winter: 'stealing as Spring / Through him, melt him but master him still' ('The Wreck of the Deutschland', stanza 10).

A person 'melted' by God's love will 'flow' towards the divinity. As Augustine writes, 'I am scattered in times whose order I do not understand. The storms of incoherent events tear to pieces my thoughts, the inmost entrails of my soul, until that day when, purified and molten by the fire of your love, I flow together to merge into you'.[48] This image of confluence is comparable to Walt Whitman's startling image of 'two cheerful waves rolling over each other and interwetting each other' ('We Two, How Long We Were Fool'd', line 15).[49] As we have seen in the Introduction, at least two bodies must exist in order to form one touch. In Whitman's poem, the two bodies, composed of the one liquid substance, intertwine, merge and yet retain their separate identities as 'two… waves'. Like Whitman, Hopkins makes a similar and evocative observation of the mutual interchange between waves. 'In the channel I saw (as everywhere in surfy water) how the laps of foam mouthed upon one another. In watching the sea, one should be alive to the oneness which all its motion and tumult receives from its perpetual balance and falling this way and that to its level' (*Journals*, 225).[50] The breaking of a wave follows a consistent pattern. When waves touch, their interaction is based on a movement of 'perpetual balance'. The impression is one of harmony, reciprocity and union. Thus, as Hopkins suggests, when one wave meets another, the two embrace in the openness and reciprocity of a kiss.

The Lover as Mirror

In the first half of the chapter, we saw how the intertwining of humans with nature is for Hopkins a reflection of God's relationship with humans. In the rest of the chapter we will see how Hopkins uses the trope of visual reflection to represent the love between humans and God. Visuality, reflection and their connection to mutual love forge a link between the two sections. Just as the sensations of heat and melting are popular in the literature of love, so, too, is the motif of the eye as a mirror reflecting the visage of the beloved, as in John Donne's poem 'The Good Morrow': 'My face in thine eye, thine in mine appears' (line 15).[51] This mutual reflection, Donne continues, makes 'our two loves…one' (line 20). Donne's image has origins in Plato's *Phaedrus*, which Hopkins studied at Oxford.[52] In the *Phaedrus*, Plato argues that the 'flashing beauty of the beloved'[53] is reflected back to him from the eyes of his lover. In the mutual gaze, 'the lover is his mirror in whom [the beloved] is beholding himself'.[54] Flowing as a stream, desire enables the lover to be his mirror:

> [T]hen does the fountain of that stream, which Zeus when he was in love with Ganymede named desire, overflow upon the lover, and some enters into his soul, and some when he is filled flows out again; and as a breeze or an echo rebounds from the smooth rocks and returns whence it came, so does the stream of beauty, passing through the eyes which are the natural doors and windows of the soul, return again to the beautiful one.[55]

The object of desire knows he is loved when he sees his reflection in the eyes of the other; through his reflection, he sees himself being loved. By reflecting the beloved, the lover makes his love known. David M. Halperin argues that the double gazing in the *Phaedrus* exemplifies Plato's treatment of the dynamic reciprocity of *eros* between the traditionally older teacher and his younger pupil.⁵⁶

In romantic discourse, reflection is linked to love, whether mutual or narcissistic. By reflecting the face of the other, we resist the narcissistic vision that sees and loves only the image of the self. By loving only himself, Narcissus rejects the love of Echo. His self-love is the act of falling in love 'with a false Other…a projection of himself, [and therefore] his desire for union with the beloved can never be satisfied'.⁵⁷ Narcissism is self-absorbed love that reflects the self rather than a true other. In contrast, Hopkins calls on us to reflect the image of the other, of God. He describes the effects of this dynamic reflection in 'As kingfishers catch fire, dragonflies draw flame'. Kingfishers and dragonflies 'catch' and 'draw' the light of the sun with the sheen of their reflective carapaces. The significance of their mirroring is clarified in the sestet:

> Í say more: the just man justices;
>   Keeps gráce: thát keeps all his goings graces;
> Ácts in God's eye what in God's eye he is –
>   Chríst. For Christ plays in ten thousand places,
> Lovely in limbs, and lovely in eyes not his
>   To the Father through the features of men's faces. (Lines 9–14)

Just as kingfishers and dragonflies reflect the light of the sun, so do the eyes of the 'ten thousand' reflect back to 'God's eye' the incarnate and 'flashing beauty' of the Son. In an earlier version of the poem, Hopkins writes that Christ 'Lives in limbs, and looks through eyes not his / With lovely yearning'.⁵⁸ The word 'lovely' combines two states: beauty and love. This idea is given credence by the play on words in the poem 'To what serves Mortal Beauty?', in which humans are both the 'World's loveliest' and 'love's worthiest' (lines 11, 10). Moreover, Hopkins associates the 'lovely' with the 'loveable' when he says, 'There met in Jesus Christ all things that can make man lovely and loveable' (*Sermons*, 35).⁵⁹ The earlier version of the kingfisher poem suggests that Christ longs for reciprocity and sees his 'lovely yearning' reflected back when humans gaze lovingly upon each 'Chríst[ed]' other. When 'God's eye' gazes on 'the features of men's faces', he simultaneously sees his own loveliness (and love) and humanity's loveliness (and love) returned to him through Christ. The reciprocal gaze between humanity and God is made possible through the person of Christ. The many and the one are united through the mediation of Christ, whose double nature, which reconciles humanity and divinity, enables him to meet the gaze of mortal and divine eyes and reconcile each with the other. As Hopkins says, 'He brings together things thought opposite and incompatible' (*Sermons*, 57).[60] His double gaze is similar to that of the guardian angels who, 'while they have us poor wretches in their sight…are at the same time gazing on the face of God' (91).[61]

Face to Face: Reflection and Likeness

In one of his early notes on Greek philosophy, Hopkins dwells on the nature of reflection and its significance to his ontology:

> The figure shewing how the Idea can be one though it exists in many is that of the sun in broken water, where the sun's face being once crossed by the ripples each one carries an image down with it as its own sun; and these images are always mounting the ripples and trying to fall back into one again. We must therefore think wherever we see many things having one idea that they all are falling back or wd. fall back but are held away by their conditions, and those philosophers have very truly said everything is becoming. (*Oxford Essays*, 305)[62]

The relationship between the one and the many is like that of the sun and its miniature reflections in rippling water. The origination of the many from the one light provides the many with their point of connection to each other and their source; the many are like the ten thousand faces reflecting the Son's face ('the sun's face') in the kingfishers poem. Not only do they partake of each other, the many also seek to return to their source. Each light, by 'mounting the ripples' and moving closer to the larger sun, reflects its corresponding advancement towards an increasing likeness to the one.

For Hopkins, the measure of our love for, and union with, God is similarly determined by the degree of our likeness to him. Our degree of likeness to God is determined by the level of our proximity. The closer we are to God, the closer the similarity will be; the further away we are from him, the greater will be the unlikeness. Augustine expresses this idea when he declares, 'One does not approach God by moving across intervals of place, but by likeness or similarity, and one moves away from him by dissimilarity or unlikeness'.[63] Hopkins writes that 'God himself…means us to copy His nature and character as well as we can and put on His mind according to our measure' (*Sermons*, 134).[64] He alludes here to Paul's call for believers to 'put on the Lord Jesus Christ'.[65] This phrase features most famously in Augustine's conversion under the fig tree.[66] This fig tree recalls the fig leaves with which the disobedient Adam and Eve clothed themselves.[67] For Augustine, however, the fig tree takes on the typological significance of putting on Christ, of becoming his likeness and redeeming ourselves to

God.⁶⁸ Christ, therefore, offers a shift in perspective on the relationship between humanity and God.

The ideal mirror is one that faithfully displays and reflects God's image. Hopkins argues that the world 'is a glass [God] looks in: what should it shew him? With praise, reverence, and service it should shew him his own glory' (*Sermons*, 239).⁶⁹ Nature praises God by reflecting his attributes:

> The sun and the stars shining glorify God… 'The heavens declare the glory of God'.⁷⁰ They glorify God, *but they do not know it*. The birds sing to him, the thunder speaks of his terror, the lion is like his strength, the sea is like his greatness, the honey like his sweetness; they are something like him, they make him known, they tell of him, they give him glory, but they do not know they do, they do not know him, they never can… (239; emphasis original)

Nature affirms, glorifies and praises God by showing him the multifaceted nature of his glory: honey reflects his sweetness; the lion, his strength; the sea, his might. Not only do they live out their being when they reflect his characteristics, they also become 'something like him'. Like the animals and the rest of creation, humans were created to give glory to God, as says Hopkins:

> BUT AMIDST THEM ALL IS MAN, man and the angels: we will speak of man. Man was created. Like the rest then to praise, reverence, and serve God; to give him glory. He does so, even by his being, beyond all visible creatures: 'What a piece of work is man!' (239; emphasis original)

Unlike animals and nature, however, humans 'can know God, *can mean to give him glory*' (239; emphasis original). Above the level of nature's unconscious imitation and praise of God is humanity's deliberate imitation and praise of him. Our relationship with God is based on consciousness and volition. Moreover, our knowledge of God and our desire to praise him place us in a unique position. Of all God's creatures, it is we who should strive to 'put on' his image.

Our privileged relationship with God and our capacity for consciousness combine to lift us above the rest of creation. But the closer we come to God, the further away we can fall from him. The more we deviate from our intended purpose, the more dissimilar our reflection of God will become. Because it reveals what we would otherwise not see of ourselves, the mirror is able to disclose the disparity between the image of God and the state of our souls. In the undated poem 'Hope holds to Christ the mind's own mirror out', Hope wishes to 'put on' Christ. She 'holds to Christ the mind's own mirror out / To take

His lovely likeness more and more' (lines 1–2). In seeking to take on his likeness, she attempts, as it were, to polish her mind's mirror:

> It will not well, so she would bring about
> A growing burnish brighter
> And turns to wash it from her welling eyes
> And breathes the blots off all with sighs on sighs. (Lines 3–6)

The combination of the 'welling eyes' and 'sighs on sighs' suggests both the mind's yearning to mirror Christ and its increasing frustration at its inability to reflect him well. In its failure to capture the light, the mind laments its darkening surface and consequent blindness:

> Her glass is blest but she as good as blind
> Holds till hand aches and wonders what is there;
> Her glass drinks light, she darkles down behind,
> All of her glorious gainings unaware.
> I told you that she turned her mirror dim
> At times, but then she sees herself, not Him. (Lines 7–12)

Darkness, the absence of light, hinders vision and reflection. While the mind's mirror 'drinks light', she paradoxically 'darkles' and becomes dimmer and more alienated from the light. A rift exists between action and realisation; she is 'unaware' of 'her glorious gainings', while the 'mirror dim' is the dimness of her mind to these gains. This unawareness typifies our blindness to the presence of Christ.

Hopkins remarks in a sermon that 'it is a dark time because the truth is either dimly seen or not seen at all' (*Sermons*, 39).[71] His words recall Paul's famous assertion, 'For now we see through a glass, darkly; but then face to face'.[72] Hopkins associates God's 'face' with light when he says, 'the true position of things between man and God appears by an immediate light at death, when man's self is set face to face with God's' (*Sermons*, 140).[73] Before the Fall, humans were able to gaze on the divine face, for 'he let himself be seen, he played his part, as we may say, in the show and pageantry of the country, he was indeed on familiar terms with all his subjects' (59).[74] Hopkins reminds his congregation that 'we read [in Genesis] of God talking with Adam; we hear of his walking in Paradise…to take the afternoon air' (59). In an effort to counter the present state of dimness, the speaker of 'The Wreck of the Deutschland' calls on Christ to 'éaster in us, be a dáyspring to the dímness of us' (stanza 35). In '*Nondum*', Hopkins connects the 'dáyspring' to the desired face-to-face encounter with God: 'to behold Thee as Thou art, / I'll wait till morn eternal breaks' (lines 53–4). This hope is likewise expressed in Hopkins' translation of the medieval Latin hymn, '*S. Thomae Aquinatis Rhythmus ad SS. Sacramentum*', in which the speaker hopes 'Some day to gaze on thee face to face in light / And be blest for ever with thy Glory's sight' (version b, lines 27–8).

We cannot love, touch and reflect Christ if we are unable to gaze upon his face. In 'Hope holds to Christ', we are told that Hope 'turned her mirror dim /…but then she sees herself not Him' (lines 11–12). This narcissistic vision from the darkened mirror is reminiscent of Christ's enemies who '*loved* darkness better than light' (*Sermons*, 40).[75] For Hopkins, the soul that turns its mirror towards itself rather than Christ, 'the light of the world' (40), is behaving illogically. In a comment to Canon Richard Watson Dixon about the latter's piece 'The Fallen Rain', he says,

> While on the one hand delighting in this play of imagination a perverse over-perspectiveness of mind nudges me that the rain could never be wooed by the rainbow which only comes into being by its falling nor could witness the wooing when made any more than the quicksilver can look from the out side [sic] back into the glass. (*Dixon*, 20)[76]

Inward-looking quicksilver is an example of unsound logic. It would be similarly irrational for people to turn their eyes away from Christ, to 'shut their eyes, their barred up doors and shutters against the daylight of the soul' (*Sermons*, 40). Teresa of Ávila compares faith to an intimate encounter between two lovers, in which the eyes of the soul are open to Christ. In her autobiography she says, 'without seeing one another, we look on one another face to face, as two lovers do. It is as the Bridegroom says to the Bride in the *Song of Songs*, I believe'.[77]

The Dim and Distorted Mirror

There is neither love nor loveliness where there is no God. For Hopkins, a life without God would literally be a life in hell. In 'Pilate', the eponymous speaker equates hell with his exile from God:

> The pang of Tartarus, Christians hold,
>   Is this, from Christ to be shut out.
> This outer cold, my exile from of old
>   From God and man, is hell no doubt. (Lines 1–4)

The distorted reflection of heaven is the face of hell whose ruler, Lucifer, is a parody of God. The darkness of hell is that which is most dissimilar to God's light. In his retreat notes on Ignatius' 'The Fifth Exercise: A Meditation on Hell', Hopkins remarks on Teresa of Ávila's vision of hell. Paraphrasing, he says, 'in spite of the darkness the eye sees there all that is most afflicting' (*Sermons*, 138). Teresa says of her vision,

> I had been put in what seemed a hole in the wall, and the very walls, which are hideous to behold, pressed in on me and completely stifled me. There is no light there, only the *deepest darkness*. Yet, although there was no light, it was possible to see everything that brings pain to the sight; I do not know how this can be.[78]

Hopkins refers to this frightening sensation of being pressed in on oneself when he recounts his bodily experience of a nightmare: 'It made me think that this was how the souls in hell would be imprisoned in their bodies as in prisons and of what St. Theresa says of the "little press in the wall" where she felt herself to be in her vision' (*Journals*, 238).[79] This wall is the very antithesis of God's wall, which returns love in mutual interchange. Instead of touching God, one touches only oneself. This touch is not a solitary pleasure but painful in the extreme. For Hopkins, the pain is a result of overabundant instress. As he argues, 'a high degree of such instress would in each case be the pain of fire' (*Sermons*, 137).[80] Instress, as we have seen, is necessary for upholding the individual; but excessive instress, particularly if it does not find external release, causes a painful surplus of energy, what Hopkins calls 'the pain of fire' and Teresa 'the inward fire'.[81] It would be like experiencing God's lightning without his love, or his arrow without the ecstasy.

Hopkins adheres to Teresa's description of hell's imprisonment and the resulting 'inward fire' when he writes that in hell 'the lost spirit dashes itself like a caged bear and is in prison, violently instresses them and burns, stares into them and is the deeper darkened' (*Sermons*, 138). This dark and inwardly burning fire is the parody of 'the fire of divine love' (208)[82] and the saints' burning love for God. The name Lucifer means 'light-bearer' or 'bringer of light', and to emphasise the travesty of Lucifer's name, Hopkins describes him in a poem as 'dark-out Lucifer' ('The dark-out Lucifer detesting this', line 1). Lucifer was believed to have been a fallen angel, and Hopkins argues that the fall of Lucifer and his angels is synonymous with the human experience of death. 'The fall from heaven', he says, 'was for the rebel angels what death is for man. As in man all that energy or instress with which the soul animates and otherwise acts in the body is by death thrown back upon the soul itself' (*Sermons*, 137). At this point, there is no longer the 'forward and perpetual motion' that Hopkins associates with *zeō* ('to boil, to be hot') and *zōē* ('life').

Lucifer's fall and human death are marked by constraint, darkness and blindness, by 'an imprisonment in darkness, a being in the dark; for darkness is the phenomenon of foiled action in the sense of sight' (*Sermons*, 137). Given this, the imprisoning pain of excessive instress, of energy gone awry, is the basis of spiritual blindness or 'foiled…sight': 'this constraint and this blindness or darkness will be most painful when it is the main stress or energy of the whole being that is thus balked' (137). What is 'balked' is the soul's 'tendency towards being, towards good, towards God' (137). The sinner's eyes are closed to God, for he or she has 'blotted out God and so put blackness in the place of light' (138). In contrast, the soul that is illuminated will be 'open wide like an eye, towards truth in God, towards light' (138). Death permanently closes the eyes of the body. This terrible fate is inflicted also on the soul that in hell finds itself imprisoned, bereft of God and doomed to the perpetual and painful instress of inward reflection.

Aside from producing a darkened surface, the dim mirror might also present a defective or impure surface. This type of mirror generates a distorted and unrecognisable face, a tarnished reflection of the ideal. It cannot offer the romantic ideal of the beautiful lover and beloved – deplorable indeed for an aesthete like Hopkins, to whom Christ is 'most beautiful' (*Sermons*, 35).[83] According to Herbert Grabes, the distorted image, a consequence of the 'soiled, tarnished, blurred or clouded mirror, [has been] used since Antiquity chiefly as an expression of a lack of moral integrity in contexts relating to knowledge of the Divine'.[84] Dissimilarity between the distorted image and the beautiful original exposes the extent to which the soul has distanced itself from the exemplary ideal. Such a mirror functions in the same manner as a conventional mirror, but instead brings to light the soul's repudiation of beauty. From his reading of her autobiography, Hopkins would have encountered Teresa of Ávila's description of the darkened soul's faulty mirror:

> Once when I was reciting the Office with the community, my soul suddenly became recollected, and seemed to me like a clear mirror; there was no part of it – back, sides, top, or bottom – that was not completely bright; and in the middle was a picture of Christ our Lord as I usually see Him. I seemed to see Him in every part of my soul as clearly as in a mirror, and this mirror – I cannot explain how – was entirely shaped to this same Lord, by a most loving communication which I could not describe… It was explained to me that when the soul is in mortal sin this mirror is covered with a thick mist and remains so dark that the Lord cannot be reflected or seen in it, even though He is always present and gives us our being. In the case of heretics, the mirror is much worse than darkened; it has the appearance of being broken.[85]

Once again, light is associated with the mirror of the soul. The soul in darkness produces a corresponding mirror that cannot reflect the image of God. Worse, still, is the mirror's 'appearance of being broken', for a broken mirror will distort Christ's beautiful face. For Hopkins, the disparity between the ideal and the reality often appears immense and irreconcilable. He, too, uses the image of the mirror to compare the unlikeness between God and the self: 'Are we his glass to look in? we are deep in dust or our silver gone or we are broken or, worst of all, we misshape his face and make God's image hideous' (*Sermons*, 240).[86] Dust prevents the clarity of reflection, while missing quicksilver permits none. Moreover, because we are made in the image of God, sin would distort and misshape his image. As sacrilege, the image would be 'hideous', monstrous, unlovely.

Hopkins' preoccupation with humanity's imperfections originates from his drive towards perfectibility in the image of Christ. His knowledge that humans are able to attain greatness runs parallel with the awareness that we have not yet achieved it, as he argues in the following quote:

> In the order of intention 'other things on the face of the earth' are created after man; the more perfect first, the less after. From this it follows that the more perfect is created in its perfection, that is to say / if perfectible and capable of greater and less perfection, it is created at its greatest. And thus it is said 'Ipsius enim sumus factura, *creati in Christo Jesu* in operibus bonis, quae praeparavit Deus ut in illis ambulemus'... (*Sermons*, 196)[87]

Humanity was created, above all creation, to be 'more perfect' and '*in Christo Jesu*', in Christ Jesus. Falling from perfection tarnishes that image. When we return to that perfect state and become his likeness, we will once again come face to face with his matchless beauty, as Hopkins asserts:

> [I]f the sinner defiles God's image so he might God's person if he could; if he takes the limbs of Christ and makes them members of a harlot so he would Christ; if he could be, as Christ was, 'in the form of God' he would make God sin and do the deeds 'of a slave'. (147)[88]

We see God's face by virtue of Christ's incarnation. Looking away from Christ distorts his image in the mind. The 'harlot' embodies a false or parodied image of love, one that is bought and sold rather than freely given; this derided figure conjures up notions of illicit sexual love, including the vanity of self-love. Thus, Hopkins charges Lucifer with 'fall[ing through] pride and selflove' (63)[89] and 'dwelling on his own beauty' (201).[90] Hopkins insists that humans should instead love Christ and 'put on' his image in order to return to him his beauty. By reflecting Christ, we will enact the movements of the miniature suns in rippling water as they return to their source. If we give back to the Son his image, we will see him face to face, as lovers do.

Chapter Two

VIRGIN MARRIAGE AND THE SONG OF SONGS

Public and Private Marriages

Hopkins and Coventry Patmore, both converts to Roman Catholicism, first met in July 1883 and exchanged letters until Hopkins' death in 1889.[1] Hopkins had admired Patmore's poetry for many years, as he readily admits to Bridges:

> I read his *Unknown Eros* well before leaving Oxford. He shews a mastery of phrase, of the rhetoric of verse, which belongs to the tradition of Shakespeare and Milton and in which you could not find him a living equal nor perhaps a dead one either after them. (*Bridges*, 93)[2]

And a few months earlier: 'But for insight he beats all our living poets, his insight is really profound, and he has an exquisiteness, farfetchedness, of imagery worthy of the best things of the Caroline age' (82).[3] Hopkins' assertion turns on his judgement that Patmore's poetry, particularly his collection, the *Unknown Eros*, offers a 'really profound' insight. While he does not elucidate the nature of the text's profundity, the volume's title provides an indication of the subject to which he was most likely referring. Aubrey de Vere, Patmore's friend and fellow Catholic, describes the *Unknown Eros* thus:

> It consists of a series of poems, many of them odes…embodying trains of very lofty and occasionally of somewhat mystical thought, in subtle, expressive, and musical language. Their chief characteristics are continuity of meditation and richness of illustrative imagery, but also bound in passion – that is, passion in its intellectual and imaginative, not sensuous form.[4]

Compared to his long poem *The Angel in the House*, these poems 'have risen into a higher region, and added to his youthful poetry a nobler though a kindred element'.[5]

Shortly after their first meeting in 1883, Patmore sought critical advice from Hopkins about his forthcoming collected edition of published poems. After reading the collection, Hopkins remarks to Patmore that the 'Psyche Odes' from the *Unknown Eros*, containing the poems 'Eros and Psyche', '*De Natura Deorum*' and 'Psyche's Discontent', 'belong to such a new atmosphere that I feel it is as dangerous to criticise them almost as the *Canticles*' (*Further Letters*, 347). Hopkins' ambivalent comparison of the Odes with the Canticle of Canticles or Song of Songs is significant and apt. J. C. Reid holds that Bernard of Clairvaux's exegesis of the Song of Songs 'excited Patmore's poetic impulse, and *Unknown Eros* is stamped with its mark'.[6] Patmore was a keen admirer of the Song of Songs, which, according to its prevailing Christian interpretation, is an epithalamion celebrating the marriage of Christ with the soul. Consider, for instance, the following Victorian hymn by Horatius Bonar:

> I rest my soul on Jesus,
> This weary soul of mine;
> His right hand me [sic] embraces,
> I on his breast recline.[7]

Bonar associates the soul with the beloved disciple at Christ's breast[8] and the lover of the Song of Songs.[9] Like the bride and the groom from the Song of Songs, the relationship between Eros and Psyche had come to represent in Christianity the union between Christ and the soul. 'The model of Eros and Psyche as allegory for God and the soul is traditional', says John Maynard.[10] In 'Eros and Psyche', Patmore alludes to the Song of Songs when his Psyche says to Eros, 'Lie like a bunch of myrrh between my aching breasts'.[11] Thus, his Psyche is based not merely on the Greek myth but also on the bride in the Song of Songs.

While Hopkins was staying in Hastings with the Patmores in August 1885, Coventry Patmore asked him to read a manuscript of his new prose work, *Sponsa Dei* ('Spouse of God'), a work that had engaged his attention for many years and which he intended to have published after his death (*Further Letters*, 361). Hopkins' cautious response to the *Sponsa Dei*, however, was stronger than it had been to the *Unknown Eros*, as Patmore informed him more than two years later:

> Much-meditating on the effect which my M.S. 'Sponsa Dei' had upon you, when you read it while staying here, I concluded that I would not take the responsibility of being the first to expound the truths therein contained: so, on Xmas Day, I committed the work to the flames without reserve of a single paragraph. (385)[12]

News of the conflagration came as an unwelcome surprise to Hopkins, who declared, 'My objections were not final, they were but consideration' (385).

Patmore's intention was for the *Sponsa Dei* to be the flowering of the ideas expounded in *The Angel in the House*, *The Victories of Love* and the *Unknown Eros*. Of its composition, Claude Colleer Abbott argues that, 'no doubt [Patmore] used the warm images of bodily love, abating none of their sensuous flush, much as he had used them in the Psyche Odes' (*Further Letters*, xxxiv). Further confirmation may be gleaned from Edmund Gosse:

> This vanished masterpiece was not very long, but polished and modulated to the highest degree of perfection… The subject of it was certainly audacious. It was not more or less than an interpretation of the love between the soul and God by an analogy of the love between a woman and a man; it was, indeed, a transcendental treatise on Divine desire seen through the veil of human desire. (Cited in *Further Letters*, xxxiv)

Patmore would have most likely accepted Gosse's assertion. In *The Rod, The Root, and the Flower*, he elaborates upon what he describes as '*the burning heart of the Universe*':

> God has declared to us His mystic rapture in His marriage with Humanity in twice saying, 'Hic est Filius meus dilectus in quo bene complacui'.[13] He expressly and repeatedly calls this marriage, and pronounces the marriage of Man and Woman to be its symbol.[14]

As the title *Sponsa Dei* suggests, the soul's union with the divinity is both proclaimed and legitimised by the sacrament of marriage. Patmore's belief in divine marriage is thus concordant with the established Christian understanding of the Song of Songs as an epithalamion.

Why, however, was Hopkins – who publicly declared Christ to be 'the truelove and the bridegroom of men's souls' (*Sermons*, 35)[15] – wary of the *Sponsa Dei*? The reason, I argue, is that he did not believe the general public could be its intended audience. Some books, he believed, are suited to a wide readership, while others are simply not. Hopkins advocates the didactic purpose of art, remarking, '[a] good book is to educate the world at large' (*Further Letters*, 362).[16] In this light, he praises *The Angel in the House*, describing it as 'in the highest degree instructive…a book of morals and in a field not before treated and yet loudly crying to be treated' (362). Given these comments, it appears Hopkins did not consider the *Sponsa Dei* to be a suitable text for 'the world at large'. In other words, he believed it had exceeded the public educational content of Patmore's previously published work. 'To Patmore's disappointment Hopkins did not approve of the book', argues Derek Patmore; 'He told Patmore that he thought it too intimate, dealing as it did with "so mystical an interpretation of the significance of physical love in religion", to be placed in the hands of the general reading public'.[17] Another letter to Patmore, composed shortly after Hopkins' stay at Hastings, sheds further light on his response to the *Sponsa Dei*. In the letter, he declares, 'anything however high and innocent may happen to suggest anything however low and loathsome' (*Further Letters*, 365).[18] In Hopkins' opinion, 'high and innocent' texts are open to textual misunderstandings and, thus, to 'abuses' (365).

Hopkins' cautious attitude towards the 'Psyche Odes' and, in particular, to the *Sponsa Dei*, provides an insight into both his poetry and his relationship with Christ. Following Hopkins' death, Patmore wrote to Bridges, recalling, 'when [Hopkins] read [the *Sponsa Dei*], he said with a grave look, "that's telling secrets"' (cited in *Further Letters*, 391n1). Hopkins' aversion to 'telling secrets' indicates the amount of tension he experienced between private feeling and public expression. This in turn sheds light on his understanding of love and the manner of its public expression (or silence). As we saw in the Introduction, Hopkins sometimes substitutes the word 'charity' for *amor*. This is apparent in a sermon delivered on 4 January 1880, in which he quotes from a hymn by St Francis Xavier:

> 'O Deus, ego amo te: Non amo te ut salves me Aut quia non amantes te Aeterno punis igne' / 'O God, I love thee, I love thée – Not out of hope of heaven for me Nor fearing nót to love and be In the everlasting burning'. (*Sermons*, 50)[19]

The word Francis uses for 'I love' is *amo*; nevertheless, Hopkins concludes the sermon, not with references to *amor*, but, rather, to 'divine charity' and a person's 'willing obedience' and 'duty' to love God (53). In the public arena, Hopkins names this love in Latin, but in English merely alludes to it by the word 'charity'. He hints at *amor* when, following his reference to 'divine charity', he alludes to the existence of

> a sweeter, tenderer love, a love more working and effectual, which may be added to [divine charity] and grow out of it, of that I shall not speak tonight, but the love I have spoken of comes first and none can be higher. [A] sovereign...will be glad of a dearer love than that but he will not insist on it... (53)

That 'sweeter, tenderer love', the 'dearer love', which Hopkins hesitates to dwell on openly, can only be *amor*. In favouring charity, the substitute word for *amor*, Hopkins maintains the division between private and public loves.

Elsewhere, Hopkins exhibits his reticence in his correspondence with Richard Watson Dixon over the poem 'At the Wedding March', composed a few months before the abovementioned sermon. The poem is perhaps the most prominent epithalamion celebrating Hopkins' marriage to Christ. Hopkins at first suggests in his letter that the poem 'might do' for inclusion in Dixon's *Bible Birthday Book*. And yet, he immediately retracts the suggestion, declaring, 'but I rather think not: it is too personal and, I believe, too plainspoken' (*Dixon*, 132).[20] We witness, therefore, another example of Hopkins' need for secrecy, the degree of which directs us to the significance he attaches to marriage. According to the poem, human marriage parallels and points us to the soul's marriage with Christ:

> Gód with honour hang your head,
> Gróom, and grace you, bride, your bed
> With lissome scions, swéet scíons,
> Out of hallowed bodies bred.
>
> Eách be other's comfort kind:
> Déep, déeper than divined,
> Divíne chárity, déar chárity,
> Fast you ever, fást bínd.
>
> Then let the Márch tréad our ears:
> Í to hím túrn with tears
> Whó to wedlock, hís wónder wedlock,
> Déals tríumph and immortal years.

The first two stanzas revolve around a wedding couple. The priest describes the couple's love as their 'fást bínd' – a reference to the sexual union and the marriage band. Mutual love is given expression by Hopkins' request that 'Eách be [the] other's comfort divined'. He insists on the sanctity of marriage from the outset: the first word he utters and stresses is 'Gód', and he wishes that from the couple's 'bed' their children be 'Out of hallowed bodies bred'. With this poem, Hopkins confirms that he is a firm advocate of human marriage. The love between the couple would most rightly be defined as *amor*. Hopkins, however, locates it within the category of 'Divíne chárity'. In the third stanza, he draws the reader's attention to himself, as he turns to Christ, his bridegroom. The phrase, 'I to hím túrn', represents the act of conversion (a topic discussed in the first chapter) and the moment when the bride and groom turn to each other to state their respective vows.

Through the device of juxtaposition, the speaker draws a parallel between his private marriage to Christ and the public marriage of the unnamed bride and groom. Even so, by refusing to submit this 'too personal' poem for publication in Dixon's book, Hopkins reveals the extent to which his 'wedlock' to Christ differs from the conventional equivalent.

Celibacy and Tractarianism

Paul promoted lifelong virginity as the ideal form of Christian existence. This ideal would later run concurrently with the concept of the bride of Christ, wherein the Song of Songs plays a crucial role.[21] Although Hopkins was a great advocate of marriage, he did not choose the path of conventional marriage. His marriage to Christ was founded not only upon notions of romantic love, but also virginity and chastity – ideals he cultivated as an Anglican at Oxford. Hopkins idealised virginity and celibacy through his association with the Oxford Movement, whose followers were known as Tractarians or Puseyites (after Revd Edward Pusey). While the Church of England traditionally gave emphasis to the authority of scripture, the Tractarians emphasised the authority of the early church, and encouraged aspects of public worship and private devotion that seemed to resemble Roman Catholic modes of practice. Hopkins' introduction to Catholicism originated from his allegiance to Tractarianism; in a letter to his father he acknowledges that the foundations of his conversion were laid down by an 'increasing knowledge of the Catholic system (at first under the form of Tractarianism, later in its genuine place)' (*Further Letters*, 93).[22]

John Henry Newman, at first the most famous Tractarian celibate, would later become one of the era's most celebrated Roman Catholics. He was a mentor to Hopkins and received him into the Roman Catholic Church.[23] Newman's name was synonymous with celibacy, no less to Protestant opponents, most notably Charles Kingsley, who strongly advocated marriage.[24] In his Tractarian days, Newman was deeply moved by the asceticism of the early Church Fathers, and believed austerities, such as the celibacy requirement imposed on Oxford fellows, could contribute to his colleagues' sense of community.[25] Unlike the Protestants who understood celibacy to be a distinctly 'Romish' practice, Newman and many of the early Tractarians hoped celibacy within monastic and conventual settings in the Anglican Church could absorb those who felt called to community life and would otherwise defect to Rome.[26] (This idea, of course, could not prevent his eventual defection on theological grounds.)

Tractarian celibacy gained much of its impetus through the Tractarian doctrine of reserve. Reserve stresses the inaccessibility and hidden nature of

God and was sometimes spoken of in the language of touch. Newman ends his poem 'Awe' thus:

> And so, albeit His woe is our release,
> Thought of that woe aye dims our earthly peace;
> The Life is hidden in a Fount of Blood! –
>   And this is tidings good,
> But in the Angels' reckoning, and to those
>   Who Angel-wise have chose
> And kept, like Paul, a virgin course, content
>   To go where Jesus went;
> But for the many laden with the spot
> And earthly taint of sin, 'tis written, 'Touch Me not'. (Lines 9–18)[27]

'Awe' was published in *Lyra Apostolica*, a collection of devotional verse by a group of founding and early Tractarians. In the poem, Newman holds that there are two discrete groups: the virgins and the non-virgins. The first is composed of the 'Angel-wise', the chaste ones who have 'kept, like Paul, a virgin course'. The second comprises 'the many', those who have been smeared with 'the spot / And earthly taint of sin'. Sinners are denied the atoning blood of Christ. Instead, they are met with the words, 'Touch Me not', which the resurrected Christ uttered to Mary Magdalene.[28] 'Awe' therefore concludes with an account of the unbridgeable difference – and distance – between Christ and the sinner.

Newman's stress on the incapacity of 'the many' to touch Christ provides an idea of the Tractarians' theories of interpretation and writing. In a sermon delivered on 22 May 1831, he says, '[Christ] does not manifest His glory to mortal sense… It is in His mercy that He hides Himself from those who would be overcome by the sensible touch of the Almighty Hand'.[29] Newman argues for the aloofness of sacred scripture. While Christ verbalised the phrase, 'Touch me not', Newman declares in 'Awe', ''tis *written*, "Touch Me not"'. The words of the Word are given in scripture, a text that to his mind is mysterious and unyielding to human touch. Tractarian poetry should likewise be 'veiled, indirect, subdued, and self-effacing'.[30] On the topic of passion in particular, the Tractarians sought to be self-controlled, contained or 'subdued' – in short, reserved. As Tractarian Isaac Williams declares, 'every thing which has God for its end gives rise to feelings which do not admit of expression'.[31] Furthermore, God, 'who is invisible, and who reads the language of the heart', is he 'to whom silence may often best speak'.[32] We see, then, that this emphasis on detachment and circumscription continued to influence several of Hopkins' post-conversion writings on the topic of *eros* and virgin marriage.

Newman and Hopkins did not consider virginity to be a temporary state preceding sexual practice. Rather, they regarded virginity as an actively maintained choice, a legitimate state of sexual and spiritual being. Michel Foucault argues such a point in *The History of Sexuality: Volume Three*. In his discussion of Heliodorus' *Ethiopica*, Foucault maintains that virginity is essential to the hero's integrity to himself and his beloved:

> We see then that virginity is not simply abstention as a preliminary to sexual practice. It is a choice, a style of life, a lofty form of existence that the hero chooses out of the regard he has for himself. When the most extraordinary occurrences separate the two protagonists and expose them to the worst dangers, the gravest will of course be that of falling prey to the sexual cupidity of others. The greatest test of their own worth and their mutual love will be that of resisting at all costs and of saving that virginity which is essential to the relationship with themselves and essential to the relationship with each other.[33]

In the tale, virginity offers proof of one's fidelity to the beloved and to one's ideals. By extension, a religious celibate who chooses the life of perpetual celibacy lays bare his or her devotion to Christ. Hopkins puts forward this view in his poem 'St. Thecla', most likely composed around 1864 or 1865, either during the height of his Tractarianism or at the start of his interest in Catholicism. The source of the poem is the apocryphal story of Thecla. Promised in marriage to a man, Thecla one day chances upon Paul preaching about chastity. Thereafter, she chooses to dedicate her life and virginity to Christ:

> Her weeds all mark her maiden, though to wed,
> And bridegroom waits and ready are bower and bed.
> Withal her mien is modest, ways are wise,
> And grave past girlhood earnest in her eyes.
>   Firm accents strike her fine and scrollèd ear,
> A man's voice and a new voice speaking near.
> The words came from a court across the way.
> She looked, she listened: Paul taught long that day.
> He spoke of God the Father and His Son,
> Of world made, marred, and mended, lost and won;
> Of virtue and vice; but most (it seemed his sense)
> He praised the lovely lot of continence... (Lines 17–28)

Ordinarily, female virginity holds worth in relation to another person for whom it is considered important, most notably, the potential husband. Thus,

Hopkins juxtaposes the reference to 'weeds', the clothes that 'mark' Thecla's virginity, with mention of the awaiting bridegroom and bed. The 'weeds' declare her present virginity, which makes possible her future marriage; they 'all mark her maiden, though to wed'. Her chance encounter with Paul wipes away this future marriage for an alternative future: conversion and 'the lovely lot of continence'. The ensuing lines exemplify the poem's central argument: 'All over, some such words as these, though dark, / *The world was saved by virgins*, made the mark' (lines 29–30; emphasis original). Here, the word 'mark' echoes its use in line 17. Like biblical types, the second 'mark' supersedes and prevails over the first 'mark'. Thecla's potential to marry a man is displaced by her desire to unite with the God of her new religion. Her resolve to remain a virgin displaces the first 'mark', the virginity that declares her fit for marriage to a man. Thecla's resolve is interwoven, as threads are in her 'weeds', with her conversion to Christianity.

Religious virginity signals an exclusive commitment to God. As Paul insists, a heart divided between a spouse and God cannot fully commit to the latter. Discussing Paul's argument, Peter Brown says, 'the fact of being married betrayed an absence of God's call to continence. The married lacked the supreme quality of the undivided heart: "the married person is anxious about worldly affairs, how to please his wife, and he is divided"'.[34] For Hopkins, betrothal and marriage to God, like human marriage, is marked by one's fidelity to the other. Unlike conventional marriage, however, it is also marked by celibacy and, ideally, perpetual virginity. Hopkins developed and nurtured these ideas through his religious contacts at Oxford. As a young undergraduate, he attended several lectures given by the Tractarian, Revd Henry Parry Liddon. Liddon's lectures and mentorship helped steer the young man closer towards the religious idealisation of virginity and lifelong celibacy. In a letter to his mother, written shortly after his arrival at Balliol, Hopkins says, '[my friend] Gurney and several others went to Liddon's lecture (one of a series on the first epistle to the Corinthians) delivered at S. Edmund's Hall. Gurney took me. The lecture, I need scarcely say, was admirable. Liddon, perhaps you do not know, is Pusey's great *protégé* and is immensely thought of' (*Further Letters*, 76–7).[35] Hopkins was evidently impressed by Liddon, who, 'After lecture, tea and coffee…goes round chatting. Gurney introduced me, and I shall now go every Sunday evening' (77).

Hopkins' extensive lecture notes record his mentor's teaching on, among other things, Paul's case for sexual self-discipline and celibacy in the first letter to the Corinthians. Paul's focus on the topic was such that Newman, as we have seen, declared him the model for those who have 'kept…a virgin course'. Although Hopkins was to break ties with Liddon by his conversion to Roman Catholicism, these lectures offer insight into how an influential figure such as

Liddon prized virginity and celibacy, and how he would become significant to Hopkins' growing concern with the ascetic and religious life.[36] As is common in lecture notes, it is at times difficult to distinguish between the voice of the lecturer and that of the student; however, on the matter of celibacy, Liddon and Hopkins are at one with Paul. Hopkins writes in his notes on 1 Corinthians 6:18–20: '18, 19, 20. General observations on fornication. i. It alone is a sin against the body; ii. the body is the temple of the Holy Ghost – the body; iii. we are not our own to take our own pleasure; we are Christ's; he has bought us'.[37] These 'General observations' impart the following unambiguous message: the body is more than flesh, for it is a 'temple' owned by Christ, who has redeemed it because he has 'bought us'. Illicit sex or 'fornication' is therefore an incursion upon the temple, 'a sin against the body'.

For Paul, fornication is a sin, while marriage is tolerable, chastity preferable, and virginity ideal. Hopkins' notes on chapter 7 of the first letter to the Corinthians are testament to Paul's (and, indeed, to his and Liddon's) preference for virginity and chastity over marriage. Paul's choice is clear in his wish for the unmarried and the widowed to remain as they are: 'ii. May or should unmarried persons marry and widows remarry? Answer. It is better not to, but there are circumstances parallel to these mentioned above, v.2, which may make it expedient for them (v.9)'.[38] The 'circumstances' for marriage in verse 9 are the following: 'if they cannot contain, let them marry: for it is better to marry than to burn'. Similarly, through Paul, Liddon argues that marriage is a pragmatic necessity rather than a desirable state: 'There are three reasons, if necessary, for marriage, – i. procreation of the race; ii. the escape it affords from fornication; iii. Mutual comfort, – which are hinted at in our Marriage Service'.[39] In verse 27, Paul says, 'Art thou bound unto a wife? seek not to be loosed. Art thou loosed from a wife? seek not a wife'. Liddon paraphrases this in the following manner: 'everyone is to remain in, not change, his state (27)'.[40] Liddon's choice of words recalls the doctrine of reserve, for 'to remain in' an unchanged state is to emulate the discipline and self-containment of which celibacy is a symbol and a practice.

Paul develops a more affirmative view of marriage in his letter to the Ephesians, wherein marriage signifies the unity between Christ and the church:

> For we are members of his body, of his flesh, and of his bones. For this cause shall a man leave his father and mother, and shall be joined unto his wife, and they two shall be one flesh. This is a great mystery: but I speak concerning Christ and the church.[41]

The idea that 'two shall be one flesh' reiterates one of his most positive messages about marriage in 1 Corinthians: 'for two, saith he, shall be one flesh'.[42]

The notion that 'two shall be one flesh' underlies Hopkins' concept of marriage to Christ, an idea he held even before his conversion. In 'He hath abolish'd the old drouth', composed between 22 and 25 July 1864 (*Journals*, 32), during which time Liddon was still lecturing on 1 Corinthians and had three months to conclude, Hopkins presents the image of wheat sheaved with Christ: 'We shall be sheavèd with one band / In harvest and in garnering' (lines 14–15). The 'one band' tying the harvested wheat symbolises the wedding ring. This wedding 'band' reifies, in the words of 1 Corinthians 6:16–17, the union of two beings into 'one flesh' and 'one spirit'. It also foreshadows the 'fást bínd' in 'At the Wedding March'. Another prefiguration is the act of turning to Christ at the wedding ceremony. The speaker addresses Christ immediately before the reference to being 'sheavèd with one band' and says,

> We meet together you and I,
> Meet in one acre of land,
> And I will turn my looks to you,
> And you shall meet me with reply,
> We shall be sheavèd with one band… (Lines 10–14)

The meeting between the individual and Christ takes place 'in one acre of land', an intersubjective space of engagement.[43] The lovers' level of intimacy is measured by their degree of spatial proximity. This correlation between physical space and emotional attachment is supported by the rhymes 'land' and 'band', as well as the repetition of 'one' ('one band', 'one acre of land'). The turning of the speaker to the other, and vice versa, brings into being the mutual gaze that enacts their reciprocal love. This account of turning and meeting eyes is cleverly given in a chiasmus (lines 12 and 13), a device that performs the very gestures that Hopkins describes. Equally important is the fact that the act of turning is a motion that lifts the veil (or vail) that prevents the believer and Christ from seeing each other face to face: '"When [the heart of the people] shall turn to the Lord, the vail shall be taken away". This was the promise'.[44] Liddon cites this phrase, from Paul, in a sermon delivered on 15 May 1864, two months before the poem's composition. For the Tractarians, the veil was an image of divine reserve:

> To refer to figurative language, it is said, does not God 'deck Himself with light, like as with a garment?' Whereas this very expression conveys it; for does not a garment veil in some measure that which it clothes? is not the very light concealment? The revelations of God must ever be to mankind in one sense mysteries; whatever He makes known, opens to view far more which we know not.[45]

God's 'garment' at once conceals what it discloses. God extends a partition between himself and humanity, just as in the Old Testament a veil stands between the people and the Ark housed within the Holy of Holies. The parting of his veil would be a crucial part of the marriage ceremony.

The veil, however, is not parted. The speaker of 'He hath abolish'd the old drouth' can only look forward to the vow exchange. While he and Christ are said to meet at this very moment ('We meet together you and I'), the acts indicating the completion of the ceremony are given in the future tense: 'I *will*', 'And you *shall*', 'We *shall* be'. The speaker is caught at the brink of the turning, the gazing and the binding. In spite of the distance crossed, and as close as they are to each other, the veil of division continues to rest between them. The Tractarian doctrine of reserve could not satisfy Hopkins' desire for emotional expression and the depiction of celibate marriage the way his later allegiance to Roman Catholicism would.

Virgin Marriage and the Society of Jesus

Hopkins made the decision to become a Jesuit in 1868, two years after his conversion to Roman Catholicism. His resolve to enter the religious life would enable him to practice lifelong virginity within the ideals of marriage and fidelity to Christ. Through his marriage to Christ, Hopkins would offer his virginity as a means of maintaining it. This understanding that one's virginity can be given to Christ in marriage parallels the example of Thecla who offers her virginity to Christ upon her conversion. Her virginity would have been lost upon her marriage to a man, but in giving herself to Christ it is retained. Hence, virginity offered to Christ is a gift that by its taking is not altered, and on these grounds is returned intact. In the marriage to Christ, virginity is both given and taken, but it cannot be lost.

Hopkins sought to serve the two masters of virginity and marriage by merging his ideals of the two. We see this at work in a poem that survives in two versions under different but related names, 'The Habit of Perfection' and 'The Kind Betrothal'. The earliest version of 'The Habit of Perfection' dates from 18–19 January 1866, six months before his final resolve to become a Catholic on 18 July. Reworked extensively following his entry into the novitiate in September 1868, it is the later version, 'The Kind Betrothal' (1870–1), that appears in *The Poetical Works of Gerard Manley Hopkins*.[46] With each subsequent version, Hopkins demonstrates his increasing idealisation of the religious life. If betrothal is the novitiate, marriage takes place when the novice makes his or her final vows. 'The Habit of Perfection' and 'The Kind Betrothal' both conclude with mention of the 'bride', the 'spouse', and either a 'marriage feast' ('The Habit of Perfection', line 25) or a 'wedding' ('The Kind Betrothal', line 26). In each version, the final stanza begins with the phrase 'And Poverty be thou the bride' (line 25), which alludes not only to the allegorical figure of Lady Poverty, the bride of both Christ and St Francis of Assisi, but also to the religious vow of poverty made alongside those of chastity and obedience.[47]

Chastity is evident in the speaker's wish for water over the lushness of wine: 'Palate, the hutch of Like and Lust, / Wish now no tasty rinse of wine; / The flask will be so clear' ('The Kind Betrothal', lines 13–15). Chastity *within* marriage is represented by the bride's production of the spouse's 'lily-coloured clothes' ('The Habit of Perfection', line 27) and 'lily-coloured wear' ('The Kind Betrothal', line 27). The 'lily-coloured' attire refers to the white flower that represents virginity. For example, Thecla is compared favourably to Mary and is described as 'next whitest after Mary's own' ('St. Thecla', line 4).[48] The reference to the spinning of 'wedding weeds' (in 'A Kind Betrothal', line 26) is also reminiscent of Thecla's 'weeds' of virginity and betrothal. The garment, to be presented as a wedding gift to the spouse, provides a double representation of the virginity of the spouses and the celibate nature of their marriage. The lily resolves the tension between virginity and marriage; in addition to virginity, it represents chastity within marriage. Hence, according to the newly converted Hopkins in a letter to his father, Joseph is '[Mary's] spouse...the lily of chastity' (*Further Letters*, 94).[49] This description recalls the Catholic belief that Joseph's marriage to the Virgin Mary was celibate.

Hopkins' declaration of marriage to Christ was neither antiquated nor eccentric in the Catholic circles he frequented. Coventry Patmore praised virginity's role in divine union in his *Unknown Eros*, a volume that, as we have seen, Hopkins admired. Ernest Fontana argues that in the poem 'The Contract', Patmore

> imagines that prelapsarian erotic desire did not lead to genital contact between Eve and Adam but instead to a heightened state of unconsummated virginal desire. Eve figures her relation to Adam in terms of the metaphor of Venus illuminated by the power of the sun's light. Patmore's metaphor suggests here intense somatic reciprocity without actual bodily contact.[50]

While the planetary bodies in the poem are separated by space, they nonetheless interact through the interplay of reflected light, the uniting qualities of which I discussed in Chapter One. The union of marriage and virginity is maintained in 'Eros and Psyche', wherein Psyche calls on Eros to 'Kiss me again, thy Wife and Virgin too!'[51] As with 'The Contract', 'Eros and Psyche', according to John Maynard, attempts to realise 'the power of virgin union with God'.[52] Maynard argues that '*Deliciæ Sapientiæ De Amore*' (The Wise Delights of Love) similarly follows Patmore's effort 'to find some way to describe God's love-making with humans'.[53] The speaker declares himself 'a beggar by the Porch / Of the glad Palace of Virginity'.[54] His assertion that 'Love makes the life to be / A fount perpetual of virginity' suggests the 'revirginalising' of believers in the afterlife.[55] Finally, the speaker declares that the lovers of God, 'The husband of the heavens', will be 'clad / With the bridal robes of ardour virginal'.[56] Several of Patmore's poems, therefore, extol love's intensity or 'ardour' within virgin marriage. In fact, Maynard speculates that the poems praising virgin marriage in the *Unknown Eros* were much inspired by Patmore's daughter Emily and her increasing interest in the religious life.[57]

Following his entry into the Society of Jesus, Hopkins' ideas of virgin marriage to Christ were most likely furthered, reinforced and validated by his contact with Father Peter Gallwey. Gallwey's *Convent Life and England in the 19th Century* was read in the refectory at Manresa House, Roehampton, in March 1869, while Hopkins was still a novice.[58] Gallwey was Hopkins' Novice Master (*Journals*, 191) and treated the young man with great consideration and kindness (404n191). A dynamic preacher, several of Gallwey's other sermons were read in the refectory during Hopkins' training.[59] As we shall see, Gallwey praises marriage in *Convent Life*, so as to defend and celebrate the celibate religious life:

> [W]as it not Christ Jesus our Lord who stood beyond the Jordan and discoursed concerning marriage and virginity? – S. Mat. xix. Was it not He who…enjoining that as now in His own person the divinity was wedded for ever to one body and one soul, so too henceforth in the new created world, the bond of marriage should be…an indissoluble bond between one and one, which God joins and no man may put asunder?[60]

Marriage is, as it was between Adam and Eve, a union 'between one and one',[61] just as Christ's incarnation is the union of divinity and flesh in one body. Gallway conflates the Incarnation with Christ's assertion that marriage is the 'cleav[ing]' of two people in 'one flesh'.[62] Gallwey acknowledges Paul's allusion to the union of two in 'one flesh' when he says, 'let the Apostle St. Paul interpret his Master's teaching'.[63] Moreover, Gallwey refers to Paul's arguments on marriage in 1 Corinthians and concludes that marriage is for Paul 'a holy state'.[64]

Gallwey's ultimate intention, however, is to assert that human marriage is 'not the only state nor the highest state appointed by Divine Providence for man'.[65] He argues that religious celibacy is not an escape from marriage but a legitimate form of union. The vow of celibacy marks a valid expression of love between a person and Christ. While the express purpose of his sermon is to defend the vow of celibacy taken by nuns, the fact that it was read in the refectory at Manresa House testifies to its direct relevance to the Jesuits:

> [I]f the Convent vow were abolished, both Christ our Lord and the Christian soul that wishes to be His Spouse, would have reason to complain that human love is allowed a privilege and a stability not granted to the Divine love which unites our Blessed Saviour and His Spouses. He loves as no man has loved. He has proved His desire of being loved intimately by giving his body and blood to be man's food; to say nothing of other countless proofs. If the constant unchanging affection of the heart is prized by man, so is it dear to Christ our Lord. He does not let mother, or wife, or father, or husband, or brother, or sister, or friend on earth boast of loving more than He does.[66]

The vow of celibacy is intertwined with the vow of marriage. Celibacy expresses the soul's desire to unite with Christ in legitimate marriage. Like Hopkins, Gallwey asserts that Christ is the greatest lover, who 'loves as no man has loved'. To refuse the union between the soul and Christ would be to presuppose the unworthiness of Christ's supreme love. The wish of a person to marry him should not be denied, just as it is not denied between humans. Indeed, Gallwey argues that Christ desires to be loved and wedded: 'He will not be content that those who love Him shall not be permitted to pledge to Him by vow, if they so please, an affection as lasting as married love'.[67]

In Memoriam, Same-Sex Desire and the Song of Songs

In the Introduction and throughout this chapter, I have spoken of the Song of Songs and its place in Hopkins' thought. In this section and the next I expand on the topic, given that the biblical text provided Hopkins and his contemporaries with an important source to validate celibate marriage. Despite the importance of the Song of Songs throughout the history of Christianity, research into its significance in the Victorian era is surprisingly scarce, and this is no different in Hopkins studies. This paucity is surprising, given that James Finn Cotter, who explores the influence of the Song of Songs in 'The Wreck of the Deutschland', notes that the allegorical exegesis of the Song of Songs 'remained live in Hopkins' day as an integral part of nineteenth-century spirituality in seminary training'.[68] The Song of Songs also played a role in poetry written by Protestant poets, such as Dixon and Dante Gabriel Rossetti, whose poetry Hopkins admired and copied by hand.[69] Tractarians such as Christina Rossetti composed religious poems infused with an eroticism linked to the tradition of the Song of Songs.[70]

Like Cotter, Aakanksha J. Virkar looks at the Song of Songs and its related commentary in 'The Wreck of the Deutschland'. Virkar provides a succinct summary of the relationship between the Song of Songs, marriage and the Incarnation in Hopkins' writings.

> For Hopkins as for the [early] Fathers, the Song is a nuptial hymn to be read in the terms of that baptismal union set out by St. Paul in Ephesians: Christ and Church are united in the washing of water by the Word (Ephesians 5.26–32); in baptism is continued the nuptial union achieved first in the Incarnation. These are the grounds by which commentaries on the Song would come to be linked with the devotion to the Sacred Heart of Christ; as the sacramental streams that flowed from Christ's wounded body directed attention to their interior source, a parallel was seen between the Church formed from the side of Christ and the dove that famously nestles in the clefts of the rock (Song 2.14), in the wounded heart of Christ.[71]

In discussing the 'nuptial union', Virkar draws the reader's attention to Hopkins' preoccupation with Christ's suffering as the supreme indication of his humanity and love. Describing the moment when Christ's side was pierced on the cross, Hopkins says, 'The sacred body and the sacred heart seemed waiting for an opportunity of discharging themselves and testifying their total devotion of themselves to the cause of man' (*Sermons*, 255).[72] This emphasis on Christ's suffering reinforces the importance of the body – of ours and of Christ's – to the utterance and comprehension of longing and its fulfilment.

Both suffering and longing provide a common language between Christ and the individual in their mutual journeys towards union. Christ's wounded heart has a parallel in the believer's own passion. The body suffers the pain of death in order to gain eternal life. Symbolically, we drown in baptismal waters in order to become members of the church, which is the bride of Christ. Furthermore, in order to grasp love, the heart becomes vulnerable to the pain of yearning and the possibility of heartbreak.[73] A believer will submit to all these hardships of the body – and the heart – to be with Christ. 'Hopkins proffers a theology of renewed Incarnations, Christ reborn in the heart', argues Virkar.[74] The erotic imagery of the hand coming through the door hole 'is understood by Christian commentators to symbolize the dwelling of the word; it is a motif of Christ's descent, with the house representing human life'.[75] The body is like a house and the door is its opening, the site of possible exchange between the private and the public, between the lover and the beloved.[76] Christ enters the open door of the heart to consummate his marriage with the bride.[77]

One of the most famous poems of the era, Alfred Tennyson's *In Memoriam*, offers perhaps a surprising, but nonetheless appropriate, starting point for my discussion of the Song of Songs in Hopkins' poetry. First published in 1850, *In Memoriam* 'made the celebration of intense male friendship one of the most prominent literary themes of the century'.[78] The elegy famously celebrates and elevates Tennyson's romantic friendship with Arthur Henry Hallam, who, at the time of his unexpected death on the continent, was engaged to Tennyson's sister Emily. On one level, this engagement plays a role in the depiction of a wedding in the Epilogue. At a more profound level, the nuptial imagery and depictions elsewhere of heterosexual lovers stand in for Tennyson's enduring love for the departed Hallam. In one section, Tennyson waits in anguish outside his dead friend's house:

> Dark house, by which once more I stand
>   Here in the long unlovely street,
>   Doors, where my heart was used to beat
> So quickly, waiting for a hand,
>
> A hand that can be clasp'd no more –
>   Behold me, for I cannot sleep,
>   And like a guilty thing I creep
> At earliest morning to the door.
>
> He is not here; but far away
>   The noise of life begins again,
>   And ghastly through the drizzling rain
> On the bald street breaks the blank day. (Section 7)[79]

If the human body is like a house then the 'Dark house' is like a corpse, a notion reinforced in the next section, in which Tennyson compares himself to 'a happy lover' who approaches a door

> To look on her that loves him well
> ……………………………..
> And learns her gone and far from home;
>
> He saddens, all the magic light
>   Dies off at once from bower and hall,
>   And all the place is dark. (Section 8)

Given that the open door can be a site of meeting and exchange, in section 7 the closed door signals the division between this world and the next, between the living and the dead, between the lover and the beloved. The dead cannot open the door and the living cannot enter.[80] Impotent in the face of loss, Tennyson can only express his distress at the absence of, and his inability to touch, the other.

James Krasner argues that the hand and door imagery in sections 7 and 8 has parallels with Song of Songs 3 and 5. He believes these biblical passages 'deal with the absence or disappearance of the beloved and contain many of the same elements as [section 7]'.[81] Krasner adds that in the Song of Songs 5:2–6, 'the beloved comes to the door briefly then disappears, forcing the narrator to search for him through the bleak urban landscape'.[82]

> I sleep, but my heart waketh: it is the voice of my beloved that knocketh, saying, Open to me, my sister, my love, my dove, my undefiled: for my head is filled with dew, and my locks with the drops of the night.
>
> I have put off my coat; how shall I put it on? I have washed my feet; how shall I defile them?
>
> My beloved put in his hand by the hole of the door, and my bowels were moved for him.
>
> I rose up to open to my beloved; and my hand dropped with myrrh, and my fingers with sweet smelling myrrh, upon the handles of the lock.
>
> I opened to my beloved; but my beloved had withdrawn himself, and was gone; my soul failed when he spake: I sought him, but I could not find him; I called him, but he gave me no answer.[83]

Like the lover in the Song of Songs who reaches out for the hand of the other in the dark, Tennyson searches for the absent hand of his beloved Hallam in the 'Dark house'. While the positioning of the pair is reversed in Tennyson's poem, so that it is the lover who stands outside the door, echoes of the Song of Songs are nonetheless present.

Tennyson's appeal to the Song of Songs conveys his passionate feelings of loss and sorrow. The allusion to a biblical text lends weight both to the sanctity of his relationship with Hallam and to his immense grief at its premature end. The deeper the passion, the stronger is the pain over its loss: 'I slept and woke with pain, / I almost wished no more to wake', he says of the first Christmas Eve following Hallam's death (section 28). Even though the relationship is rendered chaste, the poem is strikingly (homo) erotic in spirit, expressing as it does the deep ache of one man for another. Sections 7 and 8 memorialise a love that is equal parts platonic, erotic, sacred and marriage-like. Passion takes precedence and its intensity is clearly evident. Indeed, because death takes away any possibility (and associated anxiety) of physical consummation, it enables the (loftier) emotions to be felt and expressed. In the genre of the elegy, Tennyson is able to declare what would have been difficult to utter elsewhere – that Hallam was, and remains, 'The centre of a world's desire' (section 64), the beginning and the end of Tennyson's affections.[84] Christopher Craft believes the anxiety that often accompanies a reading of *In Memoriam* is attributable to the poem's unmistakable homoeroticism. As a case in point, he cites an anonymous review that appeared in *The Times* on 28 November 1851, and which is now commonly attributed to Hopkins' father, Manley. Hopkins senior, according to Craft, 'complained of the elegy's erotic metaphorics, its "strange manner of address to a man, even though he be dead." A "defect," this reviewer noted, "which has painfully come out as often as we take up the volume, is the tone of – may we say so! – amatory tenderness."'[85] Manley Hopkins added that 'Shakespeare may be considered the founder of this style in English', alluding to the bard's homoerotic sonnets.[86]

It is with 'amatory tenderness' that Tennyson waits for Hallam on the other side of the door. The oft-repeated image of hands and the expressed longing for reciprocal touch expresses a deep wanting. As we have seen, he stands outside the door, 'waiting for a hand / A hand that can be clasp'd no more' (section 7), 'hands so often clasped in mine' (section 10). The trope of touching hands had obvious resonance with Tennyson; it appears in the elegiac 'Break, Break, Break', which he began a year after Hallam's death:

> And the stately ships go on
>   To their haven under the hill;
> But O for the touch of a vanished hand,
>   And the sound of a voice that is still! (Lines 9–12)

Without the sight, touch and 'voice of the beloved',[87] the senses are bereft and the loss of the 'vanished hand' appears absolute. The absence marks the speaker, whose grief is accompanied by the loss of his voice:

> Break, break, break,
>   On thy cold gray stones, O Sea!
> I would that my tongue could utter
>   The thoughts that arise in me. (Lines 1–4)

Likewise, we witness the tongue's inability to utter the deepest thoughts, heartache and longing in *In Memoriam*, wherein Tennyson draws a parallel between verbal fluency, the flow of tears and the movement of water:

> The Wye is hushed nor moved along,
>   And hushed my deepest grief of all,
>   When filled with tears that cannot fall,
> I brim with sorrow drowning song.

> The tide flows down, the wave again
>   Is vocal in its wooded walls;
>   My deeper anguish also falls,
> And I can speak a little then. (Section 19)

Utterance, and by extension hearing, is connected with touch and, more generally, the senses:

> Descend, and touch, and enter; hear
>   The wish too strong for words to name;
>   That in this blindness of the frame
> My Ghost may feel that thine is near. (Section 93)

The body's inability to reach out to the dead with voice and hand is comparable to visual blindness. Tennyson calls on the spirit of the dead man to 'enter' a space where the dead and the living, the spirit and the flesh, can meet and 'touch'. Craft refers to the section's 'desperate mode of erotic address'.[88] Endeavouring to recover the 'unconventional desire'[89] in the poem, he critiques conventional typological interpretations. Craft believes such orthodox readings compete with, suppress and silence the elegy's language of homoerotic desire:

> A perfectly conventional trope of typological interpretation enables Tennyson to represent Hallam as a 'noble type / Appearing ere the times were ripe' (epilogue) – as, that is, a medial character whose death repeats the ontologically prior sacrifice of the other 'He that died' (84), and whose earthly presence had pointed to the superior consummation of a second coming.[90]

Craft believes that 'rush[ing] to the Christological or logocentric solution… fails to register the anxious and fluctuant interfusion of sexual desire and religious faith in a poem justly more famous for the quality of its oscillations than for the force of its closural affirmations'.[91] Soon after, he turns to a discussion of Tennyson's use of the hand: 'the Christocentric impulse works its consolatory changes largely through the extended trope by which Christ's hand comes to substitute for Hallam's own; the oft-repeated images of "clasp," "touch," and "embrace" are all local variations of this trope'.[92] He notes that the squeeze of the hand 'as a multivalent site of homosocial communion is anything but anomalous in Victorian literature, although the extraordinary repetitiousness in its use of this figure may well be so'.[93] For Craft, 'Christ's otherwise redundant presence is fathered by Hallam's absence, since it is the loss of Hallam's hand and Hallam's embrace that alone motivates the re/pair/ational touch of Christ'.[94]

I believe, like Craft, that *In Memoriam* demonstrates a certain anxiety about one man's passion for another. I would argue, however, that, by its very anxiety, the poem houses ambivalence, ambiguity and, therefore, another voice. After all, how would we know that grief and convention had silenced 'The wish too strong for words to name' (section 93) if we had not glimpsed this 'wish' and known it could speak? How could Tennyson have described himself as 'widow'd' by Hallam's death (section 9) had he not considered himself married to his friend – even if he might have realised he was wife the very moment he understood himself to be a widow? The poem validates 'amatory tenderness' by associating the love with religious feeling and the Song of Songs. The religious element does not so much diminish the passion it depicts, as Craft suggests, but serves to legitimise and elevate it, in much the same way that Oscar Wilde would appeal to the authority of the Bible and Plato to defend the love between men.[95] Reconciliation between the living and dead, between the conventional and unconventional, is represented in the touching of hands in section 119. This section is a typological repetition of section 7, which, as we have seen, alludes to the Song of Songs:

> Doors, where my heart was used to beat
>   So quickly, not as one that weeps
>   I come once more; the city sleeps;
> I smell the meadow in the street;
>
> I hear a chirp of birds; I see
>   Betwixt the black fronts long-withdrawn
>   A light blue lane of early dawn,
> And think of early days and thee,
>
> And bless thee, for thy lips are bland,
>   And bright the friendship of thine eye;
>   And in my thoughts with scarce a sigh
> I take the pressure of thine hand.

Tennyson again finds himself at Hallam's door, waiting for the hand. But something is different: it appears the door is open and he can 'take the pressure of [Hallam's] hand'. The smell of the meadow, the sound of the birds, and the sight of the dawn herald his friend's presence. Like the city, the senses – note the actions, 'I smell', 'I hear', 'I see' – are given new life by the 'early dawn' and memories of 'early days'. Healing is taking place through this reunion between the men. The handshake is gentle, tender, a mutual 'pressure'. While Craft is clearly disappointed that the 'thumpingly symbolic heterosexual marriage that so famously closes – or almost closes – the elegy…quite obviously leaves the elegy's two central lovers still halved by desire, still unwed',[96] we can see that the images of life, the sensuous language and the touching of hands in section 119 point to an unconventional union.

For Craft, the absence of sexual intimacy signifies a lack, but I would argue that in the absence of transgressive intimacy, something subversive takes place. By invoking typology and the Song of Songs, the section describes a form of same-sex marriage. In the Trinity and Lincoln manuscripts of section 93, Tennyson calls on Hallam to wed him. Instead of the phrase 'Descend, touch, and enter', he exclaims, 'Stoop soul and touch me: wed me'.[97] In stark contrast to the expansive vision in the preceding and following sections, wherein Tennyson considers the arguments of science and the nature of the world, the events of section 119 contract to the intimate and personal. The seemingly random sandwiching (or concealment) of this section between ontological speculation and scientific revelation paradoxically serves to set it apart. Likewise, the touching of hands, apparently innocuous, is in fact momentous in its fulfilment of Tennyson's longing. Nonetheless – and Craft would have reason to be disappointed – this marriage seems only to take place when the possibility of physical consummation is no longer. Just as conventional marriage signals a transition from one life stage to another, same-sex marriage in Tennyson's poem provides unequivocal proof that the beloved has moved on from this life to the next. The marriage made in heaven is possible because Hallam lies waiting beyond the threshold, and his bodily presence remains simply and forever a memory in Tennyson's mind: '*And in my thoughts* with scarce a sigh / I take the pressure of thine hand'.

Unlike his father, Hopkins admired the 'personal feeling' contained in *In Memoriam*. As he tells Dixon, '[Tennyson] will be one of our greatest poets… When the inspiration is genuine, arising from personal feeling, as in *In Memoriam*, a divine work, he is at his best' (*Dixon*, 24).[98] Hopkins felt the influence of Tennyson; Saville observes that Hopkins' undergraduate poem '*Nondum*' contains echoes of *In Memoriam*.[99] Like Tennyson in his elegy, Hopkins grapples with the absence of the male object of desire, but in the sense in that, unlike Hallam, Christ is not dead and, while incarnate, is not immediately present in the flesh. The degree to which the desire for Christ either parallels or is propelled by his attraction to men such as Digby Mackworth Dolben is something I will discuss below. While Richard Dellamora argues that Tennyson uses Christ to cloak or triangulate his passion for the deceased Hallam,[100] for Hopkins, Christ is the chief object of desire. In crucial ways, Christ is to Hopkins what Hallam is to Tennyson. Hopkins seeks the hand of God, just as Tennyson longs to hold Hallam's hand: 'and dost thou touch me afresh? / Óver agáin I féel thy finger and find thée' ('The Wreck of the Deutschland', stanza 1).

In finding the pressure of Christ's hand, Hopkins experiences the reciprocity of touch. The first stanza of 'The Wreck of the Deutschland' suggests that this touch re-enacts the divine handiwork at the beginning of time, when God created the first man. Tennyson describes it thus: 'out of the darkness came the hands / That reach through nature, moulding men' (*In Memoriam*, section 124). For Tennyson and Hopkins alike, parting does not diminish love; it simply increases it. Thus, 'lovely Death' ('The Wreck of the Deutschland', stanza 25) transforms the body of Christ into something more majestic, more desirable:

> In his Passion all this strength was spent, this lissomness crippled, this beauty wrecked, this majesty beaten down. But now it is more than all restored, and for myself I make no secret I look forward with eager desire to seeing the matchless beauty of Christ's body in the heavenly light. (*Sermons*, 36)[101]

If death separates the living from the dead, it also brings them together 'in the heavenly light', in eternal union. And so, the tall, dying nun in 'The Wreck of the Deutschland' calls emphatically on 'her lóver' (stanza 25) to reach out and take her: '"O Christ, Christ, come quickly": / The cross to her she calls Christ to her, christens her wild-worst Best' (stanza 24).

Dolben, Same-Sex Desire and the Song of Songs

The passionate friendship depicted in *In Memoriam* was not unlike many that flourished at Oxford, Cambridge and schools for boys. Dellamora describes the relationships cultivated by Hopkins and his Oxford contemporaries thus:

> He and they lived in an intense atmosphere, based in the idealization of romantic friendships in their earlier schooling and focused on religious discussion, shared prayer, and joint observance of ritual. This environment stimulated homoerotic feeling, valorized it, and provided it with a convenient alibi. Friendships in Christ also provided a defense against a specifically sexual expression of desire by stimulating intimacy in a somewhat disembodied way.[102]

Saville is in agreement: 'Victorian Oxford was idealized at mid-century as a haven for young men to pursue an idyllic contemplative life in the company of intimate friends'.[103] She argues that Hopkins' experience at Balliol 'was very much characterized by close friendships whose intimacy was intensified by shared religious and intellectual interests'.[104] Frederick S. Roden writes that 'an exploration of Hopkins' homoeroticism must begin with his religious friendships'.[105]

With these remarks in mind, I turn to Hopkins' friendship with Digby Mackworth Dolben, who, though not an undergraduate but an Etonian four years Hopkins' junior, was a cousin of Hopkins' fellow Oxonian, Robert Bridges. It was Bridges who introduced the two in February 1865, the only time Hopkins and Dolben would meet. While the details are scant, and derive mostly from Hopkins' cryptic confessional notes,[106] the majority of Hopkins scholars agree that the poet was erotically attracted to Dolben.[107] The two men began an epistolary friendship until Dolben's untimely drowning at the age of 19. Intellectually and spiritually, the two had several things in common: literature, particularly poetry, and a growing interest in Roman Catholicism, religious ritual, celibacy and asceticism. They exchanged poems and ideas. After Dolben's death, Hopkins wrote to Bridges, declaring, 'I looked forward to meeting Dolben and his being a Catholic more than to anything' (*Bridges*, 16).[108] He immediately distances himself, however, from any assertion of feeling surrounding the death and, by extension, from any strong attachment to Dolben: 'At the same time from never having met him but once I find it difficult to realise his death or feel as if it were anything to me' (16). And yet, a few sentences later his inquisitiveness betrays a depth of emotion: 'Some day I hope to see Finedon and the place where he was drowned too. Can you tell me where he was buried? – at Finedon, was it not? If you have letters from him will you let me see them some day?' (17). The burning questions and the desire to see Dolben's home, the place of his death, his final resting place and his letters suggest an undeniable sense of loss at Dolben's passing.

Dolben's beauty and mind had certainly attracted Hopkins; in the letter to Bridges he says, 'there can very seldom have happened the loss of so much beauty (in body and mind and life) and of the promise of still more as there has been in this case' (*Bridges*, 16–17). As I have discussed elsewhere, Hopkins admired beauty in the physical world, in active bodies, robust minds, and the life lived ethically.[109] He felt an erotic pull towards men, but he was also devout, strongly devoted to the celibate life and to Christ. The bulk of his erotic impulses reflect this devotion. 'There met in Jesus Christ all things that can make men lovely and loveable', he declares in his 'Christ, Our Hero' sermon (*Sermons*, 35). 'In his body he was most beautiful… He was the greatest genius that ever lived. You know what genius is, brethren – beauty and perfection in the mind' (35, 36). Consider, too, the rapturous eroticisation of male energy and Christ in 'Hurrahing in Harvest':

> Summer énds now; now, bárbarous in béauty, the stóoks ríse
> Around; up above, what wind-walks! what lovely behaviour
> Of sílk-sack clóuds! has wilder, wilful-wávier
> Méal-drift moulded ever and melted acróss skíes?

I wálk, I líft up, Í líft úp heart, éyes,
Down all that glory in the heavens to glean our Saviour;
And, éyes, héart, what looks, what lips yet gáve you á
Rápturous love's greeting of realer, of rounder replies?

And the azurous hung hills are his wórld-wíelding shoulder
Majestic – as a stallion stalwart, very-violet-sweet! –
These things, these things were here and but the beholder
Wánting; whích two whén they ónce méet,
The héart réars wíngs bóld and bolder
And hurls for him, O half hurls earth for him off under his feet.

Like lovers, the erotic comes together with the sacred. Each meets the other with such force that the syllables strain in the enjambment, 'what lips yet gáve you á / Rápturous love's greeting'. The astonishing placement of stresses renders the reader a little breathless. The encounter between heaven and earth, flesh and spirit, man and Christ, is as compelling as the poem's comparison of hills – by metaphor and simile – to a muscular, majestic shoulder and a violet, stalwart stallion.[110] The word 'majestic' also finds its way into the abovementioned sermon: 'picture him,…in his bearing how majestic, how strong and yet how lovely and lissome in his limbs' (*Sermons*, 36). By asking the congregation to 'picture' Christ in their minds, we again see how vision is important to Hopkins. In 'Hurrahing in Harvest', the beholder desires what he sees; looking – the stimulation of the eyes – is an erotic experience.[111] Seeing is a kind of touching, as I mentioned in Chapter One, and the beholder's gaze expresses his 'Wánting', his yearning to touch the other. Through the act of greeting, and indeed, of 'Rápturous love's greeting', the gaze-as-touch becomes mutual, reciprocal, erotically charged.

While a degree of Hopkins' passion for Christ might well have been ignited by his same-sex desires and the sight of beautiful male bodies and minds in action, it would be difficult for us to deny that he loved Christ – erotically, emotionally, spiritually – above all others. Within the sphere of his spiritual life, the bulk of Hopkins' erotic energies thrived and, like the 'bóld and bólder' heart, took wing. After all, the word 'Rápturous', from 'rapture', connotes the bliss of religious ecstasy and transport. As in the poem, this eroticism forms a genuine religious and romantic experience, replete with the trajectory of *eros*: interest, hesitation, a reaching out, rapture. Given this, the religious dimension of Hopkins' attraction to Dolben should not be ignored. White asserts, 'Dolben's flamboyant leanings towards Rome incarnated Hopkins's suppressed spiritual inclination'.[112] The twin attractions – Hopkins' attraction to Dolben and Dolben's attraction to Rome – were crucial in quickening

Hopkins' movement towards Roman Catholicism. Margaret Johnson argues the following:

> [He] alone of Hopkins' poetic acquaintances was most nearly contemporary, in terms both of relative age and of religious affiliation: only his early death at age nineteen prevented Dolben from being received into the Roman Catholic church. His poetry therefore covers the same time, and the same shifts in belief, that Hopkins' does.[113]

As we have seen, Hopkins praises *In Memoriam* for the fact that its inspiration arises from personal feeling. No doubt he was attracted to Dolben's verse for the same reason. Bridges, editor of Dolben's (and, incidentally, Hopkins') first edition of poetry, locates the roots of Dolben's emotionally naked poetry in his fondness for the maudlin verse of the 'Romanized clergyman',[114] Frederick William Faber. Further, while Bridges describes himself and Dolben as 'Puseyites', he also notes their poetic differences:

> Our instinctive attitudes towards poetry were very dissimilar, he regarded it from the emotional, and I from the artistic side; and he was thus of a much intenser poetic temperament than I… I should say that he liked poetry on account of the power that it had of exciting his valued emotions, and he may perhaps have recognised it as the language of faith. What had led me to poetry was the inexhaustible satisfaction of form, the magic of speech, lying as it seemed to me in the masterly control of the material.[115]

The distinction Bridges draws between his poetry and Dolben's is that which exists, in his opinion, between form and feeling. Readers of Bridges' poetry will note his attention to form and his 'masterly control of the material'; they will note his cool style, his withholding of emotional display, his reserve. In contrast, there is little in the tone of Dolben's poetry to suggest such modesty. While celibacy features in several poems such as '*Pro Castitate*' (For Chastity), in which the speaker calls on God to 'Give me, Give me only / Perfect Chastity' (lines 7–8), many of his writings are effusive displays, emotional unveilings that one might associate with Hopkins' later works. Like Hopkins, Dolben (about two months before his drowning in June 1867) wrote to Newman to discuss the possibility of his conversion.[116] Even so, one cannot imagine the pen of Newman composing the following piece of euphoric verse:

> As pants the hart for forest streams
>   When wandering wearily,
> Across the burning desert sands,
>   So pant I, Lord, for Thee!

Sweetest Jesu, Thou art He
   Whom my whole heart desires.
To love Thee, O! the ecstasy,
   The rapture, and the joy! ('Vocation', lines 83–90).

Likewise, the young poet simply cannot contain his excitement at the thought of seeing and touching Christ and his open Wounds. In 'The Prodigal's Benediction', a poem published in 1864 in a High Church periodical called the *Union Review*, the speaker proclaims to Christ,

I cannot thank Thee, I can only say,
'Take, dearest Lord, this crushed and bleeding heart,
'And lay it in Thy hand, Thy piercèd hand,
'That Thine atoning blood may mix with mine,
'Till I and my Belovèd are all one'. (Lines 58–62)

The arresting imagery, reminiscent of medieval visions, is deeply (and literally) visceral. As a result, the spilling forth of the otherwise hidden and internal invests the scene with striking emotional immediacy. Christ's skin is the veil that human hands have cut: 'Those tender hands [are] all rent with rugged nails' (line 18). When unbroken skin meets unbroken skin, touch is external, superficial. When skin is 'rent', the body discloses what it ordinarily withholds from the sight and touch of others. Through his wounds, Christ's body becomes open and his inward being revealed. His self-disclosure thus enables the sinner to touch the 'hidden Godhead' ('The Prodigal's Introit', line 48). When the blood from the 'piercèd hand' of Christ comes into contact with the bleeding and contrite heart of the believer, each of them touches the hidden parts of the other.

   In 'The Prodigal's Benediction', the altar of the Eucharistic sacrifice is also the altar at which the wedding ceremony takes place. The 'atoning blood' of Christ and the sinful blood of the speaker more than simply touch: they 'mix'. The merging of their blood makes the two 'all one'. The experience is for Dolben far from abhorrent. Instead, the confluence of blood simultaneously signals and enables virgin marriage. The poem unites the two categories that, according to Newman's poem 'Awe', cannot be reconciled: the sinner and the blood of Christ. In fact, Dolben's poem holds that sin – the cause of human separation from God – is the catalyst for reunion; it is sin that inflicts the wounds that allow for the blood of the sinner and the blood of Christ to merge. Blood from a wound holds the life of a person that can live and move within the heart of another. Blood, like the heart, is a symbol of love in Dolben's poetry. The bloodstream forms what he describes in 'A Letter' as 'the whole love-current of the human soul' (line 9). Whereas the blood may represent the sinner 'bent and rolled through fruitless ways' (line 10), it is nonetheless the very thing that draws him or her towards 'the ocean-love of Christ the Lord' (line 21). In 'The Prodigal's Benediction', the blood from the sinner's heart combines with the blood from the torn and opened veil ('the wounds of love')[117] and consummates the virgin marriage between Christ and the believer.

In several other passionate religious poems, Dolben alludes to the Song of Songs. Hopkins copied two of these, '*Brevi Tempore Magnum Perfecit Opus*' and '*Homo Factus Est*',[118] which he kept upon his entry into the novitiate. The first poem concerns virgin marriage and employs images from the Song of Songs:

> His life was in the Sanctuary, and like a fountain sealed
> He to the Master's eyes alone its height and depth revealed.
>
> Of that which in each motion spoke he seldom told in word,
> But on his face was written up the Secret of the Lord.
> ....
> We never heard him laugh aloud, we know he often wept,
> We think the Bridegroom sometimes stood beside him as he slept
>
> And set upon those virgin lips the signet of His Love,
> That any other touch but His they never should approve. (Lines 9–12, 17–20)

The image of the 'fountain sealed' is from the Song of Songs 4:12 and symbolises virginity.[119] The poem draws a link between virginity and fidelity; it is 'to the Master's eyes alone' that the protagonist's inner 'sanctuary' and 'sealed' life are revealed. Likewise, his 'virgin lips' are kept exclusively for the kiss of the bridegroom: 'any other touch but His they never should approve'. The protagonist's early death in May allows him to retain his chastity and youth and, furthermore, brings about his heavenly marriage with Christ. As the virgin bride of the 'Virgin born of Virgin' ('*Pro Castitate*', line 1), he and Christ ascend the heavenly stair to the 'Marriage and the Feast' (line 52).

In '*Homo Factus Est*', the themes of virginity and marriage are also conspicuous:

> Jesu, my Belovèd,
> Come to me alone,
> In Thy sweet embraces
> Make me all Thine own.

> By the quiet waters,
>   Sweetest Jesu, lead,
> 'Mid the virgin lilies,
>   Purest Jesu, feed.

The speaker's call for Christ to 'Come to me alone' suggests his desire for an intimate and exclusive relationship. Similarly, he wishes for Christ to 'Make me all thine own', a line that recalls the Song of Songs and the lover's declaration that 'My beloved is mine, and I am his: he feedeth among the lilies'.[120] Dolben's speaker both incorporates and furthers this reference when he asks Christ to 'lead' him and 'feed' him among the 'virgin lilies'.[121] The lilies provide an obvious sign of the couple's virgin marriage. Feeding alongside Christ allows the speaker to live in partnership with him, for the field that was Christ's, and on which he alone had fed, has become available to the bride. While the speaker may be considered masculine, he is also the bride. Taking this gender duality into account, we can see how the poem reverses the legal custom of property transference upon marriage, wherein the newly wedded bride surrenders the ownership of her property to her husband. In his poem, Christ's land is now also the bride's land. It has become their joint dwelling, the ground of their union.

The existence of the bride and groom on the same pastoral terrain is reminiscent of 'He hath abolish'd the old drouth', in which Christ and the individual 'Meet in one acre of land' and are 'sheavèd with one band'. The word 'one' is used to similar effect in 'The Wreck of the Deutschland'. In stanza 26, the speaker refers to Christ as 'the ónly one'. This expression not only foreshadows Hopkins' declaration that Christ is 'the only person that I am in love with' (*Bridges*, 66), it also recalls a phrase from the Song of Songs that describes the singularity and distinction of the bride in the eyes of her beloved: 'My dove, my undefiled is but one; she is *the only one* of her mother, she is the choice one of her that bare her'.[122] The 'undefiled' bride is not merely 'the only one' of her mother but also of the groom. Indeed, he addresses her as 'thou fairest among women'[123] and describes her as 'the lily among thorns',[124] phrases that set her apart from all others. In like manner, Hopkins was a firm believer in his marriage to Christ, 'the ónly one'.

Eros

In 'The Wreck of the Deutschland', the rain descends while the souls of the drowned nuns rise to reunite with Christ. Earlier, the speaker declares, 'I whirled out wings that spell / And fled with a fling of the heart to the heart of the Host. / My heart, but you were dovewinged, I can tell' (stanza 3). Cotter believes this reference to the dove alludes to the dove in the Song of Songs.[125] To his suggestion I would add the image of Eros from an earlier poem, 'Love Preparing to Fly'. This short poem, which begins, 'He play'd his wings as tho' for flight' (line 1), describes the god Eros immediately before and at the moment of flight. As we have seen, Eros is often associated with his beloved Psyche, and the two figures, by Hopkins' time, had come to allegorise God and the soul. Eros is love personified. Thus, the flight of the winged god is the expression of love at its fullest expansion and greatest impact. Anne Carson observes that, in classical Greek poetry, wings 'are the mechanism by which Eros swoops upon the unsuspecting lover to wrest control of his person and personality'.[126] Eros cannot be fought when his power is unleashed upon the lover, who consequently undergoes the effects of love, namely, the fluttering of the heart, the (metaphorical) sprouting of wings. For instance, when desire sweeps over Sappho in Fragment 31, she says '*eptoaisen*, which means something like "it puts the heart in my chest on wings" or "it makes my heart fly inside me"'.[127]

In 'The Windhover', a similar stirring of the heart occurs, though unaccompanied by the lover's loss of control. The speaker utters, 'My heart in hiding [is] / Stírred for a bird' (lines 7–8). This 'stir[ing]' of the heart attests to the existence of *eros*; as Hopkins declares of Christ, 'the one that I am in love with...stirs my heart' (*Bridges*, 66).[128] Under the influence of awakened feelings the heart undergoes perturbations and alterations of its calm and quiet rhythms, the steady beatings of which ordinarily go unnoticed and permit the heart to exist 'in hiding'.[129] In an early poem, 'The Elopement', the speaker utters, 'My heart irregularly shook, / I cried with my desire' (lines 9–10). In 'The Windhover', the breathtaking alliteration, irregular rhythm and metre correspond to the fervour of the heart's irregular quivering in excitation. Accordingly, the speaker's opening statement that he has 'caught this mórning morning's mínion, /...dapple-dáwn-drawn Falcon, in his riding' (lines 1–2) suggests not so much an act of grounding and restraining the bird 'in his riding'. Rather, it implies that it is the lover whose heart has 'caught' love and, thus, mastered the flight of Eros: 'My heart in hiding / Stírred for a bird, – the achieve of, the mástery of the thing!' (lines 7–8).

The winged soul features prominently in Plato's *Phaedrus*, which records a myth that the soul regenerates its wings in order to return to its original home. Carson argues that the provenance of Plato's myth of wings is the tale of Eros. 'Plato', she holds, 'takes the traditional wings of Eros and reimagines them'.[130] The Greek philosopher quotes from an alleged work by Homer, which puns on the name Eros and the word 'feather': 'Mortals call him Eros (love), / But the immortals call him Pteros (feathered dove), / Because the growing of feathers is a necessity to him'.[131] In Plato's myth, mortals once possessed the wings of immortality, but while the fallen soul has lost its wings, it remembers its home from time to time, for example, when it gazes upon beauty and falls in love.[132] This home is recoverable by means of the rejuvenated wings that will carry the exiled soul back to its origins. Rejuvenation can occur when the soul falls in love with 'any one having a godlike face or form, which is the expression of divine beauty'.[133] In other words, Plato equates the sprouting of wings with the act of falling in love. Carson explains, 'When you fall in love you feel all sorts of sensations inside you, painful and pleasant at once; it is your wings sprouting'.[134] Taking into account Plato's myth, the image of Eros and the dove of the Song of Songs, we see, then, that in 'The Wreck of the Deutschland', the heart in flight embodies the heart of the one who has fallen in love with Christ. The very sensations felt by the heart in love make possible the 'fling of the heart to the heart of the Host'. Thus, 'falling' in love with the divine other is not a 'fall' but an ascent towards redemption and marriage.

Chapter Three

CONCEPTION, PREGNANCY, BIRTH

Openness

Having looked at celibacy and marriage in the previous chapter, I now turn my attention to pregnancy. The pregnant body is full of potent significance; figuratively and literally it embodies what Anne Elvey calls 'hospitality, an openness to the other'.[1] Hopkins believed that by opening ourselves to Christ we make room for him to enter (in conception), to embrace (in pregnancy) and depart (in birth). The mother embraces the foetus within her uterus, while the foetus feels her as its second skin. Eve came out of the body of her husband Adam, but the Second Eve gave birth to her son, the Second Adam. By extension, the Second Eve, the Virgin Mary, is a mother to a legion of believers who, like her, conceive and give birth to her son. Thus, Christ is at once our son, brother and lover. This paradox rivals that of the Incarnation and Eucharist, in which God loved the world so much that he was willing to be conceived and born, to die and be consumed.

Hopkins understood that if Mary could conceive Christ through the intervention of the Holy Spirit, then it would be possible for others to do the same in their hearts. In his undated Latin hymn to Mary '*Ad Matrem Virginem*', Hopkins exalts and exhorts the woman who miraculously conceived, bore and gave birth to God incarnate:

> Teach me about Him,
> About the small sweet God.
>   How much did you love
> The One you conceived –
> Thing inconceivable! (Lines 3–7)[2]

The distinguishing feature of this hymn is that it does not reflect on Mary's conception of Christ alone; it explores also one's conception of Christ. We conceive Christ, not in the physical womb, but in the 'heart' (*cor*) (lines 12, 13). The heart in this instance alludes to the innermost and central part of me, to the soul. As Hopkins declares in a sermon on the Sacred Heart, 'in all these [figurative] expressions what we call heart is not the piece of flesh so called, not the great bloodvessel only but the thoughts of the mind that vessel seems to harbour and the feelings of the soul to which it beats' (*Sermons*, 102).³ Reference to Christ's conception in the heart follows the first mention of Mary's pregnancy in '*Ad Matrem Virginem*':

> And He does not even despise
> My own heart:
> My unworthy heart
> Which holds so great a sacrament,
> Unworthy, O, that it should carry
> The One who was this morning with me;
> He creeps in, O Mary,
> In the Eucharist.
> He Himself wishes to enter:
> I cannot deny myself to Him. (Lines 11–20)⁴

Taking the body of Christ into our own is an erotic experience – conception may well follow. Christ 'creeps' into our hearts; he seduces – 'wishes to enter' – and 'I cannot deny myself to Him'. We 'carry / The One' in our hearts, just as Mary carried him in her womb. No man has been closer to her in body, heart and mind than has Christ. His seductive entry into our hearts amounts to another virgin conception.

In '*Ad Matrem Virginem*', the speaker desires to conceive and be pregnant with Christ. Nevertheless, he fears he has denied Christ entry and has, instead, become round with 'worldliness': 'For I too swell up, yet am filled / With worldliness from the world' (lines 41–2).⁵ In this passage, Hopkins uses the word *abundo*, to which he refers in etymological speculations on the Latin word *flos*: 'Original meaning to be inflated, to swell as the bud does into the flower. Also φλέω (*abundo*) and *flaw* (storm), *flare* (English not Latin)' (*Journals*, 13).⁶ The image of the flower suggests the organic growth of the bud, culminating in its 'swell[ing]', expansion or 'flar[ing]' into flower. Hopkins' use of the word *abundo* in these two instances indicates, to his mind, a clear linguistic and visual parallel between pregnancy and expansion. And yet, as '*Ad Matrem Virginem*' reveals, not all pregnancies are desirable. Isaiah speaks out against those who 'conceive mischief, and bring forth iniquity'.⁷ In like manner, the psalmist makes reference to one who 'hath conceived mischief, and brought forth falsehood'.⁸ Augustine himself says,

> I inquired what wickedness is; and I did not find a substance but a perversity of will twisted away from the highest substance, you O God, towards inferior things, rejecting its own inner life and swelling with external matter.⁹

But if we are faithful to Christ then we will conceive only him in the heart.

Hopkins believes our souls should 'swell up' with the presence of God, whose perfection resembles that of a sphere. In three-dimensional space the sphere is completely round from every angle. Hopkins' repeated references to the perfect nature of the sphere, from his undergraduate to his later years, tell us of its importance to his conception of the divinity. In an undergraduate essay, he refers to 'the immoveable spherical One or Whole of Xenophanes' (*Oxford Essays*, 206).[10] Returning again to Xenophanes' sphere, he argues the philosopher believed in 'God eternal…one, and spherelike' (309).[11] Elsewhere, he notes that Parmenides, 'compares it [i.e., Being] like Xenophanes to a ball rounded true' (314).[12] The sphere is 'rounded and true'; its truth or exactness corresponds to its shape.

The image of the divine sphere reappears years later. In his notes on 'The Incarnation' Hopkins likens the shape of the world (*mundi*) to a pomegranate, an image of fecundity, which he compares to 'the sphere of the divine being':

> 'Magnum capacitatem et ambitum mundi' ['*the great capacity and circuit of the world*'] – This suggests that 'pomegranate', that *pomum possibilium*. The Trinity saw it whole and in every 'cleave', the actual and the possible. We may consider that we are looking at it in all the actual cleaves, one after another. This sphere is set off against the sphere of the divine being, a steady 'seat or throne' of majesty. (*Sermons*, 171)[13]

The sphere represents not merely 'the sphere of the divine being', which is the unity of the Trinity, but also perfect knowledge and vision. As Hopkins argues at the beginning of his notes, 'The divine Persons see the whole world at once' (169). The Trinity comprehends, at once, each cleave of the 'whole' pomegranate. In contrast, humans perceive but each cleave 'one after another'. Elsewhere, Hopkins reiterates this assertion, saying, 'like a pomegranate in the round, which God sees whole but of which we see at best only one cleave' (151).[14] God sees the whole, for he is whole. Hopkins concludes the final lines of 'In the Valley of the Elwy' by asking God to 'Complete thy creature dear O where it fails, / Being mighty a master, being a father and fond' (lines 13–14). For Hopkins, the 'O' in line 13 is the shape of God. In contrast, the 'creature' is a cleave, an incomplete or 'fail[ed]' sphere. God's association with fullness is that which prompts Hopkins to call on him to 'Complete thy creature dear'.

Hollows and Holes, Stress and Spirit

God 'completes' us when he enters our souls. We make room for his presence when we are receptive to him. Hopkins' etymological speculations surrounding the word 'hollow' are especially important to his notion of human openness to the divine: '*Hollow, hull* (of ships and plants), κοῖλος, *skull* (as κεφαλή and *caput* that which holds, contains), *hole, hold*, etc' (*Journals*, 12).[15] The word 'hollow' is linked to images of containers; the 'hollow' or 'hole' is that which may indeed 'hold' an object. The theological significance of these etymological speculations is evident 18 years later in his assertion that humans are 'expressly made' to harbour God's presence: 'God rests in man as in a place, a *locus*, bed, vessel, expressly made to receive him as a jewel in a case hollowed to fit it, as the hand in the glove or the milk in the breast' (*Sermons*, 195).[16] The jewel case is 'hollowed' to fit the jewel, while the glove is designed to encase the hand. Similarly, the open individual, like a 'vessel', gives space to hold the other. Hopkins' synecdoches signal our capacity to receive and contain God; the bed suggests the intimacy of that reception.

The example of the breast in the above excerpt is not as straightforward as that of the jewel box and glove, but it is no less significant. The presence of life-giving milk facilitates the breast's fullest growth, given that it swells to its greatest roundness during pregnancy. The expanded breast symbolises a person's development from lack to wholeness, from bud to bloom. In the previously mentioned notes on 'The Incarnation', the 'whole' and the 'cleave' are synonymous – in the language of Aristotle – with 'the actual and the possible', respectively. These two states allude to a person's 'great capacity' (*capacitatem*) to move towards the realisation of his or her intended purpose, which Aristotle argues is an organism's successful development from potentiality to actuality or 'form': 'The form indeed is "nature" rather than matter; for a thing is more properly said to be what it is when it has attained to fulfilment than when it exists potentially'.[17] The essence or 'nature' of a form is its end or actualised state rather than its potential or starting point. Thus, the movement towards form is a 'process of growth' towards the fulfilment of one's 'nature'. 'We also speak of a thing's nature as being exhibited in the process of growth by which its nature is attained', says Aristotle.[18] Following the Greek philosopher, Hopkins asserts that an organism's 'fullest or highest form' is the greatest possible state of which it is capable.[19] When it has achieved this state, it has successfully developed into that which it truly is. Each 'cleave', then, represents a potential or a 'possible', whereas the actual is the 'whole' and the 'sphere' (that is, the *pomum possibilium*). When each cleave or potential achieves its highest form it approaches the shape of the sphere. To Hopkins' mind, Aristotle's ontology is applicable not simply to the individual but also to the person in relation to God. Just as the breast cannot fulfil its intended purpose unless it is swollen with milk, humans cannot achieve their 'nature' without the informing presence of God.

Hopkins uses other images of vessels or 'hollow' objects to describe the fruition of humanity through the presence of Christ, such as in the following note:

> God *in forma servi* rests *in servo*, that is / Christ as a solid in his member as a hollow or shell, both things being the image of God; which can only be perfectly when the member is in all things conformed to Christ. This too best brings out the nature of the man himself, as the lettering on a sail or device upon a flag are best seen when it fills. (*Sermons*, 195)[20]

Though Hopkins mentions God and Christ, it is essentially to the workings of the Holy Spirit that he refers.[21] Given that each of us is a 'hollow or shell' – words that for Hopkins are etymologically related, as we shall see – we have the capacity to 'hold' the 'solid' presence of air, of the Spirit. The word 'solid' renders the seeming immateriality of air irrelevant: air is as the Spirit that does not lack. Only when a person has 'in all things conformed' to the Spirit's solidity can 'the nature of the man' be revealed as 'the image of God'. Just as air inflates sails and flags, thereby making them legible, the Spirit 'fills' the soul to its perfect form.

Without the Spirit, we would be mere shells without 'solid' kernels. With no support, we would 'flag' and 'droop'.[22] Even worse, each of us would become as 'the poor collapsing frame, / Hung like a wreck' ('The Escorial', lines 21–2). This poetic portrayal, written when Hopkins was 15, is comparable to his adult account of a 'nervous collapse' experienced in a nightmare: 'The feeling is terrible: the body no longer swayed as a piece by the nervous and muscular instress seems to fall in and hang like a dead weight on the chest' (*Journals*, 238).[23] This sensation of 'hang[ing]' gives the impression of the body's frame collapsing and 'fall[ing] in' on itself. Hopkins compares this state to the extreme movement of 'holding oneself at stress' and then 'suddenly go[ing] slack' (238). What is evident in his recounting of the nightmare is the degeneration from stress to slackness. This frightening event causes Hopkins to lose his ability, in the words of another poem, to 'stand at stress' and be 'beechbole firm' ('Harry Ploughman', lines 6, 9). In contrast, 'the divine nature is infinite in stress as much as in magnitude and absolute as much as infinite' (*Sermons*, 153).[24]

Aspiration and Inspiration

Mary conceived Christ through the influence of the Holy Spirit.[25] The Spirit is equally responsible for our conception of Christ. Hopkins' Marian poems and hymns are, ultimately, Christological. Mary's relation to Christ determines the nature of her maternity, setting the standard for the rest of humanity, as we likewise become mothers through the indwelling of the Spirit. In 'The Blessed Virgin compared to the Air we Breathe', Hopkins declares that 'Men here…draw like breath / More Christ and baffle death' (lines 66–7). The spiritual equivalent to the physical act of inhalation engenders Christ in our being; he is 'draw[n] like breath' into the heart. Indeed, immediately after the above lines, Hopkins states that Christ, '*born so*, comes to be / New self and nobler me' (lines 68–9; emphasis added). When referring to Mary, Hopkins argues that Christ,

> Of her flesh he took flesh:
> He does take fresh and fresh,
> Though much the mystery how,
> Not flesh but spirit now
> And makes, O marvellous!
> New Nazareths in us,
> Where she shall yet conceive
> Him, morning, noon, and eve;
> New Bethlems, and he born
> There, evening, noon, and morn –
> Bethlem or Nazareth… (Lines 55–65)

The change from the past to the present tense in line 56 is telling. It suggests that, while Christ was once conceived in the 'flesh' from Mary's 'flesh', he continues to be conceived 'fresh and fresh', that is, again and again, with each new human breath.[26] Indeed, the phrase, 'Not flesh but spirit now', reinforces the connection between the virgin conception in the past and the spiritual conception in the present. Just as Nazareth is the place of Christ's physical conception and 'Bethlem' his birthplace, our spiritual inhalation and exhalation will make in us 'New Nazareths' and 'New Bethlems', respectively. If Christ is in Mary, and if Mary is compared to the air we breathe, then she is within us conceiving and giving birth to Christ. He is conceived, as with each intake of breath, 'morning, noon, and eve', and is born, as with each departure of breath, 'evening, noon, and morn'. The chiasmus draws our attention to the antithetical and, yet, ultimately dependent acts of inhaling and exhaling.

The breath that we inhale and exhale at any one time is the very breath that has been, and will be, breathed by others. In short, a single breath may pass from one being to another, from generation to generation. Two years before he composed 'The Blessed Virgin compared to the Air we Breathe', Hopkins linked human respiration with the movement of the Spirit, saying,

> for as the breath is drawn from the boundless air into the lungs and from the lungs again is breathed out and melts into the boundless air so the Spirit of God was poured out from the infinite God upon Christ's human nature and by Christ, who said: Receive the Holy Ghost: as my Father sent me so I send you /, was

breathed into his Apostles and by degrees into the millions of his Church, till the new heavens and new earth will at last be filled with it. (*Sermons*, 98)[27]

The Spirit was 'poured...upon Christ's human nature'. From his body, the Spirit spread to the Apostles and was passed on, even today, 'into the millions of his Church'. Like water from a fountain, that which is 'drawn from the boundless air' continues to circulate when it is released 'into the boundless air'. Hopkins later argues in the sermon that this single breath passes continuously from one being to another: '[The Holy Ghost] passes like a restless breath from heart to heart and is the spirit and life of all the Church' (100). The Spirit's omnipresence makes of him 'our universal soul'; as the shared breath uniting millions, he makes each of us an 'AfterChrist' (100). God 'searches hearts' (99), and we draw him in like air.

Hopkins' terms 'aspiration' and 'inspiration' disclose the intimate and mutual exchange of breath between humans and God. As he says, 'man's responding aspiration or drawing in of breath' follows God's 'continued strain and breathing on [humanity]' (*Sermons*, 157).[28] Alive to the assorted meanings of the Latin word *spiritus*, Hopkins tells us that our 'aspiration' responds to God's 'inspiration':

> And even the sigh or aspiration itself is in answer to an inspiration of God's spirit and is followed by the continuance and expiration of that same breath which lifts it...to do or be what God wishes his creature to do or be. Cf. Eph. iii 16 'ἵνα δῷ ὑμῖν κατὰ τὸ πλοῦτος τῆς δόξης αὐτοῦ δυνάμει [the display of divine power] κραταιωθῆναι [like falling home into a fast bed] διὰ τοῦ πνεύματος αὐτοῦ [the aspiration on God's part] εἰς τὸν ἔσω ἄνθρωπον [known to God, the man created in Christ as ii 10.], κατοικῆσαι τὸν Χριστὸν διὰ τῆς πίστεως ἐν ταῖς καρδίαις ὑμῶν...ἵνα πληρωθῆτε εἰς πᾶν τὸ πλήρωμα τοῦ Θεοῦ.' This πλήρωμα τοῦ Θεοῦ is the burl of being in Christ, and for every man there is his own burl of being... (156)[29]

God and humans breathe 'that same breath', for the breath of one is 'the continuance' of the breath of the other. Certainly, we draw closer to God by responding with 'sigh or aspiration' to his 'inspiration', the source of our fullness, stress and solidity. The phrase 'πλήρωμα τοῦ Θεοῦ' ('fullness of God'), refers to 'the burl of being in Christ' and the 'burl of being' in each human. The 'burl', of course, has associations with roundness.[30] The phrase alludes also to Paul's wish 'that ye might be filled with all the fulness of God'.[31] We are '[made] known to God' when our 'inner' selves and 'hearts' are laid open to his 'fulness'.

It is through our 'aspiration' that we offer the Spirit hospitality, a 'home' in the soul. Hopkins declares that κραταιωθῆναι ('to be strengthened')[32] is 'like falling home into a fast bed'. The phrase, 'to be strengthened', recalls the idea that Christ is 'a solid' who gives meaning to the 'hollow or shell' in the same manner that air fills and keeps at stress a flag or sail. The Spirit who strengthens and upholds the individual is at home as if it has fallen into 'bed'. This curiously domestic, and faintly sexual, simile calls to mind the previously mentioned assertion that 'God rests in man as in a place, a *locus*, bed, vessel, expressly made to receive him' (*Sermons*, 195). In both descriptions, Hopkins appropriates and furthers Augustine's claim that 'our heart is restless until it rests in [God]'.[33] Just as the heart finds its rest in God, so, too, does God find his rest in the human heart. As Paul declares, 'be strengthened with might by his Spirit in the inner man; That Christ may dwell in your hearts by faith'.[34]

Echoes from Hollow Spaces

In '*Ad Matrem Virginem*', Hopkins asks Mary,

> What were you saying to Him then,
> And what were you hearing?
> For even though He was mute
> Yet (in the depths of your soul)
> He (the eternal Word) is speaking. (Lines 59–63)[35]

The divine nature of Christ as the Word overrides the physical inability of the foetus to speak. The 'Word' in Greek is *Logos*, from the verb *legein*, 'to speak'. The very nature of Christ is speech, which Hopkins affirms in the phrase, 'He…is speaking'. Speech is the incarnation of breath and thought; it has its own inscape.[36] Christ, the begotten Son, is the spoken Word from the Father's mouth. The circulation of breath between God and humans transfers the *Logos* from divine to mortal realms, and back again. As I will explore later in the chapter, God's 'inspiration' allows the believer to conceive Christ in his or her 'heart', and, by his or her 'aspiration', give birth to him.

The believer conceives the Word through, as it were, the act of hearing. We cannot discuss speech without referring to its complement: hearing. Alison G. Sulloway has explored the Victorians' penchant for reading aloud and listening. Exploring the influence of Ruskin on Hopkins, she notes,

> [Ruskin] extolled not only 'the pleasure of sight', as gifts of heaven, but the pleasures 'of hearing'; and the gifts of heaven in which Christians could take legitimate pleasure were 'the melody in the voice' and the 'majesty in the thunder'… Attending lectures was almost as fashionable a pursuit among the middle classes as reading aloud was among most classes, and many of Ruskin's works were first delivered as lectures. He designed his sonorous style to appeal

as fully to the ear as to the eye and the conscience. George Eliot described her intense pleasure in reading Ruskin aloud to George Lewes 'for an hour or so after dinner'.[37]

Poetry should likewise be uttered. In a letter to Bridges, Hopkins insists that a reader 'take breath and read ["The Loss of the Eurydice"] with the ears' (*Bridges*, 79).[38] In another letter he declares, 'My verse is less to be read than heard, as I have told you before' (46).[39] This fondness for the spoken word is more than a mere pleasure; it is a matter of theology. Through images of captured sounds in human ears and other similarly hollow spaces, Hopkins depicts the 'hollowed' believer as one who conceives the Word through *spiritus* and gives birth through utterance. Donatella Abbate Badin argues that hearing 'means being penetrated by another's words'.[40] It is, then, a prime example of our openness to Christ. According to popular medieval legend, the ear is the passage through which the Virgin Mary conceived the *Logos*. For that reason, when Hopkins asks in '*Ad Matrem Virginem*', 'what were you hearing?' (line 60), he refers not only to the eternal communication between Mary and her Son, but also to the conception of the Word through her ear.

Hopkins believes that believers must be similarly receptive with their ears. In 'The Wreck of the Deutschland', he asks, 'What bý your méasure is the héaven of desíre, / The tréasure never éyesight gót, nor was éver guessed whát for the héaring?' (stanza 26). The 'tréasure' we cannot see but only hear is the Word, an allusion to the story of Thomas.[41] The story is significant for Hopkins, as it shifts the focus of faith towards the ear. In his translation of '*S. Thomae Equinatis Rhythmus ad SS. Sacramentum*', a hymn once ascribed to St Thomas Aquinas, he writes, 'Seeing, touching, tasting, might mislead me here / But in faith I follow what is taught the ear' (version a, lines 5–6); and, later, 'I am not like Thomas, wounds I do not see, / But I can confess Thee Lord and God as he' (lines 13–14).

The nineteenth century saw the rise of photography, visual culture and advertising, which had the potential to dazzle or 'mislead' through what Dennis Denisoff calls the 'sensationalist excess' of consumerism and marketing.[42] A visual person, as we have seen in Chapter One, Hopkins nonetheless remained wary, believing sight could disengage us from the truth that is not so readily apparent. As he says in his translation of '*S. Thomae Aquinatis Rhythmus ad SS. Sacramentum*', 'Godhead, I adore Thee down on bended knee, / Who art here though hiding under things we see' (version a, lines 1–2). The idea was important enough for Hopkins to repeat at a later date: 'Since, thóugh he is únder the wórld's spléndour and wónder, / His mýstery múst be instréssed, stressed' ('The Wreck of the Deutschland', stanza 5). Etymologically, the word 'mystery' alludes to the closing of the eyes and mouth. When these organs are shut, the main aperture of sense and communication becomes the ear.

The nineteenth century witnessed not simply an increase in visual consumption, but also a rise in what John M. Picker terms 'close listening', initiated by the invention of the stethoscope in 1816 and 'perfected by the microphone'.[43] Armed with a stethoscope, a physician could become more intimate with the hitherto secret language of the body. Just as the instrument amplifies to the ear the beating of a heart beneath the skin, so Hopkins believes we need to stress God's hidden presence to our hearts. While detractors of the Sacred Heart might 'hear' in its name 'a strange sound, an unmeaning sound, or even an unpleasing and repulsive sound', Hopkins listens closely and hears 'the beating of the heart [which] is the truth of nature' (*Sermons*, 101, 103).[44]

The poet clearly privileges the ear over the eye in an early, unfinished poem, 'I hear a noise of waters drawn away':

> I hear a noise of waters drawn away,
> And, headed always downwards, with less sounding
> Work thro' a cover'd copse whose hollow rounding
> Rather to ear than eye shews where they stray,
> Making them double-musical. (Lines 1–5)

It is 'to ear [rather] than eye' that the speaking presence of the hidden water is perceived. More significantly, the sound is transformed and amplified – made 'double-musical' – by the 'hollow rounding' of the copse. Hopkins repeats this image of the hollow landscape some 14 years later in another unfinished piece, 'Repeat that, repeat', which aligns the physical landscape with the inner scape of the ear. Hopkins urges the cuckoo bird to 'open ear wells, heart-springs…/ With a ballad, with a ballad, a rebound' (lines 2–3). The repetition, 'With a ballad, with a ballad', creates a literal echo to mimic the song that 'rebound[s] / Off trundled timber and scoops of the hillside ground, hollow hollow hollow ground' (lines 3–4). The ground's hollowness provides a reflective mirror for the bird's song. In fact, 'ballad' is a pun on 'ball'; we can indeed imagine the ball(ad) 'rebound[ing]' off the 'scoops' of the 'hollow hollow hollow ground'.

Todd K. Bender notes a link between 'scoops' and 'hollow', with the two words echoing each other in meaning:

> The set of words used to signify shovelling or hollowing out, scoop, scooped, scoops, appear in three cases. In 'Il Mystico' the persona banishes 'sensual gross desires' to 'Scoop you from teeming filth some sickly hovel, / And there for ever grovel'. 'Harry Ploughman' is described as 'the rack of ribs; the scooped flank; lank / Rope-over thigh; knee-nave; and barrelled shank – '. And the cuckoo's song echoes 'Off trundled timber and scoops of the hillside ground'… In all these contexts, scoop appears to mean a '*hollow place shaped as if scooped out.*'[45]

Hopkins draws a striking parallel between the scoops of the ground and the function of ears. Compare the poem to his sermon on the deaf and dumb man – delivered at around the same time as the poem's composition – in which he says Christ's finger 'opened' the man's 'barred up' ears (*Sermons*, 18).[46] Similarly, in the poem, the bird is asked to unblock and 'open ear wells'. The suggestion is that listeners must have a receptive or 'open' ear and, that, in order to echo or return a sound, they must first be able to hear well.

Given its likeness to the ear, the 'hollow' is that which, in a sense, conceives by catching words (and the Word). This process is similar to how a scoop catches a ballad, a well rainwater, and a hand a ball. In his observation of another cuckoo call, Hopkins likens an echoing, hollow ground to the catching and throwing function of the hand: 'Sometimes I hear the cuckoo with wonderful clear and plump and fluty notes: it is when the hollow of a rising ground conceives them and palms them up and throws them out' (*Journals*, 232).[47] By using the word 'conceives', Hopkins compares the reception of sound to an act of conception. Catching is both active and receptive,[48] and it implies a degree of agency. In order to catch, the hand must have the potential to grasp the object it gets (or begets) in the hand. A flat hand is unlikely to catch a ball, but once it is made hollow, it becomes receptive. By its ability to receive and hold, the hand is able to grasp the object.

The act of holding precedes, and is necessary to perform, the act of throwing. The theological implication is evident: spiritual conception is the catching of the Word, pregnancy the holding, and birthing the echoing of the Word back to God. Hopkins uses the image of the ball and the act of catching in several poems. For instance, 'The Windhover' begins, 'I caught this morning morning's minion, kingdom of daylight's dauphin, dapple-dáwn-drawn Falcon, in his riding' (line 1). Daniel Brown argues that in this poem, 'The object "caught" by the poet-persona…is effectively the Parmenidean ball of Being, which is identified in Hopkins' Christian ontology with that great ball of fire, the sun'.[49] This 'great ball of fire' is the person of Christ; in 'The Blessed Virgin compared to the Air we Breathe', the brilliant sun, her Son, is referred to as a 'blinding ball' (line 197). To the eyes of the earthbound looking up, the air to which Mary is compared certainly appears to be carrying this fiery foetal ball, the ball from which kingfishers 'catch fire' ('As kingfishers catch fire, dragonflies draw flame', line 1). The significance attached to 'catching' the 'ball' is traceable to Hopkins' etymological speculations that draw on and extend his speculations of the word 'hollow':

> *Gulf, golf*. If this game has its name from the holes into which the ball is put, they may be connected, both being from the root meaning hollow. *Gulp, gula, hollow, hold, hilt*, κοιλός, *caelare* (to make hollow, to make grooves in, to grave)[,] *caelum*

[heaven], which is therefore same as though it were what it once was supposed to be a translation of κοιλόν, *hole, hell*, ('The hollow hell') *skull, shell, hull* (of ships and beans). (*Journals*, 25)[50]

Elsewhere, Hopkins alludes to receptive containers when he describes eye sockets as the 'Cups of the eyes' (72).[51] The eyes are held in these 'cups' because an eye is a ball, as he makes clear in 'Binsey Poplars': 'this sleek and seeing ball / But a prick will make no eye at all' (lines 14–15). This discussion of eyeballs and hollows might seem trivial, but we should remember that it is in the etymological richness and playfulness of words that many of Hopkins' ideas take root and flourish. Of course, these concepts very often revolve around the indwelling presence of Christ in the individual, 'as a solid in his member as a hollow or shell' (*Sermons*, 195).

The individual, 'as a hollow or shell', is like a bell that rings from its concavities. As Kunio Shimane explains,

> The metaphor of the bell in *The Deutschland* [sic] is based on a comparison between the human body and the actual bell, as both are resonators. The head, containing the skull, nasal cavity, mouth and tongue, is rightly compared with the bell, for the sound made by the tongue and other organs resonates in the mouth, nasal cavity, and even the skull itself, just as the sound made by the tongue resonates in the bell.[52]

'The Wreck of the Deutschland' contains the following description of a bodily bell:

> Fínger of a ténder of, O of a féathery délicacy, the bréast of the
>   Maiden could obey so, be a bell to, ring óf it, and
> Startle the poor shéep back! (Stanza 31)

The divine 'Fínger' delicately touches the nun's 'bréast', which responds as a bell to the touch of a hand. In his reading of this passage, Shimane holds,

> The breast here is identical with the chest cavity that functions as a bell. Confined with ribs, as a *bower of bone*, it amplifies the vibrations of the ribs and the spinal cord caused by the vocal cord vibration. Generally speaking, bones are compared to tuning forks, and the cavities to bells. In this sense, the human body itself is a resonator. An experienced stage actor, for instance, makes full use of his entire body to convey his speech; the head and the chest cavity are especially ideal resonators. It was quite natural that Hopkins used them in the nun to signify the two kinds of bells.[53]

Shimane cites an earlier example of a bodily bell in the unfinished poem 'Pilate'.[54] Unlike the nun from 'The Wreck of the Deutschland', Pilate's tongue does not create a ring: 'My tongue strikes on the gum / And cleaves, I struggle and am dumb' (lines 69–70). The 'tongue' – which signifies both the body part and the striking implement of a bell – 'cleaves' to a surface, hindering the vibration of sound. Pilate's silence exemplifies his status as an outcast 'exile[d]…/ From God and man' (lines 3–4).

The virtuous have the capacity to resonate with God's name. Hopkins believes one such person is the recusant Margaret Clitheroe, arrested in 1586 for sheltering persecuted priests. For subsequently 'standing mute', that is, for refusing to plead guilty or allowing her case to go to trial, she was subject to the old penalty of being crushed to death.[55] Hopkins suggests in a poem that Margaret Clitheroe's silence before the law gives her the capacity to speak the name of God: 'She caught the crying of those Three, / The Immortals of the eternal ring, / The Utterer, Utterèd, Uttering' ('Margaret Clitheroe', lines 29–31). Like the 'hollow hollow ground', which has caught the sounds of the cuckoo bird, Margaret has 'caught' the Trinity's 'eternal ring', a pun that implies both the sound and the 'sphere of the divine being' (*Sermons*, 171).[56] The word 'ring' suggests also an open mouth; we recall the round edge of a bell is known as the 'lip'. Unlike the 'selfbent' sinner ('Ribblesdale', line 11) whose attention focuses narcissistically inwards, '[Margaret's] will was bent at God' ('Margaret Clitheroe', line 7), enabling her to catch his name and return it at the moment of death: 'When she felt the kill-weights crush / She told his name times-over three; / *I suffer this* she said *for Thee*' (lines 55–7; emphasis original). Her final three breaths bear the 'aspiration' which echo the divine 'inspiration, just as the word 'told' is a verbal echo of 'tolled', the past tense of the (bell) toll. This use of 'told' references its prior use in 'The Wreck of the Deutschland': 'A próphetess tówered in the túmult, a vírginal tóngue tóld' (stanza 17).[57] By tolling/telling 'his name times-over three', Margaret's virtuous tongue does indeed 'fling out broad [his] name' ('As kingfishers catch fire, dragonflies draw flame', line 4).

Uttering Christ

Like Margaret Clitheroe, the tall nun in 'The Wreck of the Deutschland' is struck with divine speech, and in no less dramatic fashion. Her vocalisations are contrasted to the sounds of human distress:

> The woman's wailing, the crying of child without check –
>   Till a líoness aróse bréasting the bábble,
> A próphetess tówered in the túmult, a vírginal tóngue tóld. (Stanza 17)

The sudden introduction of rhythmic, accented stress in the final two lines, particularly of the first syllables, suggests the striking of a bell. If the nun is a 'prophetess', and if prophets were traditionally assumed to be the mouthpiece of God, then her utterances evidently resonate with divine inspiration. The human 'bábble' comprises the confusing sounds of a woman's wailing and the child's cry. Indeed, 'bábble' – inarticulate sounds – refers directly to the Tower of Babel and the confusion of tongues. The Hebrew verb for Babel (*Balal*) means 'to confuse', and Hopkins refers to this definition when he says that Lucifer 'is always…brought to confusion and vice… And God is continually confounding the builders of Babel or of Babylon' (*Sermons*, 180).[58] In Genesis, God created the confusion of languages to confound the hubristic builders of the tower of Babel.[59] By describing the nun's 'tóngue' as 'vírginal', therefore, Hopkins implies her speech is pre-Babel, pristine, like the legendary language of Adam.[60] By 'bréasting the bábble', the nun rides over what Hopkins calls 'the stórm's brawling' (stanza 19). This 'brawling' is the linguistic disorder into which humanity has fallen. The storm parallels the universal chaos before creation. In fact, stanzas 17 and 19 allude to the movement of the Holy Spirit upon the waters of chaos and the subsequent initiation of order at creation.[61] By associating the ontological turmoil of the pre-created world with the linguistic confusion of Babel, Hopkins equates divine order with linguistic order. The nun's tolling tongue is thus an echo of God's speech at creation.

The nun bears a suitable linguistic disposition to give tongue to the Word. Her 'vírginal tóngue', the linguistic equivalent to Mary's physical virginity, is the organ capable of giving birth to the Word. The 'Fínger' of 'a féathery délicacy' (stanza 31), which touches the nun, alludes to the Annunciation, when the Virgin Mary conceived Christ through the influence of the Spirit.[62] The 'Fínger' is undoubtedly the Spirit, for the 'féathery délicacy' refers to the tender beating of his wings. Moreover, in the same stanza, Hopkins says the nun is 'not uncomforted', a reference to the Spirit as the Paraclete or Comforter.[63] In stanza 30, Hopkins alludes to the Feast of the Immaculate Conception, which commemorates the Virgin's freedom from original sin or 'stáin'. Celebrated on 8 December, the day after the nuns are believed to have drowned in 1875, the two events are clearly married in the poem. Like Mary at the Annunciation, the tall nun in 'The Wreck of the Deutschland' conceives the spoken word:

> For so concéivèd, so to conceive thee is done;
> But here was heart-throe, birth of a brain,
> Wórd, that héard and képt thee and úttered thee óutríght. (Stanza 30)

The phrase, 'birth of a brain', could well refer to the birth of the *Logos* from the Father's head, reminiscent of Athena's birth from the head of Zeus. Our understanding of the phrase, however, is enlightened by Hopkins' previously mentioned etymological speculations, wherein the word 'skull' is linked to 'hollow' and 'hold'. To give 'birth' to the 'brain' is to deliver it from the skull. This delivery is made possible by the act of utte*ring*. The 'brain' refers most conspicuously to the *Logos*, which can be defined as meaning, thought, account and reason. It is worth noting, though, that the common translation of *Logos*, for example in the gospel of John, is 'Word'. By his use of the word 'brain', Hopkins attempts to incorporate these definitions to suggest that Christ is the thought or Idea uttered in the mind of God. In this way, the *Logos* is the divine and incarnate equivalent of a concept posited in his notes on Greek philosophy, in which he says 'the word is the expression, uttering of the idea in the mind' (*Oxford Essays*, 307).[64] Hopkins has faith in the ability of words to materialise thought. Thus he says, 'God's utterance of himself in himself is God the Word, outside himself is this world' (*Sermons*, 129).[65] In 'The Wreck of the Deutschland', the 'brain', birthed by utterance, is literally the flesh enmeshed with thought. The materialisation of verbal expression is suggested in an image from an original version of stanza 8: 'We mouth, and the blue flesh burst / Gushes – it flushes the being with it sour and sweet'. Sound is the incarnation of breath, and the words we 'mouth' are like hidden juices suddenly and visibly gushing from the bitten 'blue flesh' of a fruit. When we 'mouth', we open our lips to an 'O' shape in order to expel utterance and give birth to the Word.

Before Christ can be born as utterance, he must be conceived in the listener. Christ was 'conceivèd' by Mary, but the nun conceives him in the present time. Indeed, the transition from the use of the past tense, 'conceivèd', to the present tense, 'conceive', confirms this idea (stanza 30). The Word gestates within the nun who has 'képt' it. The word 'képt' is significant in terms of catching and holding. According to the *Oxford English Dictionary*, the obsolete definitions of 'keep' include catching, seeking, receiving, holding, taking with the ears and mind, and caring. At the conclusion of her pregnancy the nun gives birth by uttering the Word back to God. Since Christ is later called the 'heaven-flúng' (stanza 34), the neologism, 'heart-throe', may well be a pun on 'heart throw'. We can therefore say that the human heart, in the 'throe[s]' of giving birth, 'throws' back to God the 'heaven-flung' Word it has caught and kept.

God's ear catches our sounds in his listening. In the next chapter, I will further discuss the act of listening, but in the meantime I will look at the following description from 'The Wreck of the Deutschland':

>...she réars hersélf to divíne
> Éars, and the cáll of the táll nún
> To the mén in the tóps and the táckle rode óver the stórm's brawling. (Stanza 19)

God's opened 'divíne / Éars' are not unlike our 'open[ed] ear wells'. Just as we are required to listen in order to conceive the Word, God's auditory receptiveness is equally important to our reciprocating utterance, to our giving birth. God's 'Éars' are hollows receiving us when, by the exertion of 'heart-throe', we fling to his 'H*ear*t' not only the Word but also ourselves. As Hopkins says, 'I whirled out wings that spell / And fled with a fling of the heart to the heart of the Host' (stanza 3). By listening, God opens his heart to our hearts. This relationship between listening and speaking, between giving breath and receiving the other, leads me to the exploration of conversation and kissing in the next chapter.

Chapter Four

CARESSING, CONVERSING, KISSING

Breath, Speech, Caress

Images of breath exchange form some of Hopkins' most effective and beautiful portrayals of union between God and humanity. For Hopkins, breathing involves not only the individual but also another who sustains the breath by returning it to him or her. In his writings, this other being, more than any other, is God. In the previous chapter, I explored breath exchange in relation to conception, pregnancy and birth. In this chapter, I develop an understanding of this exchange in relation to touching, communicating and kissing. In Genesis, God's act of breathing into the body of Adam initiated the first intimate exchange between God and humanity.[1] Hopkins reminds us of this first contact in his description of the deity as the 'giver of breath and bread' ('The Wreck of the Deutschland', stanza 1). Breath may be intangible to the naked eye, but it caresses us in ways that we do not immediately recognise. The breath that we inhale, and to which we are thus open, touches, passes through, and sustains every living cell in our bodies. It reaches us from the bodies of other living and breathing beings; in this way, others touch us in a most intimate manner. Similarly, others inhale our exhalations, and as a consequence, we touch them. In other words, by our exhalations and inhalations, we caress, and are caressed by, others.

'Speech', notes Friedrich Max Müller, 'is pre-eminently significant sound'.[2] Giving weight and volume to breath, speech is the incarnation of our thoughts and the verbal expression of our exhalations. Within the structure of conversation, it promotes the necessary openness for meaningful relations with others. As Catherine Belsey argues,

> Speech is a 'relation', the possibility of dialogue, of demand, of community, reciprocity, love. As the condition of subjectivity, permitting a difference between 'I' and 'you', speech is also necessarily the possibility of intersubjectivity, of address and response, question and answer.[3]

So as to realise its unitive potential, speech must be given to, and returned by, another in dialogue. That is, it must be offered in the reciprocity of conversation. Conversation initiates and sustains one's verbal, intellectual and emotional engagement with another because speech moves outward from the utterer until it physically and mentally touches the listener. Dialogue facilitates a dynamic exchange of action and reception, of speaking and listening. During the course of a conversation, the listener replies to the speaker who in turn becomes the listener, thereby ensuring the ebb and flow of exchange. Conversation enables us to embrace the words of the other and, by so doing, inhale the other's breath. In the mutual embrace, I am both the enfolded and the enfolder. As the embraced, I am within the embrace of the other; as the embracer, I am outside that embrace. Through this interpenetration, I am simultaneously within and outside the other, equally the recipient and the giver, the listener and the speaker, the one who inhales and the one who exhales. In the intimacies of conversation, each person inspires, and is inspired by, the other.[4]

By this shared experience of conversation, this exchange of breath, each person reaches into, and touches, the heart of the other. When two beings touch, they produce the one touch that declares their union. Think of Rainer Maria Rilke's image of the two strings that meet to fashion a single sound: 'Yet everything that touches us, you and me, / takes us together as a bow's stroke does, / that out of two strings draws a single voice' ('Lovesong', lines 8–10).[5] For Hopkins, the union between the soul and God is initiated by the exchange that enables each to touch and affect the other. As he asserts, 'inspiration' and 'aspiration' form '*that touch* which only God can apply and the response which only God can perceive' (*Sermons*, 158).[6] God's 'touch', the 'inspiration' that he alone can apply, is intended for, and felt by, the soul alone. In like manner, the soul's signature response, its 'aspiration', is intended for, and felt by, God alone. God's desire for us to aspire towards him is set in motion by his touch. He touches in order to be touched; he longs for 'the aspiration in answer to his inspiration' (158).

Hopkins describes our response to the 'inspiration' as our 'sigh of correspondence' (*Sermons*, 156). A 'sigh' may be an inarticulate sound to most, but to Hopkins it expresses its speaker's 'aspiration'. Likewise, we could call poetry a series of spoken 'sighs' rather than words on paper: 'só sighs déep / Poetry', says the poet in 'Ashboughs' (lines 2–3). Poetry is thus a way of communicating with God. Hopkins' theory of sprung rhythm gives reason to his emphasis on breath, speech, and the articulate sighs of poetry. This theory is voiced in his mature poetry, for example, in 'Ashboughs' and his first poem written in sprung rhythm, 'The Wreck of the Deutschland'. In the 'Author's Preface on Rhythm' (which accompanies the latter poem), he declares sprung rhythm to be 'the most natural of things', for it is the rhythm, first, of common speech and some prose, second, of almost all music, and, third, of nursery rhymes.[7] Nevertheless, Hopkins contends, sprung rhythm ceased to be used after the Elizabethan Age.[8] The name sprung rhythm denotes its relationship to rhythm, what Hopkins describes as the movement of 'stress' and 'slack', of the accented and unaccented syllables, respectively.[9] Hopkins reveals a propensity for stress in his various discussions of sprung rhythm. For instance, he asserts that the basis of a metrical foot is not the standard rhythm or metre, but stress: 'This then', he confirms to Dixon, 'is the essence of sprung rhythm: *one stress makes one foot*, no matter how many or few the syllables' (*Dixon*, 23).[10] He reiterates the important association between stress and sprung rhythm in a letter to his brother Everard when he declares, 'sprung rhythm makes verse stressy'.[11] Stress is crucial because it brings to the fore the 'meaning and feeling' of terms: 'And so throughout let the stress be made to fetch out both the strength of the syllables and the meaning and feeling of the words'.[12] Similarly, in a letter to Patmore, he argues that stress is 'the making a thing more, or making it markedly, what it already is; it is the bringing out of its nature' (*Further Letters*, 327).[13]

The importance of stress is equalled and complemented by the weight of poetry's utterance. To Hopkins' mind, the two chief characteristics of poetry, stress and speech, draw together in sprung rhythm. He reiterates the importance of speech when he argues that sprung rhythm perfects 'the true nature of poetry, [which is] the darling child of speech, of lips and spoken utterance'.[14] For Hopkins, speech is the apex of sprung verse, while stress is its foundation. 'As poetry is emphatically speech, speech purged of dross like gold in the furnace', he says, 'so it must have emphatically the essential elements of speech. Now emphasis itself, stress, is one of these'.[15] As we have seen in the previous chapter, Hopkins believes poetry does not exist without speech; it is speech, rather than silence, which is golden. The written, silent poem is mere potential waiting to be actualised by vocalisation:

> The play or performance of a stageplay is the playing it on the boards, the stage: reading it, much more writing it, is not its performance. The performance of a symphony is not the scoring of it however elaborately; it is in the concert room, by the orchestra, and then and there only.[16]

Like a play or a musical score, a poem must be given breath and sound in order to realise its latent capacity. It achieves its purpose, its reason for being, through 'the playing it' to an audience. Hopkins' audience, as we shall shortly see, is God.

Sprung rhythm is a means of conveying the poet's 'aspiration'. This is because the two important aspects of poetry, stress and speech, converge in the 'sigh'. A sigh is a lengthened stress, and a stress is a syllable that 'the voice dwells on'.[17] A sigh in everyday discourse is expelled without poetic intent. In Hopkins' verse, however, a sigh is a deliberately weighed and timed sound that imparts a deep and expressive exhalation. 'To utter the word ["sigh"]', as Miller notes, 'is to do what it names'.[18] As he says, 'One of the ways to sigh is to say "Sigh" or "Sss-iii-gh," drawing out the initial sibilant, prolonging the "i" and then cutting off the expiration of breath with the "gh" at the end, before all breath has been expelled'.[19] In Hopkins' poetry, the sigh is given equal prominence as, if not more so than, other words. Previous commentators have explored his frequent use of exclamations, ejaculatory interjections, cries and apostrophic addresses of 'O's, 'Oh's and 'ah's.[20] Cotter associates them with the primal 'Om' of human breath, as well as the Alpha and the Omega.[21] Miller associates these sounds with sprung rhythm and the sigh, arguing they exemplify Hopkins' attempts to 'keep the words at the level of sound'.[22] Brown also links these exhalations with sprung rhythm, along with the 'ur-words from which all language develops'.[23] These commentators emphasise that breath, sound and stress are as significant to Hopkins as dictionary meanings are to words.

Hopkins argues that sprung rhythm 'lends itself to expressing passion' (*Bridges*, 92).[24] Sighs have the ability to communicate 'passion' because they are expressive, primal sounds that convey and, indeed, stress the speaker's feelings. As we have seen, stress, of which a sigh consists, brings out 'the meaning and *feeling* of the words'. In 'Duns Scotus's Oxford', Hopkins deploys a sigh, an 'ah!', to great effect: 'Yet ah! This air I gather and I release / He lived on' (lines 9–10). Hopkins' sigh expresses his intense delight and wonder at the realisation he is inhaling the very breath his role model Duns Scotus had 'lived on' centuries ago. In order to proclaim the 'ah!', the reader must open his of her mouth to its roundest capacity, which works to facilitate the greatest exhalation. Hopkins' use of the exclamation is thus a clever device enabling readers to actively exhale the very breath of which he speaks. In like manner, his 'ah!' in 'God's Grandeur' successfully expresses his heightened emotions at the sight of dawn: 'Because the Holy Ghost óver the bent / World broods with warm breast and with ah! Bright wings' (lines 13–14). As in 'Dun Scotus's Oxford', the 'ah!' forces the lips into a round and verbal smile. This sigh, which has no dictionary meaning, eloquently articulates Hopkins' joy and awe at the brightness that has banished 'the black West' ('God's Grandeur', line 11).

Poetry, Hopkins believes, has the power to touch its audience; he is critical when it does not achieve this potential. Commenting on an excerpt from Tennyson's 'Enoch Arden', he tells his friend Alexander William

Mowbray Baillie, 'the words are choice and the description is beautiful and unexceptionable, but it does not *touch* you' (*Further Letters*, 218).[25] Poetry-writing (more specifically, poetry-speaking) is for Hopkins an act of love that 'express[es] passion' and offers a means of touching the divine other. Giving breath, and therefore life, to a poem allows him to stroke the work with the tongue and mouth before offering it to God. Poetry comprises Hopkins' distinct form of 'aspiration', just as the cries of the tall nun in 'The Wreck of the Deutschland' convey her own 'aspiration' and, ultimately, her final expiration to her 'lover', Christ: 'Breathe, arch and original Breath. / Is it lóve in her of the béing as her lóver had béen? / Breathe, body of lovely Death' (stanza 25). Hopkins rhymes 'Breath' with 'Death' to reinforce the relationship between the soul's 'aspiration' and its final breath.[26] The rhyme is redolent of that in stanza six of John Keats' 'Ode to a Nightingale', a poem about poetry and expiration. In a similar but less dramatic manner, poetic creation is an act in which Hopkins offers his *spiritus* to, and in praise of, God. A poem can be a prayer, which, once uttered, is informed by the essence that impels its speaker's life; 'This air, which, by life's law, / My lung must draw and draw / Now but to breathe its praise', says Hopkins in 'The Blessed Virgin compared to the Air we Breathe' (lines 13–15). We are reminded of George Herbert's description of prayer as 'God's breath in man returning to his birth' ('Prayer', line 1).[27] Poetry is like Adam breathing into the mouth of God.

Hopkins' poetry is a composition of sighs and a series of stresses that dwell upon God's creative 'inspiration' and offer him the author's 'aspiration'. The 'aspiration' is indeed 'the counter stress which God alone can feel' (*Sermons*, 156).[28] The soul's 'counter stress' is its answer to 'God's finger touching the very vein of [its] personality' (158). This 'finger' is the sigh of the Spirit, which moves through the world and touches each mortal being. As the instrument of God's caress, the Spirit is the means by which he communicates his love. Like the air we breathe, the Spirit reaches into the heart and, indeed, 'the very vein of [one's] personality'. It is through our 'aspiration' that we caress God in return. The nun's 'bréast', caressed by the Spirit's 'Fínger of a ténder… féathery délicacy', quivers and 'ring[s]' like a 'bell' ('The Wreck of the Deutschland', stanza 31). Hopkins expresses his poetic 'aspirations' to God in another poem written in sprung verse, 'The Leaden Echo and the Golden Echo'. The Golden Echo calls on the reader to 'deliver' his or her 'Winning ways' (line 31) with 'sighs':

> Resign them, sign them, seal them, send them, motion them with breath,
> And with sighs soaring, soaring sighs, deliver
> Them; beauty-in-the-ghost, deliver it, early now, long before death… (Lines 33–4)

The chiasmus of 'sighs soaring, soaring sighs' renders the sigh a pneumatic reflection, a 'ghost' of God's original breath or 'inspiration'. The word 'deliver' draws a comparison between 'soaring sighs' and letter-writing. In the poem, however, the 'sigh of correspondence' is not written expression, but living speech 'motion[ed]...with breath'. As the Golden Echo says, 'Resign them, sign them, seal them, send them, motion them with breath' (line 32). Once again, Hopkins rhymes 'breath' with 'death' (line 34) in order to foreshadow and reinforce the relationship between the soul's 'aspiration' and its final expiration. The Golden Echo calls on one to 'resign', that is, to yield and 'sign' away, one's best actions or 'Winning ways'. Hopkins' metaphor of letter-writing provides further insight into the significance of sprung rhythm to one's relationship with God. As with a signature, one offers to God one's unique being, perhaps at first expressed through the poetic work of one's hands, yet, finally, uttered and set in 'motion...with breath'. The 'motion' of spoken poetry returns to God his stress and 'inspiration'. The Golden Echo says, 'Give beauty back, beauty, beauty, beauty, back to God, beauty's self and beauty's giver' (lines 34–5). Through echoes or verbal reflection, the Golden Echo gives back to God the 'beauty, beauty, beauty' of his Trinitarian voice.

Sympathetic Vibration and the Science of Attraction

The circular movement of 'inspiration' and 'aspiration' creates a dialogue between God and humans. God initiates this dialogue when he calls on us to convert. His 'call into being' is his call to conversion or vocation (*Sermons*, 200).[29] We engage in this dialogue when we convert or answer the call to the religious life. Hopkins' first words in his sermon 'On St. Matthew's Calling' are, '*Suddenness of the call*; a casual-seeming thing, "as Jesus passed thence"' (23).[30] This sermon is devoted to vocation, a word the *Oxford English Dictionary* defines as, 'The action on the part of God (or Christ) of calling persons or mankind to a state of salvation or union with Himself; the fact or condition of being so called'. 'Vocation' is composed of the Latin words *vox* ('voice'), *vocatio* ('bidding, invitation') and *vocare* ('to call, summon'). In the above sermon, Hopkins emphasises in equal measure God's calling and our hearing and response. He says, '[St. Jerome] was not prepared to be called but he was prepared to obey the caller, of whose miracles he had heard', and 'to hear God's voice and obey his will...is spiritual and saving prudence' (*Sermons*, 23). Still, not all who hear his voice will answer to his call: '[some] do not follow [Christ], yet they look wistfully after him...wish they dared answer to his call' (35).[31] Vocation is an answer to a call, a response to 'that beckoning finger' (25); it is participation in a dialogue, an effort at communication and harmonious interaction.

The word 'vocation' implies that sounds can resonate within us in a manner that objects of vision cannot. David Michael Levin describes our connection with sound this way:

> It is easier for us to remain untouched and unmoved by what we see than by what we hear; what we see is kept at a distance, but what we hear penetrates our entire body… Hearing is intimate, participatory, communicative; we are always *affected* by what we are given to hear.[32]

Our positive response to God's call declares, in a sense, our deep attraction to his voice. The concept of resonance attraction continued to hold currency in the nineteenth century. Texts such as George Eliot's *The Mill on the Floss* explored its protagonist's undeniable attraction to the voice of her lover.[33]

John M. Picker and Delia da Sousa Correa have discussed the theory of sympathetic vibration to which Eliot was drawn through her reading of the natural philosopher Hermann von Helmholtz.[34] Experimenters since Galileo have observed the occurrence of sympathetic vibration, in which sound waves of a particular pitch emanating from a source cause distant materials such as strings, bells, and glass to sound at the same pitch. Helmholtz was not the first to describe this phenomenon, but he was the first to situate it within a theory of hearing. Comparing the ear to a piano, Helmholtz reasoned in the following manner: 'The end of every fibre of the auditory system is connected with small elastic parts, which we cannot but assume to be set in sympathetic vibration by the waves of sound'.[35] Says Picker,

> Uniting established acoustical phenomena with recent breakthroughs in mathematics (Ohm's principle of wave analysis as derived from Fourier's theorem), physiology (Müller's doctrine of specific nervous energies), and anatomy (Corti's cochlea discoveries), Helmholtz set forth a resonance theory of hearing that was both revolutionary and elemental: it posited that hearing, a form of sensory excitation by the external stimuli of sound waves, is nothing less than a bodily form of sympathetic vibration, and the ear a kind of microscopic Aeolian harp wired to the brain.[36]

In *Problems of Life and Mind*, George Henry Lewes, George Eliot's partner, evinces the influence of Helmholtz: 'When a note is sounded by one chord it will set vibrating any other chords which are in sympathy with it… It is thus also that external voices awaken sympathetic tones in us'.[37] As Hopkins puts it in 'Repeat that, repeat', 'The whole landscape flushes on a sudden at a sound' (line 5). The song of the cuckoo bird has 'awaken[ed] sympathetic tones', and the word 'flushes' suggests an instant, 'sudden' wave of response.

In *The Mill on the Floss*, we witness the play of sympathy in the romantic and musical attraction between Eliot's heroine, the 'highly-strung' Maggie Tulliver, and Stephen Guest, 'a rather striking young man'.[38] Maggie's undeniable attraction is exposed by her powerful response to Stephen's voice. His singing voice tempts and draws Maggie away from her renunciation of the world towards a semblance of her former vibrancy:

> The music was vibrating in her still – Purcell's music, with its wild passion and fancy – and she could not stay in the recollection of that bare, lonely past. She was in her brightest aërial world again.[39]

Maggie believes that Stephen's glance, furtively directed at her during his singing, had sympathetically 'caught the vibratory influence of [his] voice'.[40] At another time, she, who had 'always tried in vain to go on with her work when music began',[41] succumbs entirely to the seductive strength of Stephen's voice. Eliot's narrator describes Maggie's helpless emotional and physiological response thus:

> Poor Maggie! She looked very beautiful when her soul was being played on in this way by the inexorable power of sound. You might have seen the slightest quivering through her whole frame as she leaned a little forward, …her eyes dilated and brightened.[42]

Maggie's body is like a musical instrument being 'played on' by Stephen's voice. Eyes 'dilated' with desire, she leans forward, drawn to him through his voice. Her 'slightest quivering' culminates in ever greater stirrings at another performance: 'Maggie, in spite of her resistance to the spirit of the song and to the singer, was taken hold of and shaken by the invisible influence – was borne along by a wave too strong for her'.[43] The word 'influence' is particularly rich in this context, given its relationship to 'influential' and the notion of sound as an influx. Foreshadowing the devastating flood of the final chapter and Maggie's 'strong resurgent love towards her brother',[44] this scene illustrates the extent to which her equanimity could be 'shaken' by 'wave[s]' of sound sweeping her up and bearing her away. The irresistible lure of music exemplifies the laws of attraction, the impact of which Stephen defends to Maggie: 'We have proved that the feeling which draws us towards each other is too strong to overcome: that natural law surmounts every other; we can't help what it clashes with'.[45] With these words, Eliot draws a link between sympathetic vibration, magnetic attraction and romantic passion.

The equation of desire with magnetic attraction is a cliché nowadays, but in the nineteenth century it was a relatively fresh concept, for electromagnetism was only in the initial stages of scientific investigation.[46] Commentators and writers used the trope of magnetic attraction for religious illustration. In his explication of the line 'Draw me after thee', from the Song of Songs 1:4, Richard Frederick Littledale says,

> Thou has said in Hosea the Prophet, 'I drew thee with cords of a man, with bands of love;'[47] and in Jeremiah, 'I have loved thee with an everlasting love, therefore with loving-kindness have I drawn thee.'[48] And in this drawing, which consists of leading the human will into union with the Divine will, as the magnet draws the iron to itself, the Three Persons of the Holy Trinity co-operate…[The] cord…will not be broken.[49]

Littledale ties the tangible qualities of the binding cord with the invisible drawing power of the magnet. God's love, he asserts, is magnetic; it draws and binds us irresistibly to him. Similarly, Patmore says in '*Deliciæ Sapientiæ De Amore*', 'The magnet calls the steel: / Answers the iron to the magnet's breath'.[50] The magnet 'calls' out to the other; equally attracted, the iron reponds. This responding 'answer', this drawing of the iron to the magnet, is for Hopkins a 'yes' to God's call: 'It would seem that there must be some revelation of himself by God to the soul to awake the strain or *nisus* which is either to be gratified or denied… [I]t is one of attraction or repulsion, of yes or no' (*Sermons*, 139).[51] The sinner who says 'no' to God 'is carried and swept away to an infinite distance from God' (139). Conversely, sympathetic reception carries us towards God. Like Maggie Tulliver 'borne along by a wave too strong for her', unable to resist the voice of Stephen Guest, Hopkins is compelled, drawn to God's call, that voice 'awaken[ing] sympathetic tones in us'. Soon after his conversion, Hopkins admits to his mother, 'I cannot fight against God who calls me to His Church' (*Further Letters*, 92).[52] Likewise, in his sermon on vocation he argues that Christ magnetically captivates the believer with the voice of his calling. In contrast to Lucifer's 'enchantment' (*Sermons*, 201)[53] (a word derived in part from the Latin *cantare*, 'to sing'), Christ's 'spell' is a blessing, the call to vocation: 'Christ exerted a magnetic spell, as the saint says. What was this spell? – The grace of vocation' (23).[54]

Silence and Speech

What happens when God no longer calls to us? What if he no longer offers his 'inspiration'? If Christ is the eternally speaking Word, then silence spells his absence. In '*Nondum*', a silent God is as uncomforting as an absent one. Expressing dejection, the speaker declares, 'though to Thee our psalm we raise / No answering voice comes from the skies' (lines 1–2); 'Thou art silent' (line 31). Urged on by God's silence, he seeks reassurance, urging God to 'Speak! whisper to my watching heart / One word – as when a mother speaks / Soft, when she sees her infant start' (lines 49–51). Ordinarily, a loving mother would respond kindly to the child who seeks her. In this poem, her responsive voice exemplifies the love, attentiveness and concern of one being for another. Just as a mother responds to her child, so the speaker wishes the same of God. Earlier, he laments,

> I move along life's tomb-decked way
> And listen to the passing bell
> Summoning men from speechless day
> To death's more silent, darker spell. (Lines 39–42)

No divine finger beckons and no comforting voice calls out in the dark. The absence of light and love leaves only darkness; the silence of God serves to spell his absent affections. The 'spell' is not Christ's call but death's bell. '*Nondum*' thus reminds us of Hopkins' later description of hell as a benighted place far removed from God. The poem's title, which translates as 'not yet', alludes to the adjournment of God's voice and love.

In one of the so-called sonnets of desolation, Hopkins' speaker expresses similar despair over a silent God. In 'I wake and feel the fell of dark, not day', conceived 19 years after '*Nondum*' he bemoans that 'my lament / Is cries countless, cries like dead letters sent / To dearest him that lives alas! away' (lines 6–8). The absent recipient, the 'dearest' one who 'lives alas! away', does not receive, or is unreceptive to, the letters of the lover. The lover's words are like unreturned 'dead letters' because the intended addressee no longer corresponds with him. His misery is comparable to that of the Leaden Echo, which, at the prospect of death and loss, utters, 'O there's none; no no no there's none: / Be beginning to despair, to despair, / Despair, despair, despair, despair' ('The Leaden Echo and the Golden Echo', 13–15). In 'I wake and feel the fell of dark, not day', the circuit of correspondence is broken; the lover and beloved are no longer in touch. Hopkins laments with an 'O' reminiscent of the Leaden Echo's 'O' of emptiness and desolation: 'What hours, O what black hours we have spent / This night!' (lines 2–3).

In 'I wake and feel the fell of dark, not day' and '*Nondum*', silence and broken communication exemplify the separation between God and the soul.

However, in 'He hath abolish'd the old drouth', the deity's response recommences his correspondence with the believer. In the poem, the speaker's greeting is met not with Christ's silence but with his reply. The speaker addresses Christ and declares,

> We meet together, you and I,
> Meet in one acre of one land,
> And I will turn my looks to you,
> And you shall meet me with reply,
> We shall be sheavèd with one band
> In harvest and in garnering... (Lines 10–15)

If seeing is a form of touching (as I have argued), then eye contact is mutual touching. As we have seen, the image of turning and facing Christ foreshadows the wedding vow exchange in 'At the Wedding March'. To utter a wedding vow is to initiate a conversation. During the ceremony, the vows uttered by one party are repeated and, in a real sense, replied to, by the other. Indeed, a mutual declaration of love is necessary for the couple's union to be binding. The speaker addresses Christ as if to exchange vows: 'And I will turn my looks to you, / And you shall meet me with reply, / We shall be sheavèd with one band'. In this instance, to 'meet' refers not simply to the couple's coming together in 'one acre of land', but also to the response of one person to the looks and speech of the other. The exchange of looks and replies enables the subject and Christ to unite through the 'one band' of the harvest sheaf, a signifier of the wedding ring. The gathering of the harvest into sheaves, the culmination of agricultural labour, symbolises the fullness of communication between the soul and Christ.

The speaker of 'Hurrahing in Harvest' likewise salutes Christ at the instant when they 'ónce méet' (line 12). Greeting Christ, he offers his looks, the feelings from his heart and the words from his lips: 'And, éyes, héart, what looks, what lips yet gáve you á / Rápturous love's greeting of realer, of rounder replies?' (lines 7–8). Brown argues that the description of the rounded lips 'suggests the curve of a smile'.[55] A smile, Anna Wierzbicka observes, 'sends a message, and...this message has meaning'.[56] For Hopkins, the smile is a gesture that wordlessly expresses love. A face that offers 'looks' and 'lips' of 'á / Rápturous love's greeting' expresses intense pleasure at meeting the other. Resembling a drawn bow, the smile actualises the mouth from a state of rest and slackness to one of stress and tautness. The broadest smile, the mouth at its greatest stress, fully communicates the emotional content behind the speaker's 'looks' towards Christ. Given that the gestures of the speaker's face are referred to as 'replies', we see, then, that Christ is witnessing the reflection of his smile in the one who returns his greeting.

'Kisses meant for your mouth'

Lips offer smiles. They also offer kisses. In 'Hurrahing in Harvest', the association between 'greeting' and 'replies' suggests an exchange of friendly salutations. And yet, since the 'replies' are described as 'realer' and 'rounder' and are, furthermore, aligned with 'love's greeting', they also suggest the kiss of greeting. The kiss is one of the most intimate forms of touch and, as such, presents a significant gesture of love and welcome. In 'The Wreck of the Deutschland', Hopkins introduces the fifth stanza by declaring, 'I kiss my hand / To the stars, lovely-asunder / Starlight, wafting him out of it'. He concludes the stanza with the declaration, 'For I greet him the days I meet him, and bless when I understand'. An outstretched hand to the stars provides the body with its greatest vertical extension. Unsurprisingly, it is his own hand that Hopkins kisses to extend his greeting to the approaching Christ. Moreover, because Hopkins associates a hand with its fingers, and the fingers with the Spirit, the hand also signifies the speaker's *spiritus*. As he asserts, the Spirit 'is called the finger of the Father's right hand, that is all the fingers, for the fingers are to the hand or arm as many things are to one' (*Sermons*, 99).[57] Thus, when the speaker touches Christ with the hand that he has kissed, he communicates to him his breath and being. We come across another kiss of greeting in 'The Soldier', in which Christ greets the soldier thus: 'For lóve he leans forth, néeds his néck must fáll on, kíss' (line 12). This seemingly odd description of greeting alludes to the reunion of Esau with his estranged brother Jacob.[58] Hopkins' use of this biblical greeting suggests that the soldier is redeemed at the moment of greeting. The reconciliation between the two men is all the more poignant when we recall that Christ was tormented and crucified by Roman soldiers. As the poem makes clear, redemption is an act of love: it is 'For lóve' that Christ draws closer to the soldier in an embrace and a kiss. This kiss of greeting seals the love between the two who meet.

Writers have long believed that something more than breath might be given in a kiss; that the essence of a person might pass from one pair of lips to another. In Ben Jonson's early seventeenth-century play, *Volpone*, which Hopkins read (*Bridges*, 237), the eponymous character promises Celia the pleasures of kissing: 'I will meet thee in as many shapes: / Where we may, so, transfuse our wandering souls, / Out at our lips, and score up sums of pleasures'.[59] A kiss makes possible the exchange of souls. Jonson suggests the physical act of touching lips ends in literal ecstasy, such that one's 'soul' can pass into the body of another. Christopher Marlowe argues a similar notion in *Doctor Faustus*, another early seventeenth-century play with which Hopkins was almost certainly familiar (*Bridges*, 227). Faustus utters the famous lines,

> Sweet *Hellen*, make me immortall with a kisse:
> Her lips sucke forth my soule, see where it flies!
> Come *Hellen*, come, give me my soule againe.
> Here will I dwell, for heaven be in these lippes,
> And all is drosse that is not *Helena*!⁶⁰

Here, the desire to kiss is again expressed in religious language. Similar sentiments are espoused in Shakespeare's *Henry VI*, which Hopkins probably first read in 1864 (*Journals*, 35). In *The Second Part of King Henry VI*, Suffolk despairs over leaving his mistress, Queen Margaret. He expresses his wish to die by exhaling his soul into her body – his 'Elysium' – through a kiss:

> Where, from thy sight, I should be raging mad,
> And cry out for thee to close up mine eyes,
> To have thee with thy lips to stop my mouth;
> So shouldst thou either turn my flying soul,
>   [*He kisses her*]
> Or I should breathe it, so, into thy body,
> And then it liv'd in sweet Elysium.⁶¹

Volpone, Faustus and Suffolk link the kiss to respiration, arguing it is breathed into the 'body' of the other in the act of kissing. Hopkins would have also encountered contemporary Victorian examples of the pneumatic kiss. For instance, Tennyson's 'Fatima' refers to the soul's exit through the kiss of the mouth: 'O Love, O fire! Once he drew / With one long kiss my whole soul thro' / My lips, as sunlight drinketh dew' (lines 19–21).

The kiss features in the erotics of spiritual engagement. The Latin text of the Song of Songs begins with a kiss: 'Osculetur me osculo oris sui' (Let him kiss me with the kiss of his mouth). Bernard of Clairvaux describes this kiss as 'the breath of life':

> Joining his mouth to this dead mouth of mine, [Christ] gave the kiss of peace, for while we were yet sinners and dead to righteousness, he reconciled us to God. Setting his mouth to mine he breathed into it a second time the breath of life.⁶²

This kiss is for Bernard a typological re-enactment of God's inspiration in Adam. The notion of the kiss as a pneumatic exchange is likewise found in the

Apostles' encouragement of the 'kiss of peace' among early Christians. This kiss on the mouth, however, is not merely allegorical; it is also literal. Peter exhorts his fellow Christians to 'Greet ye one another with a kiss of charity'.[63] For Paul, the 'holy kiss' encourages closeness and community among fellow Christians.[64] The 'kiss of peace' facilitates unity, for, in the kiss, the believers are 'all made to drink into one Spirit'.[65] Among the early Christians, the kiss of greeting was understood to transmit the unitive qualities of the Spirit, as Nicholas James Perella argues: 'When the individual bodies kiss, they give evidence of being knit together by virtue of the Spirit they have in common. It may be said that they kiss one another with that Spirit'.[66]

Two people must meet in order to form a kiss. In the caress of the kiss, one kisses, and is kissed by, another. The kiss provides an intimate example of one's openness to the other. The kiss on the mouth undoubtedly circulates 'inspiration' and 'aspiration', enabling two subjects to share and exchange the same breath. For Hopkins, this kiss is synonymous with the transference of the Spirit, breath, and speech. In 'Hurrahing in Harvest', the speaker describes his greeting as both 'realer' and 'rounder', thereby suggesting an unusually abundant exchange of *spiritus*. In the kiss, as with conversation, breath circulates from the open lips of the one who breathes to the other who replies in kind. By opening his mouth to a 'rounder' capacity, the speaker increases his ability to inhale and, indeed, return to Christ his breath, speech and kiss.[67] The kiss allows Hopkins and Christ to simultaneously unite and retain their otherness. This idea of difference within unity is exemplified by the nature of the Trinity, the Three in One. The Spirit forms the kiss that unites the Trinity. According to Bernard of Clairvaux, the Father is the kisser, the Son is the kissed, while the Spirit is the kiss that unites them:

> [T]ruly the kiss…is common both to him who kisses and to him who is kissed…
> If, as is properly understood, the Father is he who kisses, the Son he who is kissed, then it cannot be wrong to see in the kiss the Holy Spirit, for he is the imperturbable peace of the Father and the Son, their unshakable bond, their undivided love, their indivisible unity.[68]

Hopkins holds to the Spirit's unitive character when he declares that the Spirit is 'the bond and mutual love of Father and Son, so of God and man' (*Sermons*, 195).[69]

Hopkins makes important use of the pneumatic kiss in an early ballad, 'The Queen's Crowning', which he composed the same year he read *Henry VI*. This poem presents the earliest sign of his preoccupation with breath exchange and foreshadows his later concepts of 'inspiration' and 'aspiration'. The poem tells the story of Alice who weds William, heir to the English throne. Following their wedding night, William leaves his new wife and returns to England. He is killed by his brothers after informing them of his marriage to a woman of lowly status. Two years later, a stranger knocks at Alice's door. When she asks him where he is from, he replies,

> 'I am not come from English land,
>   Nor yet from over the sea.
> If I were come from Paradise,
>   It were more like to be.' (Lines 125–8)

He bears a lily and a rose from Paradise. Hopkins continues,

> The more she ask'd, the more he spoke,
>   The fairer waxèd he.
> The more he told, the less she spoke,
>   The wanner wanèd she. (Lines 141–4)

The more one speaks, the more the other weakens. The suggestion is that, during the course of their conversation, the stranger inhales Alice's breath, leaving her with less and less, and thereby drawing her closer to death. Certainly, the entrance at which Alice meets the stranger is as much the threshold between life and death as it is between her and him.

The stranger asks Alice whether she will follow him and accept his 'kisses three'. She replies,

> 'O I will follow thee, my true love.
>   Give me thy kisses three.
> Sweeter thy kisses, my own love,
>   Than all the crowns to me.' (Lines 149–52)

The poem concludes thus:

> He gave her kisses cold as ice;
>   Down upon the ground fell she.
> She has gone with him to Paradise.
>   There shall her crowning be. (Lines 153–6).

The stranger's trinity of kisses completes what was begun with the verbal exchange: namely, it allows him to suck the breath and soul out of Alice. His kisses are described as being 'cold as ice', an allusion to a version of the ballad 'Sweet William's Ghost', upon which 'The Queen's Crowning' is based.[70]

'Sweet William's Ghost' is a supernatural ballad, which concludes with Margaret spurning the cold kisses of the dead lover. In contrast, the climax of Hopkins' ballad has clear theological significance, with its suggestion that Alice's 'true love' is Christ, the king of Paradise, whose three kisses exchange her mortal breath for eternal life. Just as Christ is the Second Adam, in the ballad he is the Second William. The Second William's reunion with his bride offers an alternative vision of the Second Coming.

In '*Ad Matrem Virginem*', the kiss at once initiates and exemplifies the conversational exchange between the self and the Christ. The speaker asks Mary for the embrace and kisses of her Son: 'Allow me to embrace Him, grant me a little of the love [*amore*] given to you, and kisses meant for your mouth'.[71] Speech and breath enter and leave through the mouth, helping to account for the speaker's request for 'kisses meant for your mouth'. We can say, then, that Mary conceived her Son, the Word, through kisses. This idea of conceiving through the mouth is reminiscent of certain Renaissance depictions of the Annunciation, which show a sequence of Hebrew letters emanating from the angel's mouth and reaching Mary's head.[72] These renderings gesture towards God's act of breathing his Spirit into the mouth of Adam. The angel of the Annunciation breathes the life of the Second Adam into the mouth of Mary. In Hopkins' hymn, the speaker yearns for the kisses from the mouth of this new Adam, Christ:

> The One who wishes to be given for me,
> Unspeaking, to speak to me,
> To converse with me,
> Do you give to me that I may contemplate Him too… (Lines 67–70)[73]

The Word is transmitted and 'given for me' through kisses, kisses originally given by the Spirit to Mary's mouth and, later, by the Word in conversation. By asking Mary, 'Do you give to me that I may contemplate Him too', the speaker reiterates his desire for the kisses that bear the Word. Christ willingly seeks to fulfil his yearning; as the speaker says, 'The One…wishes to be given for me', so that he might 'speak to me, to converse with me'. But the unborn Word is yet 'Unspeaking'. Physically incapable of speech, he may only 'speak' and 'converse' through kisses, kisses exemplifying and transcending speech. In this way, the kiss is necessary for the speaker to 'converse' with Christ. The speaker's reply would be his own kisses, because if the speech of Christ were given in kisses, the conversation between Christ and the speaker would be made possible only through the kisses given and responded to. This act requires face-to-face intimacy, and confirms the conversation of kisses as a demonstration of love. Certainly, when the speaker asks for 'a little of the love given to [Mary]' and the kisses meant for her mouth, he reveals that the word *ore* (from your mouth) is given in *amore* (out of your love). The kiss creates a circle of touching, a sharing of breath between the individual and Christ. It enables each participant to caress the other, to become one, and yet remain two.

Irigaray argues that, despite the teachings of the Christian tradition, we have forgotten about the importance of the breath in human and divine life.[74] 'With whom do I cultivate the breath?' she asks. And continuing:

> Who will allow me to remain two: the one, the other, and the air between us? Life is taken from no one. Each one safeguards it for him or herself and for the other, existing in solitude thanks to nature, but still wanting to live with the other. Each one, therefore, trains the breath in order to be, to be and to become: divided between us, perhaps, but together at the same time. Distanced by our difference, but present to each other.[75]

In a relationship of mutual interchange, what is the thing that distinguishes us from, and unites us with, the other? What enables us to touch, and be touched, in equal measure? For Hopkins, the spring of mutual caress, of otherness and unity, is the breath that moves between God and us.

Chapter Five

HOMECOMING

'Journeys end in lovers meeting'
—Shakespeare. *Twelfth Night*[1]

Return to Virgin Terrain

The word 'emotion' is etymologically linked to 'motion', as Giuliana Bruno notes:

> The Latin root of the word *emotion* speaks clearly about a 'moving' force, stemming as it does from *emovere*, an active verb composed of *movere*, 'to move,' and *e*, 'out.' The meaning of emotion, then, is historically associated with 'a moving out, migration, transference from one place to another.'[2]

Love and desire, as I have argued, compel us to reach out and touch the other; in 'The Windhover', even a 'heart in hiding' can be moved and 'Stírred for a bird'. The epigraph from Shakespeare suggests that the object of (e)motion is union with the beloved. With union comes home, rest and the end of the journey. Love is to home what a journey is to its destination: one leads to the other.

In this chapter, I concentrate on home as the thing for which we most yearn. Home satisfies several desires; it provides sanctuary, a place of belonging, a haven of intimate relationships. The hunger of the adult draws on the desires of the child. The adult, like the child, longs for shelter and tenderness, and finds it in the arms of a lover or a mother figure – or in objects of home standing in for them.[3] In a world of pollution, disease and death, Hopkins sees parallels between the lost youth of the earth and that of the individual. For the poet, home is not so much a middle-class abode of husband, wife and children, but a time and place of intense nostalgia and longing. As we see in the poem 'In the Staring Darkness', it is a moment in time, a golden past, like memories of childhood keeping the darkness out:

> In the staring darkness
> I can hear the harshness
> Of the cold wind blowing.
> I am warmly clad,
> And I'm very glad
> That I've got a home.

At the same time it is a place, Eden, a material yet virgin body. Necessary to the idea of home is the possibility of its recovery. To return home is to rediscover what we had lost in leaving it. Without home there is simply homesickness. As Hopkins writes in Ireland, 'To seem the stranger lies my lot, my life / Among strangers' ('To seem the stranger lies my lot', lines 1–2).

For Hopkins, our truest home is the Holy of Holies; at its centre dwells the divine other. In thinking of home in relation to bodies, emotion and motion, we will see that homecoming involves a journey to the most inward and intimate place, to the heart of Christ. Until the crossing is complete, we are displaced souls, moving restlessly until reaching our final destination. In Augustine's view, each human is *peregrinus*, a word that Robert J. O'Connell translates and interprets as

> the foreigner, the one who is traveling or perhaps residing 'abroad' and hence in alien surroundings, 'not at home'; so, it comes to mean one who 'feels like a foreigner,' experiences the pang of being far from one's native city or homeland, one's *domus*, *civitas*, or *patria*.[4]

Of the eternal Jerusalem, Augustine declares, 'your pilgrim people yearn [for it], from their leaving it to their return'.[5] The yearning is bound to the greatest longing: the desire to reunite with God and, finally, complete the circle of the touched and the touching.

Hopkins' poems '*Ad Mariam*', '*Rosa Mystica*' and 'St. Winefred's Well' help us understand the extent to which his awareness of suffering and death influenced his desire for an eternal home. Composed in the time between his entry into the Society of Jesus and his composition of 'The Wreck of the Deutschland', these poems express the notion of home in relation to Eden and the feminine. As we shall later see, this feminisation of home leads us to a feminised Christ. In '*Ad Mariam*', Eden is located with the newness of spring and the body of the Virgin Mary, whereas the Fall sits alongside the darkness of winter. Addressing Mary, the speaker says,

'For the fallen rise and the stricken spring to thee, / Thee, May-hope of our darkened ways!' (lines 39–40). Just as the ancient Romans associated May with Flora, the goddess of spring and flowers, so Hopkins associates the month of renewal with Mary. An anthropomorphic description confirms this link:

> And May has come, hair-bound in flowers;
> With eyes that smile thro' the tears of the hours,
> With joy for today and hope for tomorrow
>   And the promise of Summer within her breast!
>
> And we that joy in this month joy-laden,
>   The gladdest thing that our eyes have seen,
> Oh thou, proud mother and much proud maiden –
>   Maid yet mother as May hath been –
> To thee we tender the beauties all
> Of the month by men called virginal... (Lines 13–22)

Mary is paradoxically 'mother' and 'maiden'. Such motherhood is 'virginal' and redemptive. Evoking a life unblemished by sin and death, virginal fecundity is life as it was before the incursion of disobedience, sickness and decay. It is maidenly Eden, *virga* (maid) and *virgo* (meadow).[6] In these descriptions of a smiling Mary and May, Hopkins expresses childlike and naïve wistfulness for the end to 'tears'.

In another Marian poem, '*Rosa Mystica*', both *virgo* and *virga* form the heavenly paradise to which the speaker seeks to return. Like his counterpart in '*Ad Mariam*', the speaker situates himself, along with the reader, in the position of a child. This is achieved through the poem's catechism-like structure and simple rhyme scheme. The refrains anticipate the future fulfilment of present desires, a future in which the child is granted its wish to be with its mother:

> The rose in a mystery, where is it found?
> Is it anything true? Does it grow upon ground? –
> It was made of earth's mould but it went from men's eyes
> And its place is a secret and shut in the skies.
> Refrain –
> *In the gardens of God, in the daylight divine*
> *Find me a place by thee, mother of mine.* (Lines 1–6; emphasis original)

Mary dwells in the heavenly '*gardens of God*'. In this paradise the speaker will be with Mary. In the garden, Mary is 'the mystery, she is that rose' (line 22).

But she is more than the rose; foreshadowing the cross, she is also 'the tree' holding 'her rose', Christ:

> Is Mary the rose then? Mary the tree?
> But the blossom, the blossom there, who can it be? –
> Who can her rose be? It could be but one:
> Christ Jesus our Lord, her God and her son. (Lines 24–9)

The speaker asks of Christ, 'How many leaves had it? – Five they were then, / Five like the senses and members of men' (lines 37–8). The simile renders the rose an emblem of Christ and humanity alike. Indeed, this stanza concludes with the refrain, '*In the gardens of God, in the daylight divine / Make me a leaf in thee, mother of mine*' (lines 41–2; emphasis original). Just as Mary is the parent plant of the five-leaved Christ, she is also the mother of each fallen 'leaf'.[7] The speaker reiterates his earlier declaration of longing for the maternal home: '*I shall come home to thee, mother of mine*' (line 24; emphasis original).

In '*Rosa Mystica*', the speaker wishes to be a leaf '*in*' Mary. For Hopkins, our return to the Virgin's womb heralds our 'revirginalisation' (a term coined by Lloyd Davis and introduced in the second chapter). In other words, our return to Mary will enable us to return to that place of innocence and youth: Eden. In '*Rosa Mystica*', Mary is the rose and the tree, whereas in '*Ad Mariam*' her womb is a microcosm of paradise, a vaginal, 'deep-groved Aidenn' (line 23). Like the 'virginal' month that gives birth to a renewed world, Mary's virginal motherhood gives birth to the revirginalised individual. Hopkins draws a connection between innocence and youth in 'On the Portrait of Two Beautiful Young People', in which he declares, 'corruption was the world's first woe' (line 33). The poem celebrates virginal youth as the antithesis of decay, ruin and 'corruption' (the root of the word deriving from the Latin verb *rumpere*, 'to break', 'to break down'). And certainly, the Hebrew word *alamoth* implies a connection between virginity and youth.[8]

Similarly, in the nostalgic poem 'Spring', the renewal of the earth is depicted as a typological 'strain of the earth's sweet being in the beginning / In Eden garden' (lines 10–11). Through its celebration of spring, the poem expresses the speaker's yearning to return to a world 'before it cloy, / Before it cloud…sour with sinning' (lines 11–12). This 'sweet being' of the world 'before it cloy' is complemented by humanity's return to a state of 'Innocent mind and Mayday in girl and boy' (line 14). Clearly, the boy and girl represent Adam and Eve in the purity of their 'Mayday', the time before the Fall. This is the world before procreation, for reproduction is one of the surest signs of mortality and its attendant suffering. Just as Hopkins' experience of 'tears' helps define his ideal home as a place without distress, so the acute awareness of pain and death defines this home as a place without procreation.

Hopkins' awareness of death and mortality can be situated within a broader social context. In *Death and the Future Life in Victorian Literature and Theology*, Michael Wheeler refers to the 'Victorian cult of death' and the Victorians' 'obsessive interest in death'.[9] No figure embodied this 'obsessive interest' more than Queen Victoria, the most famous mourner of the era following the death of her husband, Prince Albert. Victoria's attempts to keep Albert alive through extensive mourning rituals gave death a certain cultural pre-eminence. Tennyson's *In Memoriam*, 'Victoria's favourite poem for comforting herself',[10] served also to keep death firmly in the nation's psyche. These royal and literary spectacles of mourning contributed to the spectre of death gaining a greater hold on the consciousness of the queen's subjects. On the minds of many Victorians was the question, at which point does growth end and death begin? 'The most resonant connection made by nineteenth-century physiological inquiry was between growth and death', notes Carolyn Steedman.[11] The figure of death looms larger with increasing age. 'Áh! ás the heart grows older / It will come to such sights colder', says Hopkins in 'Spring and Fall' (lines 5–6). The beating heart sustains life in the body, but it, too, 'grows older' and eventually fails.

Hopkins often places death alongside its dialectic other to bring out the significance of each. In 'Spring', he represents childhood as a state of pre-decay and growth before its inevitable decline. Youth is the pristine, virginal state of existence, like the 'sweet being' of the fragrant bloom before it withers and decomposes. In 'The Bugler's First Communion', the young bugler's nature is one that 'Breath[es] bloom of a chastity in mansex fine' (line 16). His 'bloomfall' (a literal deflowering) is itself a little death portending the body's death: 'freshyouth fretted in a bloomfall all portending / That sweet's sweeter ending' (lines 30–1). The neologism, 'freshyouth', underscores the association between the words 'fresh' and 'youth' in Hopkins' theology; the loss of one causes the loss of the other. Death, the 'sweeter ending', brings welcome relief to old age. As readers, we sense that fruit, a symbol of fecund adulthood, is simply not 'fresh' enough for Hopkins, to whom 'Nothing is so beautiful as Spring' ('Spring', line 1). Indeed, he appears to bypass the fruiting period altogether, ascribing the bloomfall to the stage succeeding the virgin bloom. Thus, in 'St. Winefred's Well', the virgin's beheading cuts short her 'fresh… bloom' and leads to the onset of deathly winter: 'her bloom, fast by | her fresh, her fleecèd bloom, / Hideous dáshed down, leaving | earth a winter withering' (B., lines 51–2).[12]

Returning to one's 'freshyouth' and 'fresh…bloom' signals the return of one's youthful 'chastity'. This return is restorative to body and soul. Hopkins believed that Winefred's Well, the healing spring named after the martyr, could hasten such a rebirth. Hopkins bathed in the spring (*Further Letters*, 154) and believed that it could recover a person's bloom (just as Winefred was revived when her decapitated head was reattached to her body). According to 'St. Winefred's Well', those who enter the waters 'go rich as roseleaves' (C., line 25) and leave it by exuding the fresh aroma of vitality. In the process, bathers shall rediscover the longed-for past and revive themselves among the 'come-back-again things, | things with a revival, things with a recovery' (C., line 29). The well's inviolate core is comparable to nature's 'dearest freshness deep down things' ('God's Grandeur', line 10), which prevents it from succumbing to corruption. In another poem, 'On St. Winefred', the well is described as an eternal spring that 'wish[es] all about us sweet' (line 1) and promotes what Hopkins calls 'virgin freshness' (line 6). The reiteration of the word 'sweet' at the start of the penultimate line complements the word 'sweat' at its end, and suggests that the latter, usually acrid and sour, has recovered its purity or 'virgin freshness': 'Sweet soul! Not scorning honest sweat / And favouring virgin freshness yet' (lines 5–6).[13] The pristine essence of the individual is like flowers guarded by a walled garden or as nectar hidden in a flower: 'His brightest blooms lie there unblown, / His sweetest nectar hides behind' ('On a Piece of Music', lines 40–1).

Sex and the City

Sexual virginity was once associated with fragrant scents, for it was thought a virgin's body was uncorrupted by the fluids of sexual intercourse.[14] For instance, it was believed Teresa of Ávila's virginity prevented her corpse from decaying, enabling her body to retain its floral fragrance.[15] Virtues possess their own distinctive smell. In his gloss on Ignatius' exercise by means of the five senses, Hopkins writes, 'You may suppose each virtue to have its own sweetness – one rich, another fresh, a third cordial, like incense, violets, or sweet-herbs, or, for taste, like honey, fruit, or wine' (*Sermons*, 176).[16] Hopkins links smell and taste here as elsewhere. Smell is crucial to the sense of taste, a word etymologically related to touch. Pleasant smells in the nose promote a sweet taste in the mouth. Both are highly attractive. In contrast, an unpleasant taste is repellent. When we say something tastes 'good' or 'bad' we imbue it with moral and emotional associations. Moral corruption, like physical putrefaction, exudes malodours tasting nothing like honey, fruit or wine in the mouth. Hopkins believes our sweet odours turn foul through sinning: 'Are we his censer? we breathe stench and not sweetness… If we have sinned we are all this' (240).[17] Similarly, he imagines the excremental stench of hell to be 'like vomit and like dung' (242).[18]

Naturally, Christ exemplifies sanctified sweetness. The medieval hymn 'S. Thomae Aquinatis Rhythmus ad SS. Sacramentum', translated by Hopkins, declares Christ to be 'the sweetness man was meant to find' (version b, line 20). Christ's sweet taste and odoriferousness mirrors that of paradise: 'Does it smell sweet too in that holy place? – / Sweet unto God, and the sweetness is grace: / O breath of it bathes great heaven above' ('Rosa Mystica', lines 42–4).[19] Hopkins associates St. Winefred, like Christ and paradise, with the sweet odour of sanctity and bloom. Hence, in 'St. Winefred's Well', Teryth refers to 'this bloom, this honeysuckle, | that rides the air so rich about thee' (A., line 17), and Caradoc describes her as 'time's one rich rose' (B., line 49).

The theological emphasis on smell might appear to us excessive. In Hopkins' time, however, smells – stench in particular – were pervasive and often overwhelming, especially in the expanding industrial cities. Hopkins writes, for example,

> I was yesterday at St. Helen's, probably the most repulsive place in Lancashire or out of the Black Country. The stench of sulphuretted hydrogen rolls in the air and films of the same gas form on railing and pavement. (*Bridges*, 90)[20]

Malodour was believed to cause disease. This concept of miasma (from the Greek word meaning, 'to pollute') was both a theory of disease causation and a description of polluting matter or filth.[21] According to the theory, disease is a response to decomposition, human waste, accumulated dirt, stagnant water and foul air. Thus, smell and noxious gases, results of putrefying matter, are either or both the causes and carriers of disease.[22] Subscribing to such a theory, Hopkins declares, 'the air and water carry in their currents the poison of disease' (*Sermons*, 90).[23] It was clear in the nineteenth century that English towns and cities were becoming progressively unhealthier habitations, and the ill effects of pollution were partly accounted for by the theory of miasma. Overcrowded cities such as London were increasingly prone to outbreaks of infectious diseases, such as cholera, and stench – most notoriously 'The Great Stink' of 1858 and 1859, the result of pollutant waste in the Thames. The growth of these cities was founded on the spiritually numbing work and polluting exertions of 'trade' and 'toil', antithetical to the rest and play of home life and the country: 'And all is seared with trade; bleared, smeared, with toil; / And wears man's smudge and shares man's smell: the soil / Is bare now' ('God's Grandeur', lines 6–8).

London in Hopkins' time was imagined as a Victorian Babylon, 'a city whose splendour was its downfall'.[24] This vision was not new, of course. William Blake and William Wordsworth had painted a vision of decadence and decay in 'London' and 'London, 1802', respectively. For Hopkins, the very exploitations driving urbanisation and typifying a metropolis will, in due course, stifle the body, mind and soul:

> What I most dislike in towns and in London in particular is the misery of the poor; the dirt, squalor, and the illshapen, degraded physical (putting aside moral) type of so many of the people, with the deeply dejecting, unbearable thought that by degrees almost all our population will become a town population and a puny unhealthy and cowardly one. (*Further Letters*, 293)[25]

Betraying his middle-class origins, and perhaps his anxieties about his own health and short stature, Hopkins feared the ugly, overcrowded and festering slums – which promoted the 'degraded', 'ill-shapen' and unhealthy state of the working-class masses – might infect and corrupt the rest of the country.[26] As a city-bound aesthete prone to nostalgia, he preferred robust bodies – such as that of Harry Ploughman – devoted to (agricultural) labour in healthier and aesthetic rural landscapes.[27] In mind and body, Hopkins experienced the side effects of living in large cities and yearned for country life. As he says, while 'My muse turned utterly sullen in the Sheffield smoke-ridden air' (*Bridges*, 48),[28] the Welsh landscape is 'always to me a mother of Muses' (227).[29] In short, 'Wild Wales breathes poetry' (*Dixon*, 142).[30] And elsewhere:

> I love country life and dislike any town and that especially for its bad and smokeful air... I think that very much may be said for life in London; though my dream is a farm in the Western counties, glowworms, new milk...but in fact I live in Dublin. (*Further Letters*, 292–3)[31]

A few years earlier, he had told his mother, 'I felt wretched for some time. Neither am I very strong now and as long as I am in Liverpool I do not see how I can be' (157).[32]

To Hopkins' mind, the scent of heaven and the stench of hell find their respective earthly counterparts in the country and city. 'Now at Liverpool one can *not* see the sun. Not but what for Liverpool too, "hellhole" though it is, something can be said', he says to Francis de Paravicini (*Further Letters*, 63; emphasis original).[33] Of the city's Italian inhabitants, he says to his mother, 'I do not know how they can bear such an air and sky. No, I see nothing of the Spring but some leaves in streets and squares. It is good, and I advise it, to get out of town and breathe fresh air' (157).[34] Escaping the city for the country is as returning to a remembered country home of sweet and comforting smells.

Discussing the importance of smell in Victorian gardens, Michael Waters argues,

> Odorous gardens are connected…with Proustian forms of temporal experience – with past times and the recollection of past times. The garden of childhood, particularly in its literal sense, can more easily be recalled or recaptured by the adult who in former times imbibed its associated scents.[35]

Hopkins' 'In the Valley of the Elwy' corroborates this very association between scent and a recollected rustic childhood:

> Í remémber a house where all were good
>   To me, God knows, deserving no such thing:
>   Cómforting smell bréathed at very entering,
> Fetched fresh, as I suppose, off some sweet wood. (Lines 1–4)

By remembering the 'Cómforting smell', the speaker momentarily recaptures the place in its springtime. He remembers that, in such a place and time, 'all were good'. In one sense, the place is the childhood country home in 'this world of Wales' (line 10), recollected in adulthood. In another sense, it is the paradise to which the speaker seeks to return; here, he will be reunited with the divine other. The poem concludes thus: 'God, lover of souls…/ Complete thy creature dear O where it fails, / Being mighty a master, being a father and fond' (lines 12–14).

Home is Where the Sacred Heart Is

Hopkins' Marian poems are Christocentric. Ultimately, they lead the believer to the most important figure, Christ. In '*Ad Mariam*', the significance of spring is that it heralds the summer. May gives birth to, and makes way for, summer, just as Mary gives birth to Christ, 'the promise of Summer within her breast!' (line 16). For Hopkins, our return to Mary is ultimately driven by our desire to reunite with Christ, he who dwelled in Mary's 'breast'. In Roman Catholicism, the Sacred Heart is associated with Christ's Five Wounds, comprising the four nail wounds in his hands and feet and the lance wound in his heart. These Wounds were instrumental in drawing Hopkins to the faith he believed would bring him closer to Christ. In a letter to his father, written shortly after his conversion, Hopkins implores him to

> approach Christ in a new way in which you will at all events feel that you are exactly in unison with me, that is, not vaguely, but casting yourself into His sacred

broken Heart and His five adorable Wounds. Those who do not pray to Him in His Passion pray to God but scarcely to Christ. (*Further Letters*, 94–5)[36]

Utterly devoted to Christ's Heart and Wounds, Hopkins believed that praying to God alone would be to ignore the incarnate Christ and his Passion. Hopkins' entry into the Society of Jesus, which held a special reverence for the Sacred Heart, enabled him to continue 'one of the dearest devotions of the Church' (*Sermons*, 101).[37] Texts devoted to the Sacred Heart, including the periodical *The Messenger of the Sacred Heart*, and books *The Life of the Venerable Mother Margaret Mary Alacoque* and Pierre Arnold's *The Imitation of the Sacred Heart of Jesus* were read in the refectory in the first two years of his training.[38]

The Wounds, particularly the one leading to the Sacred Heart, are the sites of Christ's outpouring of blood. Providing potent manifestations of his love, they offer invitations to reciprocate. As it is said in *The Life of the Venerable Mother Margaret Mary Alacoque*,

> the heart is the most natural symbol of love, and consequently it ought to be that of a devotion which is all love. Love is the object, love is the motive, love is the end of it… [U]nder the name and symbol of the sacred wounds of Jesus Christ the Church honours His suffering: it is in the same spirit that we find the representation of the heart of Jesus Christ, and in the symbol of that adorable heart, the remembrance of His love, and a fit object to awaken our own tenderness and gratitude.[39]

Margaret Mary was one of the greatest champions of the Sacred Heart, and Hopkins was certainly well acquainted with her *Life*. He says in his sermon on the Sacred Heart,

> we find [the Sacred Heart] in St. Gertrude's prayers and in St. Bernard's sermons, but little notice was in their days taken of it, and when the Bd. Margaret Mary said that our Lord himself had revealed it to her it struck people as a new thing and many called it a dangerous or a foolish one and spoke and wrote against it and opposed it with all their power… (*Sermons*, 100)[40]

Bernard's writings on the Sacred Heart, mentioned above, include this vivid and visceral description:

> the nail that pierced him has become for me the key to unlocking the sight of the Lord's will. Why should I not gaze through the cleft? The nail cries out, the wound cries out that God is truly in Christ reconciling the world to himself.[41] 'The iron pierced his soul'[42] and his heart has drawn near,[43] so that he is no longer one who cannot sympathise with my weaknesses.[44] The secret of his heart

is laid open through the clefts of his body; that mighty mystery of loving is laid open,[45] laid open too the tender mercies of our God, in which the morning sun from on high has risen upon us. Surely his heart is laid open through his wounds! Where more clearly than in your wounds does the evidence shine that you, Lord, 'are good and forgiving, abounding in steadfast love'?[46]

Like Margaret Mary, Bernard emphasises that the Wounds and the Heart supply ample 'evidence' of Christ's 'steadfast love'. Their meaning is 'laid open' to the intimate, piercing 'gaze' of the believer. The Wounds are the orifices in which the individual finds sanctuary, embrace, *eros*. 'Where then', Bernard asks, 'is the soul of the martyr?'[47] His answer? 'In a safe place,...in the heart of Jesus,...in wounds open for it to enter'.[48] The Wounds are the sites of Christ's abundant hospitality; they literally mark his openness to others, and it is through them that we enter into the very essence, the very Heart, of Christ.

The gaping bosom, the Wounds and the vital fluids flowing from them evoke the relationship between the curative, the corporeal and unconditional *eros*. In contemplating these Wounds, we are drawn to a feminised, sacrificial Christ whose agony and death have in the past been identified with the physical suffering of female martyrs, and vice versa. 'Through suffering', says Amanda Porterfield, 'the humanity of the [female] saint and the humanity of Jesus coincided, body to body and soul to Spirit, each contributing to a mystical relationship that reveals the other's humanity'.[49] Bodily pain and mutilation, however, do not point directly to inherent weakness. Maureen F. Moran convincingly argues that the women in Hopkins' poetry who willingly undergo suffering – notably St Winefred, Margaret Clitheroe and the tall nun of 'The Wreck of the Deutschland' – provide models of courage, righteousness and sacrifice that Hopkins and other religious thinkers would have considered 'manly'.[50] These heroic qualities, demonstrated by example, could thus belong to both men and women. Christ is the 'mártyr máster' ('The Wreck of the Deutschland', stanza 2), whose submission to bodily suffering furnishes the clearest evidence of nobility of character and strength of mind.

For Hopkins, this willingness to suffer is heroic and stoic, inspired by unswerving devotion and a willingness to convey vulnerability in the name of love: 'The piercing of Christ's side. The sacred body and the sacred heart seemed waiting for an opportunity of discharging themselves and testifying their total devotion of themselves to the cause of man', he says (*Sermons*, 255).[51] Christ is 'the world's hero', who sets an example by his suffering and death: 'He is the truelove and the bridegroom of men's souls...[T]he martyrs follow him through a sea of blood, through great tribulation' (35).[52] Christ's Passion testifies to his humanity, humility and love, to his divine otherness made accessible through his body's abjection. The model for the Christian martyr, he became flesh so that he might love us all the more and then die to prove his love.

Christ is the wounded healer whose healing touch comes from his own experiences of suffering, from his own com*passion*. As Porterfield puts it,

> In John, the suffering and humiliation that Jesus endures is part of a metaphysical process in which the Logos and Son of God take on human flesh and its vulnerabilities in order to redeem the world. In this context, the sicknesses and debilities that Jesus treated are symbols of mortality, and his miraculous healings are symbols of salvation from death.[53]

In Hopkins' words, the 'Heavenly physician' (*Sermons*, 19)[54] cures believers 'with his hands hardnailed out and appealingly stretched on the cross' and 'by the shedding of all his precious blood' (18).[55] Hopkins' translation of '*S. Thomae Aquinatis Rhythmus ad SS. Sacramentum*' speaks of a Christ who redeems the world through his suffering and *kenosis* (self-emptying):

> Make the tender tale true of the Pelican:
> Nurse me weak and naked at Thy breast that ran
> Blood one single drop of has the worth to win
> All the world redemption from a world of sin. (Version a, lines 21–4)

The early Christian tale of the pelican, said to have cut her own breast to sustain her young with her blood, paints her as a Christ-like figure. The 'tender tale' of the pelican (literally) expresses the Sacred Heart humanised by love: 'No heart as his was ever so tender' (*Sermons*, 37).[56]

Augustine famously declares to God, 'our heart is restless until it rests in you'.[57] Our spiritual journeys end when we find repose in the heart of the divine other. God himself wishes us to return to our rightful place, with him: 'He is very close to the heart; but the heart has wandered from him... Rest in him and you will be at rest'.[58] While Augustine spoke metaphorically of the reunion of hearts, Margaret Mary comprehended such a thing in a literal manner. In her vision, Christ 'took her heart, and placed it within His own, which she saw through the wound in His side, and which appeared to her brilliant as the sun, or as a burning furnace, whilst her own seemed but a little atom in the midst of that furnace'.[59] Christ's Heart is essentially on fire with his tremendous love. The love it inspires within Margaret Mary renders her heart a microcosm of its 'furnace':

> [A]fterwards, our Lord appeared to draw [her heart] from Him so inflamed that it resembled a furnace, and replacing it in the side of His servant, He said, 'Behold,

My beloved, a precious token of My love, which encloses within thy bosom a small spark of My charity to serve thee as a heart, and to consume thee to the last moments of thy life'.[60]

In 'The Wreck of the Deutschland', Hopkins describes the hearts of the believer and Christ as similarly 'inflamed' organs:

> My heart, but you were dovewinged, I can tell,
>   Cárrier-wítted, I am bóld to bóast,
> To flash from the flame to the flame then, tower from the grace to the grace.
> (Stanza 3)

The human heart reflects back to the Sacred Heart its divine 'flame'. The 'tower' suggests the lofty altitude of the Sacred Heart, which is filled with the 'grace' of love.

Like the winged Eros or the dove from the Song of Songs, the human heart, charged with love and (e)motion, rises. Like mounting flames, love carries us towards the divine other. As Augustine puts it, the heart that burns with love ascends to its rightful place in God:

> A body by its weight tends to move towards its proper place. The weight's movement is not necessarily downwards, but to its appropriate position: fire tends to move upwards, a stone downwards. They are acted on by their respective weights; they seek their own place… Things which are not in their intended position are restless. Once they are in their ordered position, they are at rest. My weight is my love. Wherever I am carried, my love is carrying me… Lit by your fire, your good fire, we grow red-hot and ascend, as we move upwards 'to the peace of Jerusalem'.[61]

In our journey from Eden to redemption, we return full circle into the embrace of the beloved, 'the ónly one', God.

NOTES

Introduction: Love and Touch

1 Armstrong's *Victorian Poetry* and Brown's *Gerard Manley Hopkins* and *Hopkins' Idealism* have examined intellectual and philosophical influences in Hopkins' writings. Beer's *Open Fields*, Brown's *Hopkins' Idealism*, Nixon's *Gerard Manley Hopkins and His Contemporaries* and Zaniello's *Hopkins in the Age of Darwin* have discussed the influence of nineteenth-century scientific thought. I engage with some of these issues when they advance a science of erotic engagement. Armstrong's *Victorian Poetry* also deals with the political background, Johnson's *Gerard Manley Hopkins and Tractarian Poetry* with the Tractarian heritage, Muller's *Gerard Manley Hopkins and Victorian Catholicism* with the Catholic climate, Zonneveld's *The Random Grim Forge* with social ideas and Ward's *World as Word* with philosophical theology.
2 Most recently, Bristow's 'Churlsgrace', Dellamora's *Masculine Desire*, Kaylor's 'Beautiful dripping fragments', Roden's *Same-Sex Desire in Victorian Religious Culture*, Saville's *A Queer Chivalry* and Sobolev's 'Hopkins's "Bellbright Bodies"'.
3 See Kitchen's *Gerard Manley Hopkins*, Martin's *Gerard Manley Hopkins* and White's *Hopkins*. Hopkins' latest biography, Mariani's *Gerard Manley Hopkins*, does not add to the debate.
4 Hopkins, *The Early Poetic Manuscripts*. Most of the items listed are not so much 'sins' as common or undesirable personal habits, such as idleness.
5 Saville, *A Queer Chivalry*, 6.
6 Saville, *A Queer Chivalry*, 7.
7 Saville, *A Queer Chivalry*, 3.
8 Saville, *A Queer Chivalry*, 3.
9 Dau, 'Beautiful Action', 4.
10 See Bristow's 'Churlsgrace', Dellamora's *Masculine Desire*, Higgins' '"Bone House" and "Lovescape"', Moran's 'Lovely manly mould', Overholser's 'Looking with terrible temptation', Roden's *Same-Sex Desire in Victorian Religious Culture*, Saville's *A Queer Chivalry* and Sobolev's 'Hopkins's "Bellbright Bodies"'.
11 From a sermon dated 23 November 1879.
12 Sobolev, 'Hopkins's "Bellbright Bodies"', 119.
13 Bristow, 'Churlsgrace', 709.
14 See Dellamora *Masculine Desire*, 86–93; Herrington, 'Hopkins and Whitman', 39–57; Kaylor, 'Beautiful dripping fragments', 157–87; and White, *Hopkins*, 110. Herrington focuses less on Hopkins' and Whitman's affinities in sexuality than on the similarities and influences of poetic and literary styles: 'the "heart" and "mind" the poets share is witnessed not just in their shared sexuality, to which critics have liked to limit themselves, but in their politics, philological interests, verse forms, and subjects for poetry' (54).

15 From a letter dated 18 October 1888.
16 Dacey, *Gerard Manley Hopkins Meets Walt Whitman in Heaven and Other Poems*.
17 From a letter dated 15 February 1879.
18 Higgins, '"Bone House" and "Lovescape"', 12.
19 Hopkins first alludes to the *Confessions* in an undergraduate essay, 'The Life of Socrates' (*Oxford Essays*, 131). Augustine will be discussed throughout this study, particularly in Chapter One.
20 Foltz and Bender, *A Concordance to the Sermons of Gerard Manley Hopkins*, 156–8. In addition, the word 'loveable' occurs twice, 'loved' 25, 'lovely' 7, 'lover' 4, 'loves' 13, and 'loving' 6 times (158–9).
21 In addition, a greater comprehension of love in Hopkins' thought will allow us, as readers, to better understand his poetic theory and practice. Hopkins believed love to be vital to his art, such that without it there would no art at all: 'Feeling, love in particular, is the great moving power and spring of verse', he wrote to his friend Robert Bridges (*Bridges*, 66). From a letter dated 15 February 1879. As I will demonstrate in Chapter Four, such a concept of love can help us comprehend Hopkins' theory of 'sprung rhythm'.
22 From a letter dated 16 October 1866.
23 From a letter dated 1 June 1864; emphasis original.
24 Hopkins, *The Poetical Works of Gerard Manley Hopkins*. Unless otherwise stated, future references to Hopkins' poems are to this edition. Line or stanza numbers will follow in brackets.
25 Carr, *The Erotic Word*, 10.
26 Nygren places a divide between the common Christian concept of love, *agape*, and the Greek or Platonic concept of desire, *eros*. 'There cannot actually be any doubt', he says, 'that Eros and Agape belong originally to two entirely separate worlds, between which no direct communication is possible' (*Agape and Eros*, 13).
27 See Rist, *Eros and Psyche*, 26, 69–70, 204–7.
28 From a sermon dated 31 August 1879.
29 Thomas à Kempis, *The Imitation of Christ*, 99–100.
30 Bell, 'A Bibliography of English Translations', 85. For a list of works translated between 1813 and 1891, see pages 101–11.
31 Hopkins translated '*Jesu Dulcis Memoria*' in 1866, a hymn that at the time was attributed to Bernard. Hopkins was also familiar with Bernard's *On the Song of Songs*, as his own sermons testify (*Sermons*, 100, 282n100). While Hopkins was in training at St Mary's Hall, Stonyhurst, a selection of Bernard's writings was read in the refectory in 1871, and the library contained Bernard's most important writings, including *On the Song of Songs* (Thomas, *Hopkins the Jesuit*, 237, 299).
32 Bernard of Clairvaux, *On the Song of Songs*, vol. 4, 83.2.4.
33 Bernard of Clairvaux, *On the Song of Songs*, vol. 4, 83.3.5.
34 Srivi, 'The Song of Songs', 50; emphasis original.
35 John of the Cross, *Dark Night of the Soul*, 166.
36 Saville, *A Queer Chivalry*, 67.
37 From a letter dated 6 January 1865.
38 Origen, *Song of Songs*, 29. In the *Symposium*, the term 'heavenly eros' occurs in the speech of Pausanius, 'signifying a practice of desire that begins with physical love but ultimately transcends the physical' (Boyarin, 'What Do We Talk About When We Talk About Platonic Love?', 4).

39 Osborne, *Eros Unveiled*, 72–3.
40 Origen, *Song of Songs*, 30.
41 Origen, *Song of Songs*, 31; emphasis original.
42 Origen, *Song of Songs*, 35.
43 During Hopkins' final year at St Bueno's College, the topic at the College's 'Essay Society' on 27 January 1877 was 'St Augustine's *City of God*' (Thomas, *Hopkins the Jesuit*, 173). Hopkins attended these fortnightly meetings and on 28 April 1877 read the final paper of the year's session, a piece entitled 'The composition of place in the Spiritual Exercises' (173).
44 Titus 1:8
45 John 21:15.
46 Augustine *City of God* (trans. Bettenson) 14:7.
47 Augustine *City of God* 14:7.
48 From a sermon dated 14 December 1879.
49 From a sermon dated 14 December 1879; emphasis added. Hopkins elsewhere calls God 'a master, being a father and fond' ('In the Valley of the Elwy', line 14).
50 Ignatius of Loyola, 'Contemplation for Obtaining Love', cited in *Sermons*, 192–4.
51 From notes on 'Contemplation for Obtaining Love', dated 14 August 1882; emphasis original. Unless otherwise stated, Hopkins' spiritual notes concern sections of Ignatius of Loyola's *Spiritual Exercises*.
52 Irigaray, *To Be Two*, 25.
53 Merleau-Ponty, *The Visible and the Invisible*, 142.
54 Merleau-Ponty, *The Visible and the Invisible*, 143. He also declares, 'Speaking-listening, seeing-being seen, perceiving-being perceived circularity (it is because of it that it seems to us that perception forms itself *in the things themselves*) – *Activity = passivity*' (265; emphasis original).
55 Merleau-Ponty, *The Visible and the Invisible*, 263.
56 Irigaray, *To Be Two*, 12.
57 Irigaray, *To Be Two*, 16.
58 Irigaray, *To Be Two*, 11.
59 Joy, O'Grady and Poxon, 'Editors' Introduction', xvi.
60 Irigaray, 'Introduction', 5.
61 Irigaray, 'Introduction', 1.
62 Irigaray, 'Introduction', 8.
63 Irigaray, 'Introduction', 4.
64 Jowett, 'Introduction', 246. From Plato, *The Dialogues of Plato*, vol. 4, 3rd ed. Hopkins attended lectures given by Jowett, was a member of at least one of his tutorials almost every term and 'was virtually in daily contact with [him]' (Higgins, 'Hopkins and "The Jowler"', 149, 143).
65 Stewart, *Poetry and the Fate of the Senses*, 162.
66 Augustine *Confessions* (trans. Chadwick) 10.27.38.
67 Colligan and Linley, *Media, Technology, and Literature*, 4.
68 Colligan and Linley, *Media, Technology, and Literature*, 4.
69 Rudy, *Electric Meters*, 131. Rudy regards lightning as destructive, whereas I see it in relation to emotional passion.
70 Acts 9:3–9.
71 'Feeling, love in particular, is the great moving power and spring of verse' (*Bridges*, 66). From a letter dated 15 February 1879.

Chapter One: Confluence and Reflection

1 Johnson, 'Introduction', xix.
2 'There is a circle of the touched and the touching, the touched takes hold of the touching; there is a circle of the visible and the seeing, the seeing is not without visible existence; there is even an inscription of the touching in the visible, of seeing in the intangible' (Merleau-Ponty, *The Visible and the Invisible*, 143).
3 Johnson, 'Introduction', xx.
4 Merleau-Ponty, *The Visible and the Invisible*, 154.
5 Merleau-Ponty, *The Visible and the Invisible*, 139.
6 Merleau-Ponty, *The Visible and the Invisible*, 153–4.
7 Cotter, 'Hopkins and Augustine', 79.
8 White, *Hopkins*, 21, 22, 88.
9 From a journal entry dated March 1871.
10 From a journal entry dated 19 July 1872.
11 From a journal entry dated 12 December 1872.
12 'The ashtree growing in the corner of the garden was felled… [S]eeing it maimed there came at that moment a great pang and I wished to die and not to see the inscapes of the world destroyed any more' (*Journals*, 230). From an entry dated 8 April 1873.
13 The last phrase originates from an essay by Monika Langer, which discusses Merleau-Ponty's philosophy in relation to deep ecology. For Merleau-Ponty, 'self and nonself, human and nonhuman, intertwine in a mutual enfolding, such that comprehension itself becomes a relation of "embrace" with the other' ('Merleau-Ponty and Deep Ecology', 115). For more on ecology and visual perception in the poem, particularly from a Scotist and Ignatian perspective, see Day, 'Hopkins' Spiritual Ecology in "Binsey Poplars"', 181–94. Day also notes the pun on the word 'scene' (185).
14 Essay written between winter 1866 and winter 1867.
15 Miller, *The Disappearance of God*, 291–2.
16 From the notes 'Parmenides', written between 9 February 1868 and Spring 1868. This is the first time Hopkins uses the word 'instress'.
17 From a journal entry dated 18 July 1868.
18 From a journal entry dated 1 August 1868.
19 From a journal entry dated 20 July 1873.
20 From a journal entry dated 31 May 1866.
21 From a journal entry dated July 1871.
22 From a journal entry dated 3 September 1866.
23 From a journal entry dated 13 August 1874.
24 From notes on 'The Rules for the Discernment of Spirits', dated 25 November 1881.
25 Aristotle *De Anima (On the Soul)* (trans. Lawson-Tancred) 1.2.405b. Hopkins refers to *De Anima* in his Dublin lecture notes on the *Nicomachean Ethics* (G.I, fos.11, 20, 28).
26 From notes on 'Creation and Redemption: The Great Sacrifice', dated 8 November 1881.
27 Heraclitus, 'B125', cited in and translated by David Wiggins, 'Flux, Fire and Material Persistence', 12. Heraclitus' philosophy is crucial to one of Hopkins' later poems, 'That Nature is a Heraclitean Fire and of the Comfort of the Resurrection'.
28 Bernard of Clairvaux, *On the Song of Songs*, vol. 4, 83.2.4.
29 Dolben, *The Poems and Letters of Digby Mackworth Dolben 1848–1867*. Unless otherwise stated, future references to Dolben's poems are to this edition. The handwritten poem is in MS Eng. Poet. e. 90.

30 Song of Songs 4:12, 4:16, 5:1, 6:2, 6:11.
31 F. fo. 83; emphasis original. Hopkins had originally written 'refresh its thirst'.
32 From notes on 'Contemplation for Obtaining Love', dated 8 December 1881.
33 'There is beauty in lovely physical objects, as in gold and silver and all other such things. When the body touches such things, much significance attaches to the rapport of the object with the touch... Human friendship is also a nest of love and gentleness because of the unity it brings about between many souls' (Augustine *Confessions* 2.5.10).
34 Augustine *Confessions* 2.6.13.
35 From undated notes on 'On Personality, Grace and Free Will'.
36 From notes on 'First Principle and Foundation', dated 20 August 1880.
37 Augustine *Confessions* 3.6.11.
38 Madison, 'Flesh as Otherness', 29.
39 From notes on 'Contemplation for Obtaining Love', dated 8 December 1881.
40 Loughlin, *Alien Sex*, x.
41 Augustine *Confessions* 10.27.38.
42 Compare this to Augustine: 'As an adolescent I went astray from you (Ps.118: 76), my God, far from your unmoved stability. I became to myself a region of destitution' (*Confessions* 2.10.18).
43 John of the Cross, 'The Dark Night of the Soul', translated by Paul Mariani, *God and the Imagination*, 219, 221.
44 Augustine *Confessions* 3.3.8.
45 Augustine *Confessions* 10.29.40.
46 Carson, *Eros the Bittersweet*, 115. The example by Sappho is from Fragment 130. For more on Hopkins' knowledge of Sappho and Pindar, see *Dixon*, 150, and *Bridges*, 49, 123, 147, 157, 159, 228–9, 233–4 and 239. Yopie Prins argues that the Victorian period saw 'an increasing number of scholarly editions, poetic translations, and other literary imitations' of Sappho's surviving work (*Victorian Sappho*, 3).
47 'And hard men feel a softening touch', Hopkins writes in '*Il Mystico*' (line 30).
48 Augustine *Confessions* 11.29.39.
49 Whitman, *Complete Poetry and Collected Prose*.
50 From a journal entry dated 16 August 1872.
51 Donne, *John Donne*.
52 Hopkins' lecturer, Robert Williams, taught him that the *Phaedrus*, along with the *Phaedo*, *Symposium* and *Republic*, was one of the 'Purely Platonic dialogues' (*Oxford Essays*, 236).
53 Plato *Phaedrus* (trans. Jowett) 254b. From Plato, *The Dialogues of Plato*, vol. 2, 2nd ed. Future references to the text are to this edition.
54 Plato *Phaedrus* 255d.
55 Plato *Phaedrus* 255c.
56 Plato's Socrates 'claims that the beloved youth comes to participate in his lover's passionate desire for him. The younger partner no longer feels mere honor or esteem for his lover but is said to return his desire – though more weakly, Socrates hastily adds in an effort to square his account with contemporary moral standards and unwritten rules of social behaviour. What the beloved experiences, according to Socrates in the passage from the *Phaedrus* quoted above, is not philia but *erōs*, specifically *anterōs* ('counter-love' in Hackforth's translation) – that is, an *erōs* in return for *erōs*, which is an image or replica (*eidōlon*) of his lover's *erōs*' (Halperin, 'Plato and Erotic Reciprocity', 67).
57 Astell, 'Kristeva and Bernard of Clairvaux', 127.
58 Hopkins, *The Poetical Works of Gerard Manley Hopkins*, 369.

59 From a sermon dated 23 November 1879.
60 From a sermon dated 11 January 1880.
61 From a sermon dated 25 October 1880.
62 The entirety of D.XII.3, written between Autumn 1867 and 9 February 1868.
63 Augustine *The Trinity* (trans. Hill) 8.4.
64 From undated notes on the *Spiritual Exercises*.
65 Romans 13:14. Unless otherwise stated, biblical quotes will be from the King James Version, given its general prominence and the fact that it was known to Hopkins since childhood.
66 Augustine *Confessions* 8.12.28–9.
67 Genesis 3:7.
68 A typological relation between the fig tree and Paul's declaration is argued for by Garry Wills in *Saint Augustine*, 46–7.
69 From undated notes on 'Principle or Foundation'.
70 Psalm 19:1.
71 From a sermon dated 30 November 1879.
72 1 Corinthians 13:12.
73 From spiritual notes dated 7 September 1883.
74 From a sermon dated 18 January 1880.
75 From a sermon dated 30 November 1879; emphasis added.
76 From a letter dated 10 March 1879.
77 Teresa of Ávila, *Life*, 191.
78 Teresa of Ávila, *Life*, 234; emphasis added.
79 From a journal entry dated 18 September 1873.
80 From notes on 'The Fifth Exercise: A Meditation on Hell', dated 1881.
81 Teresa of Ávila, *Life*, 233.
82 From notes on 'The Rules for the Discernment of Spirits', dated 13 August 1882.
83 From a sermon dated 23 November 1879.
84 Grabes, *The Mutable Glass*, 105.
85 Teresa of Ávila, *Life*, 308.
86 From undated notes on 'The Principle or Foundation'.
87 From notes on 'Creation and Redemption: The Great Sacrifice', dated 8 November 1881; emphasis added. The Latin translates as, 'For we are his workmanship, created in Christ Jesus unto good works, which God hath before ordained that we should walk in them' (Ephesians 2:10).
88 From undated notes on 'On Personality, Grace and Free Will'. Hopkins is quoting in part from 1 Corinthians 6:15: 'Know ye not that your bodies are the members of Christ? shall I then take the members of Christ, and make them the members of an harlot? God forbid'. He is also quoting from Philippians 2:6: '[Christ] being in the form of God, thought it not robbery to be equal with God'.
89 From a sermon dated 25 January 1880.
90 From notes on 'Creation and Redemption: The Great Sacrifice', dated 8 November 1881.

Chapter Two: Virgin Marriage and the Song of Songs

1 Hopkins describes their first meeting in a letter dated 12 August 1883 (*Dixon*, 111–12).
2 From a letter dated 16 October 1879. The reference to the *Unknown Eros* is a slip on Hopkins' part; he completed his studies in 1867, whereas the text was published a decade later in 1877. He is therefore referring to either *The Angel in the House* or

The Victories of Love. Nevertheless, after its publication he did indeed read, and admire, the *Unknown Eros*; in a letter to Patmore, dated 4 April 1885, he compares the *Unknown Eros* to Bridges' *Eros and Psyche* (*Further Letters*, 359).
3   From a letter dated 26 May 1879.
4   de Vere, *Essays*, 139–40.
5   de Vere, *Essays*, 149.
6   Reid, *The Mind and Art of Coventry Patmore*, 90–1.
7   Horatius Bonar, 'I lay my sins on Jesus'. From *The English Hymnal*.
8   John 13:23–5 and 21:20.
9   'His left hand is under my head, and his right hand doth embrace me' (Song of Songs 2:6) and 'His left hand should be under my head, and his right hand should embrace me' (8:3).
10 Maynard, 'Like a Virgin', 139.
11 'A bundle of myrrh is my wellbeloved unto me; he shall lie all night betwixt my breasts' (Song of Songs 1:13).
12 From a letter dated 10 February 1888.
13 'This is my beloved Son, in whom I am well pleased' (Matthew 3:17). These words were spoken by God at Christ's baptism. See also Mark 9:11 and Luke 3:21–2.
14 Patmore, *The Rod, The Root, and the Flower*, 213; emphasis original.
15 From a sermon dated 23 November 1879.
16 From a letter dated 14 May 1885.
17 Patmore, *The Life and Times of Coventry Patmore*, 199.
18 From a letter dated 21 August 1885.
19 From a sermon dated 4 January 1880. This translation is included in *The Poetical Works of Gerard Manley Hopkins* under the title '*O Deus, Ego amo te*'.
20 From a letter dated 30 June 1886.
21 Bugge, *Virginitas*, 59.
22 From a letter dated 16 October 1866.
23 The surviving letters from Newman to Hopkins are collected in *Further Letters*, 404–14. For more on the relationship between Hopkins and Newman, see Nixon, *Gerard Manley Hopkins and his Contemporaries*, 51–107. See also Johnson, *Gerard Manley Hopkins and Tractarian Poetry*, 166–200.
24 For more on Kingsley's antagonism towards Newman and Tractarianism, see Adams, *Dandies and Desert Saints*, 65, 80, 84, 98–102, 187, 209.
25 Dowling, *Hellenism and Homosexuality in Victorian Oxford*, 42.
26 Kollar, 'The Oxford Movement and the Heritage of Benedictine Monasticism', 284.
27 Newman, *et al.*, *Lyra Apostolica*. Poems from the text will be taken from this edition. The volume was originally published in 1836.
28 John 20:17.
29 Newman, *Sermons Bearing on Subjects of the Day*, 139.
30 Tennyson, *Victorian Devotional Verse*, 106.
31 Williams, 'Tract 80', 53. From Members of the University of Oxford, *Tracts for the Times*, vol. 4.
32 Williams, 'Tract 80', 53.
33 Foucault, *The Care of the Self*, 230.
34 Brown, *The Body and Society*, 56. The quotation is from 1 Corinthians 7:33–4.
35 From a letter dated 4 May 1863. Hopkins entered Balliol in April 1863 and began attending the lectures on 4 May that year. The lectures on 1 Corinthians ended on 30 October 1864 (Nixon, *Gerard Manley Hopkins and His Contemporaries*, 29).

36 For instance, Hopkins' journals record his severe curtailment of food during Lent in 1866 (*Journals*, 72).
37 MS Eng. Poet. e. 90, fo. 108v.; emphasis original. The notes are reproduced in Nixon, 'Gerard Manley Hopkins and Henry Parry Liddon', 101–8.
38 MS Eng. Poet. e. 90, fo. 107v.
39 MS Eng. Poet. e. 90, fo. 108v.
40 MS Eng. Poet. e. 90, fo. 106v.
41 Ephesians 5:30–2.
42 Paul says, 'for two, saith he, shall be one flesh. But he that is joined unto the Lord is one spirit' (1 Corinthians 6:16–17).
43 The phrase, 'intersubjective space', is from J. E. Malpas, who discusses the encounter between the self and the other in *Place and Experience*, 138.
44 Liddon, *Sermons Preached Before the University of Oxford*, 80. The quotation is from 2 Corinthians 3:17.
45 Williams, 'Tract 87', 42–3. From Members of the University of Oxford, *Tracts for the Times*, vol. 5.
46 Hopkins, *The Early Poetic Manuscripts*, 219.
47 Francis of Assisi's marriage to Lady Poverty symbolises his renunciation of wealth and entry into the religious life. His marriage makes him a figure of Christ, the first spouse of Lady Poverty (Dante, *Paradiso*, 11.49–99). From Dante, *The Divine Comedy*.
48 Hopkins describes Mary as an 'immaculate white' rose in '*Rosa Mystica*' (line 32). The rise of the cult of the Virgin Mary among the early Christians was due in part to the belief that virgins of the Church 'bore bodies analogous to that of Mary: unshaken by intercourse and childbirth' (Brown, *The Body and Society*, 444).
49 From a letter dated 16 October 1866.
50 Fontana, 'Patmore, Pascal, and Astronomy', 283.
51 Patmore, *Poems*, 338. Further references to Patmore's poems are to this edition. In the absence of line or stanza numbers, page numbers will be cited.
52 Maynard, 'Like a Virgin', 139.
53 Maynard, *Victorian Discourses on Sexuality and Religion*, 250.
54 Patmore, *Poems*, 330.
55 Patmore, *Poems*, 334. Lloyd Davis coins the word 'revirginalized' in 'The Virgin Body as Victorian Text', 22. In the final chapter, 'Homecoming', I examine the concept of redemption as a state of 'revirginalisation'.
56 Patmore, *Poems*, 334.
57 Maynard, *Victorian Discourses on Sexuality and Religion*, 196. According to Maynard, Emily 'loved the poem ["*Deliciæ Sapientiæ De Amore*"]' (196).
58 Thomas, *Hopkins the Jesuit*, 220.
59 Thomas, *Hopkins the Jesuit*, 219. Gallwey is also featured in *Sermons by Fathers of the Society of Jesus*, which was read on 13 August 1869 (223).
60 Gallwey, *Convent Life*, 17.
61 'And Adam said, This is now bone of my bones, and flesh of my flesh: she shall be called woman, because she was taken out of man. Therefore shall a man leave his father and his mother, and shall cleave unto his wife; and they shall be one flesh' (Genesis 2:23–4).
62 'Have ye not read, that he which made them at the beginning made them male and female, and said, For this cause shall a man leave his father and mother and shall

cleave to his wife: and they twain shall be one flesh? Wherefore they are no more twain but one flesh. What therefore God hath joined together, let no man put asunder' (Matthew 19:4–6).

63 Gallwey, *Convent Life*, 17. See 1 Corinthians 6:16 and Ephesians 5:31.
64 Gallwey, *Convent Life*, 18.
65 Gallwey, *Convent Life*, 18.
66 Gallwey, *Convent Life*, 40.
67 Gallwey, *Convent Life*, 40.
68 Cotter, 'The Song of Songs and "The Wreck of the Deutschland"', 57. See also his short article, 'Orion Behind the Lattices', 24–6.
69 Shortly before his entry into the Society of Jesus, Hopkins copied poems by Dixon and D. G. Rossetti as a keepsake (MS Eng. poet. e. 90 and MS Eng. poet. e. 91).
70 Barfoot, 'In This Strang Labourinth How Shall I Turne?', 243. Hopkins' 'A Voice from the World' is a poetic response to Christina Rossetti's 'Convent Threshold'.
71 Virkar, 'Gerard Manley Hopkins and the Song of Songs', 195.
72 From 'Dublin Meditation Points', dated 22 February 1884 to 25 March 1885.
73 The word 'vulnerable' has roots in the Latin word for 'wounding'.
74 Virkar, 'Gerard Manley Hopkins and the Song of Songs', 202
75 Virkar, 'Gerard Manley Hopkins and the Song of Songs', 205. 'My beloved put in his hand by the hole of the door, and my bowels were moved for him' (Song of Songs 5:4).
76 'A human body is like a house. Private and public life, inward and outward worlds, meet there. It, not banks or money, is the primary place and means of exchange. It encloses our inmost thoughts and feelings. It also lets them out and reveals them. It "deals out that being indoors each one dwells" (G. M. Hopkins, "As Kingfishers Catch Fire")' (Drury, *Painting the Word*, 50).
77 Virkar, 'Gerard Manley Hopkins and the Song of Songs', 204.
78 Oulton, *Romantic Friendship in Victorian Literature*, 46.
79 Tennyson, *The Poems of Tennyson*, vol. 2. Future references to Tennyson's poems are to this edition.
80 Tennyson again uses the image of the door to represent separation and express grief during the first Christmas following Hallam's death. The Christmas bells from the hamlets 'Answer each other in the mist'; they 'Swell out and fail, as if a door / Were shut between me and the sound' (section 28).
81 Krasner, '*In Memoriam* 7 and the Song of Solomon', 93.
82 Krasner, '*In Memoriam* 7 and the Song of Solomon', 93.
83 Song of Songs 5:2–6. A shorter version of the same incident can be found in the Song of Songs 3:1–2. Similarly, Tennyson represents variations of same incidents and examples throughout the elegy.
84 'The cultural status of death in the mid-Victorian period allows for strong expressions of intense feeling, as historians point out' (Oulton, *Romantic Friendship in Victorian Literature*, 57).
85 Manley Hopkins cited in Craft, *Another Kind of Love*, 47.
86 Craft, *Another Kind of Love*, 47.
87 Song of Songs 5:2.
88 Craft, *Another Kind of Love*, 52.
89 Craft, *Another Kind of Love*, 53.

90 Craft, *Another Kind of Love*, 53. Tennyson imagines that at the end of time, 'He that died in Holy Land / Would reach us out the shining hand, / And take us as a single soul' (section 84).
91 Craft, *Another Kind of Love*, 53.
92 Craft, *Another Kind of Love*, 55.
93 Craft, *Another Kind of Love*, 56.
94 Craft, *Another Kind of Love*, 58.
95 'Even during the second trial, when Wilde made his impassioned speech about the "love that dare not speak its name", his terms of reference were to the Bible and to Plato: texts to which he naturally turned to uphold forms of intimate homosociality, which had long gained legitimacy among the Oxford faculty' (Bristow, *Effeminate England*, 5).
96 Craft, *Another Kind of Love*, 63.
97 Tennyson, *The Poems of Tennyson*, 410.
98 From a letter dated 27 February 1879.
99 Saville, *A Queer Chivalry*, 54–6.
100 Dellamora, *Masculine Desire*, 31–2.
101 From a sermon dated 23 November 1879.
102 Dellamora, *Masculine Desire*, 46.
103 Saville, *A Queer Chivalry*, 32.
104 Saville, *A Queer Chivalry*, 32–3.
105 Roden, *Same-Sex Desire in Victorian Religious Culture*, 85.
106 Reproduced throughout Hopkins, *The Early Poetic Manuscripts*.
107 Dolben also appears to have been drawn to men. He addressed some of his early love poems to his Eton contemporary, Martin Le Marchant 'Marchie' Hadsley Gosselin, whom Bridges renamed 'Archie Manning' in his introduction to Dolben's collection of poetry (Dolben, *Poems and Letters*, 2–3).
108 From a letter dated 30 August 1867.
109 See Dau, 'Beautiful Action', 3–18.
110 Compare this description of the landscape to 'the loins of hills' (line 5) in Hopkins' poem 'Epithalamion'.
111 See Najarian, *Victorian Keats*, 108–10. In 'Looking with Terrible Temptation', Overholser provides a long list of the sexual temptations that Hopkins the undergraduate associated with the sense of sight. Citing an early poem, 'The Alchemist', and later meditation notes, Overholser contends that 'Christ's body was…to act as an example of purity toward which to aspire and as an aid to self-control; meditation notes made in 1885 show that Hopkins continued to use "The sight of our Lord's body as a remedy for temptation" [S, 255]' (37, 40). However, Hopkins' mature poetry openly revels in the sight of mortal men's bodies, suggesting a delight unhampered by the earlier fear of 'temptation'. In 'Harry Ploughman', the speaker invites the reader to 'look' (and presumably join him in the act): 'He bends to it, Harry bends, look' (line 11). In 'Epithalamion', a stranger happens upon a group of boys swimming: 'unseen / Sees the bevy of them' (lines 15–16). He then proceeds to strip, with 'fingerteasing task' (line 33), in front of the eyes of the admiring speaker.
112 White, *Hopkins*, 110.
113 Johnson, *Gerard Manley Hopkins and Tractarian Poetry*, 133.
114 Bridges, 'Memoir', xx.
115 Bridges, 'Memoir', xiv, xxii.

116 Dolben, *Poems and Letters*, 170–1. From a letter dated 20 March 1867.
117 Keble, 'Poem 162' (line 3), *Lyra Apostolica*.
118 MS Eng. poet. e.91, fos. 48–51, 90.
119 See Bernard of Clairvaux's 'Aqueduct' Sermon: 'Exceedingly high though it is, it has preserved its integrity inviolate. This Virgin is in truth 'a garden enclosed, a fountain sealed up' (Cant. iv. 12), the living temple of the Lord, the sanctuary of the Holy Spirit' ('Sermon of the Feast of the Nativity', 89). See also Pope, *The Anchor Bible: Song of Songs*, 488–90.
120 Song of Songs 2:16. See also the line, 'I am my beloved's, and my beloved is mine: he feedeth among the lilies' (6:3).
121 Hopkins' handwritten copy contains the phrases, 'lead me' and 'feed me' (MS Eng. poet. e. 91, fo. 42).
122 Song of Songs 6:9; emphasis added.
123 Song of Songs 1:8.
124 Song of Songs 2:2.
125 Cotter, 'The Song of Songs and "The Wreck of the Deutschland"', 69. Song of Songs 1:15, 2:13–4, 4:1. As I have cited earlier, the bridegroom describes the bride as 'My dove, my undefiled' (6:9).
126 Carson, *Eros the Bittersweet*, 155–6.
127 Sappho cited in Carson, *Eros the Bittersweet*, 156.
128 From a letter dated 15 February 1879. This letter was composed at around the time of the poem's completion.
129 In her discussion of the poetic and spiritual rhythm to which John Keble aspires in his volume *The Christian Year*, Kirstie Blair argues, 'This rhythm is apparent only by its lack of visible, audible or tangible pulsation; like the normal beat of the heart, it goes unnoticed' ('John Keble and the Rhythm of Faith', 144).
130 Carson, *Eros the Bittersweet*, 157.
131 Plato *Phaedrus* 252b.
132 Plato *Phaedrus* 246a–52b.
133 Plato *Phaedrus* 251a.
134 Carson, *Eros the Bittersweet*, 157. See Plato *Phaedrus* 251a–e.

Chapter Three: Conception, Pregnancy, Birth

1 Elvey, 'The Material Given', 201. Such a body 'calls into question these assumptions of separateness and sameness. When I am pregnant, "my" body is both "I" and "not I"' (203).
2 Unless otherwise indicated, the translation of '*Ad Matrem Virginem*' will be from Robert Boyle in Hopkins, *The Poetical Works of Gerard Manley Hopkins* (302) and will be given in the body of my text, while the Latin will be given in the footnotes: 'Doce me de Eo, / De parvo dulci Deo. / Quantum amavisti / Quem tu concepisti / Non concipiendum'.
3 From a sermon dated 26 June 1881.
4 'Et contemnit idem / Ne cor meum quidem: / Meum cor indignum / Quod capiat tantum signum, / Indignum O quod gerat / Qui mane mecum erat, / Subit, O Maria, / Un eücharistia. / Ipse vult intrare: / Nolo me negare.'
5 'Nam tumeo et abundo / Immundo adhuc mundo'.
6 From a diary entry dated 1863.

7   Isaiah 59:4.
8   Psalm 7:14.
9   Augustine *Confessions* 7.16.22.
10 From the essay 'How far may a common tendency be traced in all pre-Socratic philosophy?' written between winter 1866 and winter 1867.
11 From the notes 'Xenophanes', written between 9 February 1868 and Spring 1868.
12 From the notes 'Parmenides', written between 9 February 1868 and Spring 1868.
13 From notes on 'The Incarnation', dated 26 August 1885. The translation is from 'The Incarnation' (*Sermons*, 169); emphasis original. See also the sermon from 25 October 1880: 'God knows infinite things, all things, and heeds them all in particular. We cannot "do two things at once", that is cannot give our full heed and attention to two things at once' (89).
14 From 'On Personality, Grace and Free Will'.
15 From a diary entry dated 1863; emphasis original.
16 From notes on 'Contemplation for Obtaining Love', dated 8 December 1881.
17 Aristotle *Physica* (trans. R. P. Hardie and R. K. Gaye) 2.1.193b6–8. From Aristotle, *The Works of Aristotle*, vol. 2. Hopkins discusses Aristotle's metaphysics in his essay 'Connection of Aristotle's metaphysics with his ethics', written between autumn 1866 and spring 1867. 'There are three stages in the conception of all Being – the Potential, the actual, and the passing fr. the one to the other: these answer to the Not-Being, Being, and Becoming wh. appear in various philosophies fr. Heraclitus to Hegel', he says (*Oxford Essays*, 263–4). 'The passing over or becoming is called by Aristotle κίνησις {process} defined as ἐνέργεια τοῦ δυνάμει ᾗ δυνάμει {the actuality of what exists in potential insofar as it is potential}' (264).
18 Aristotle *Physica* 2.1.193b12–3.
19 'Now all through nature we have found the action of some efficient cause wh. drove matter towards its fullest or highest form, the fullest or highest that is of wh. the particular matter was capable. Can this principle fail in man? On the contrary as man is the highest organisation of nature, it must be eminently true of him' (*Oxford Essays*, 264). From 'Connection of Aristotle's metaphysics with his ethics', dated Autumn 1866 to spring 1867.
20 From notes on the 'Contemplation for Obtaining Love', dated 8 December 1881.
21 Hopkins acknowledges the etymological link between the Spirit and breath when he declares the Holy Ghost's 'name and the manner of being…is Spirit or Breath' (*Sermons*, 98). From a sermon dated 15 May 1880.
22 According to Hopkins' early etymological speculations of 1863, 'flag' means '(droop etc), *flaccere*, notion that of waving instead of rigidity' (*Journals*, 11). Flaccid is compared to flabby: 'Cf. the connection between flag and *flabby*' (12; emphasis original).
23 From a journal entry dated 18 September 1873.
24 From 'On Personality, Grace and Free Will', dated 30 December 1881. For more on the relation between stress and slack, Kooistra, 'The Proportion of the Mixture', 113–25.
25 'And the angel answered and said unto her, The Holy Ghost shall come upon thee, and the power of the Highest shall overshadow thee: therefore also that holy thing which shall be born of thee shall be called the Son of God' (Luke 1:35).
26 Similarly, 'God has not only created us but every moment preserves us, giving us ever fresh and fresh being, whereas an earthly father begets but once upon a time' (*Sermons*, 54). From a sermon dated 11 January 1880.
27 From a sermon dated 15 May 1881. The quote is from John 20:22.

28 From 'On Personality, Grace and Free Will', dated 30 December 1881.
29 The Greek references span Ephesians 3:16–19. The translations in brackets are from the original text.
30 As he says elsewhere, 'I marked the bole, the burling and roundness of the world' (*Journals*, 251). From a journal entry dated 8 August 1874. For a reading of the 'burl of being' in relation to 'instress', the Parmenidean sphere of being, and the '*pomum possibilium*', see Brown, *Hopkins' Idealism*, 229–37.
31 Ephesians 3:19.
32 '…to be strengthened with might by his Spirit in the inner man' (Ephesians 3:16).
33 Augustine *Confessions* 1.1.1.
34 Ephesians 3:16–17.
35 The bracketed phrases are interpolations by the translator. 'Quae tu tum dicebas / Et quae audiebas? / Etsi fuit mutus / Tamen est locutus'.
36 'The utterance of the word for Hopkins marks the incarnation of the idea' (Brown, *Hopkins' Idealism*, 311). In the undated 'Poetry and Verse', Hopkins says, 'Poetry is in fact speech only employed to carry the inscape of speech for the inscape's sake' (*Journals*, 288).
37 Sulloway, *Gerard Manley Hopkins and the Victorian Temper*, 67.
38 From a letter dated 22 April 1879.
39 From a letter dated 21 August 1877.
40 Badin, 'Uttering and Wording', 258.
41 John 20:24–31.
42 Denisoff, *Sexual Visuality*, 6.
43 Picker, *Victorian Soundscapes*, 6.
44 From a sermon dated 26 June 1881.
45 Bender, 'Scope, Scape, and Word Formation', 121–2; emphasis added.
46 From a sermon dated 11 August 1879.
47 From a journal entry dated 16 June 1873.
48 Brown, *Hopkins' Idealism*, 290.
49 Brown, *Hopkins' Idealism*, 291.
50 From a diary entry dated 1864; emphasis original
51 From a diary entry dated 1866.
52 Shimane, *The Poetry of G. M. Hopkins*, 174.
53 Shimane, *The Poetry of G. M. Hopkins*, 176; emphasis original.
54 Shimane, *The Poetry of G. M. Hopkins*, 174.
55 Hopkins, *The Poetical Works of Gerard Manley Hopkins*, 358.
56 God is the 'Utterer', Christ is the 'Utterèd', and the Spirit is the 'Uttering'. This trinity will be discussed in more detail in the next chapter. Shimane notes that 'uttering' is a pun on 'utter + ring' (*The Poetry of G. M. Hopkins*, 174).
57 Shimane notes the pun on tóld/tolled in 'The Wreck of the Deutschland', but does not refer to its repetition in 'Margaret Clitheroe' (*The Poetry of G. M. Hopkins*, 171).
58 From notes dated 20 November 1881.
59 Genesis 11:7–9.
60 When Adam 'named' the animals, he is said to have uttered their true names (Genesis 2:19–20).
61 Genesis 1:2.
62 'No not uncomforted: lovely–felicitous Providence, / Fínger of a ténder of, O of a féathery délicacy, the bréast of the / Maiden could obey so, be a bell to, ring óf it' (stanza 31).

63 'For God the Holy Ghost is the Paraclete, but what is a Paraclete? often it is translated Comforter' (*Sermons*, 70). From a sermon dated 25 April 1880.
64 From D.XII.5, dated 9 February 1868; emphasis original.
65 From notes on 'The First Principle and Foundation', dated 7 August 1882.

Chapter Four: Caressing, Conversing, Kissing

1 'And the Lord God formed man of the dust of the ground, and breathed into his nostrils the breath of life; and man became a living soul' (Genesis 2:7).
2 Müller, *The Science of Language*, vol. 2, 371. Hopkins was familiar with this text by the eminent mythologist and linguist (White, *Hopkins*, 105).
3 Belsey, *Desire*, 56.
4 'The common implications of the word "intercourse" are not totally out of place in interpreting Hopkins' need for sounding words' (Badin, 'Uttering and Wording', 258). 'Hearing means being penetrated by another's words... Dialogue is a sublimation of the sexual act' (258).
5 Rilke, *Translations From the Poetry of Rainer Maria Rilke*.
6 From 'On Personality, Grace and Free Will', dated 30 December 1881; emphasis added.
7 Hopkins, *The Poetical Works of Gerard Manley Hopkins*, 117. Many of the arguments from the 'Author's Preface on Rhythm' can be found in a letter dated 14 January 1881 (*Dixon*, 39–42).
8 Hopkins, *The Poetical Works of Gerard Manley Hopkins*, 117.
9 Hopkins, *The Poetical Works of Gerard Manley Hopkins*, 115.
10 From a letter dated 27 February 1879; emphasis original.
11 Bischoff, 'Hopkins's letters to his brother', 1511. From a letter dated 5 November 1885.
12 Hopkins, *The Poetical Works of Gerard Manley Hopkins*, 118.
13 From a letter dated 7 November 1883.
14 Bischoff, 'Hopkins's letters to his brother', 1511.
15 Bischoff, 'Hopkins's letters to his brother', 1511.
16 Bischoff, 'Hopkins's letters to his brother', 1511.
17 Hopkins, *The Poetical Works of Gerard Manley Hopkins*, 118.
18 Miller, 'Naming and Doing', 188.
19 Miller, 'Naming and Doing', 188.
20 Cotter, *Inscape*, 288–9, and Miller, 'Naming and Doing', 184–5, include an extensive list of these occurrences in Hopkins' poems.
21 Cotter, *Inscape*, 286–7. See also Cotter, 'Sounding Alpha and Omega in Dante, Milton, and Hopkins', 164–72.
22 Miller, 'Naming and Doing', 187–8.
23 Brown, *Hopkins' Idealism*, 320–2.
24 From a letter dated 8 October 1879.
25 From a letter dated 10 September 1864.
26 This rhyme is repeated in 'The Leaden Echo and the Golden Echo'.
27 Herbert, *George Herbert*. Herbert's description resonates with Psalm 150:6: 'Let every thing that hath breath praise the Lord'. Hopkins owned a copy of Herbert's collection *The Temple* (containing this poem), which he gave to his sister Millicent in September 1868, shortly before his entry into the Society of Jesus (House, 'Books Belonging to Hopkins and his Family', 30).

28 From 'On Personality, Grace and Free Will', dated 30 December 1881.
29 From 'Creation and Redemption the Great Sacrifice', dated 8 November 1881. The term *conversio* has an underlying meaning of vocation or of deciding to enter a religious order.
30 From a sermon dated 21 September 1879; emphasis original.
31 From a sermon dated 23 November 1879.
32 Levin, *The Listening Self*, 32; emphasis original.
33 Hopkins listed this novel in February 1865 as one of his books to be read (*Journals*, 56).
34 Eliot's is a combination of Romantic and contemporary Victorian acoustic theories. See Picker, *Victorian Soundscapes*, 82–109 and da Sousa Correa, *George Eliot, Music and Victorian Culture*, 110–18.
35 Helmholtz cited in Picker, *Victorian Soundscapes*, 87. While there is no direct evidence to suggest that Hopkins read Helmholtz's work, Gillian Beer speculates on the possibility in *Open Fields*, 242–72. Hopkins was well acquainted with at least one work by Lewes, his *Biographical History of Philosophy*, which was an important source of some of his undergraduate essays on psychology and philosophy (Brown, *Hopkins' Idealism*, 56, 67–8, 79). Regardless, Hopkins would have come across the theory of sympathetic vibrations in Eliot's *The Mill on the Floss*.
36 Picker, *Victorian Soundscapes*, 87.
37 Lewes cited in da Sousa Correa, *George Eliot, Music and Victorian Culture*, 113.
38 Eliot, *The Mill on the Floss*, 385, 364.
39 Eliot, *The Mill on the Floss*, 385. Coincidentally, Purcell was one of Hopkins' favourite composers (White, *Hopkins*, 23).
40 Eliot, *The Mill on the Floss*, 384.
41 Eliot, *The Mill on the Floss*, 416.
42 Eliot, *The Mill on the Floss*, 416.
43 Eliot, *The Mill on the Floss*, 418.
44 Eliot, *The Mill on the Floss*, 518. 'Maggie is a resonant listener, and Stephen's song generates a seductive sound wave, the effect of which aurally foreshadows that of the surging river current that ultimately engulfs her' (Picker, *Victorian Soundscapes*, 89).
45 Eliot, *The Mill on the Floss*, 475. Chapter Six of Book Six is entitled 'The Laws of Attraction'.
46 For more on the findings of electromagnetism and field theory, see Brown, *Hopkins' Idealism*, 211–12, 216–17, 238–43, 245, 250, 278. See also Rudy, *Electric Meters*, 137–8. Of course, the *effects* of magnetism had been observed long before the nineteenth century. According to Aristotle, Thales 'seems, from what is reported of him, to have supposed that the soul is something productive of movement, if he really said that the magnet has a soul because it produces movement in iron' (Aristotle *De Anima* 405a).
47 Hosea 11:4.
48 Jeremiah 31:3.
49 Littledale, *A Commentary on the Song of Songs*, 15–16. There is no evidence to suggest that Hopkins was familiar with this text. I use it as an example of how, like Hopkins, contemporary Christian commentators held Christ to be a magnetic personality. Littledale was a prominent Anglo–Catholic and a close friend and confessor to Christina Rossetti, whose work Hopkins admired (Arseneau, *Recovering Christina Rossetti*, 34).
50 Patmore, *Poems*, 331.
51 From notes on 'A Meditation on Hell', dated 5 September 1883.
52 From a letter dated 16 October 1866.

53 From 'Creation and Redemption the Great Sacrifice', dated 8 November 1881. In the same notes, Hopkins uses the related word 'incantation' to describe Lucifer's magnetic power: 'it was a sounding, as they say, of his own trumpet and a hymn in his own praise. Moreover it became an incantation: others were drawn in; it became a concert of voices, a concerting of selfpraise, an enchantment, a magic' (*Sermons*, 201).

54 Similarly, Hopkins' father Manley, in his volume of poetry *Spicilegium Poeticum*, compares Christ to a 'lode-stone' with the ability to magnetise Christians (Hopkins cited in Feeney, 'His Father's Son', 285).

55 Brown, *Hopkins' Idealism*, 284. The gesture of the smile enables Hopkins to anthropomorphise God, for he states elsewhere that 'the face of the eternal father smiles' (*Sermons*, 236). From a sermon scrap, dated 14 September 1879.

56 Wierzbicka, *Emotions Across Languages and Cultures*, 174.

57 From a sermon dated 15 May 1880.

58 'And Esau ran to meet him, and embraced him, and fell on his neck, and kissed him' (Genesis 33:4). Similarly, although in the context of a farewell, the Ephesians farewelled Paul in the following manner: 'all wept sore, and fell on his neck, and kissed him' (Acts 10:37).

59 Johnson, *Volpone*, 3.7.232–4. From Jonson, *The Complete Plays of Ben Jonson*, vol. 3.

60 Marlowe, *Doctor Faustus*, 5.1.1770–4; emphasis original. From Marlowe, *The Complete Works of Christopher Marlowe*, vol. 2.

61 Shakespeare, *The Second Part of King Henry VI*, 3.2.394–9.

62 Bernard of Clairvaux, *On the Song of Songs*, vol. 1, 16.3.3.

63 1 Peter 5:14.

64 Romans 16:16; 1 Corinthians 16:20; 2 Corinthians 13:12; 1 Thessalonians 5:26.

65 1 Corinthians 12:13.

66 Perella, *The Kiss Sacred and Profane*, 15.

67 This reading of the 'realer, rounder replies' is inspired by E. Ann Matter's exploration of the relation between the 'O', the mouth and the kiss. Matter briefly discusses an illuminated capital of a Cambridge manuscript of Bede's commentary on the Song of Songs, 'which exploits the O of "osculetur" ["kiss"] by portraying a mouth in which Christ and the Church sit locked in a kiss' (*The Voice of my Beloved*, 101). The Latin rendering, '*O*sculetur me *o*sculo *o*ris sui', she argues, 'repeats related words for kiss and mouth three times' (126; emphasis original). Her translation invokes this: 'Let him kiss me with the kiss of his kisser' (126).

68 Bernard of Clairvaux, *On the Song of Songs*, vol. 1, 8.I.2.

69 From notes on 'Contemplation for Obtaining Love', dated 8 December 1881.

70 Hopkins, *The Poetical Works of Gerard Manley Hopkins*, 262.

71 'Da complecti Illum, / Mihi da pauxillum / Tuo ex amore / Et oscula ab ore'. I thank one of Anthem's anonymous readers for informing me that 'oscula ab ore' should be translated as 'kisses from his mouth'. I have given here the translation from Hopkins, *The Poems of Gerard Manley Hopkins*, 337–8. The translation in *The Poetical Works of Gerard Manley Hopkins* is ambiguous: 'Grant that I may embrace Him / And give me a little out of the store of your love/ And of your mystic kisses' (lines 64–6). Subsequent translations of '*Ad Matrem Virginem*', however, will be from *The Poetical Works of Gerard Manley Hopkins*.

72 See example 91, by Simone Memmi, in Jameson, *Legends of the Madonna as Represented in the Fine Arts*, 275.

73 'Qui pro me vult dari, / Infans mihi fari, / Mecum conversari, / Tu da contemplari'.

74 Roy, 'Women and Spirituality in the Writings of Luce Irigaray', 23.

75 Irigaray, *To Be Two*, 11.

Chapter Five: Homecoming

1. Shakespeare, *Twelfth Night*, 2.3.44.
2. Bruno, *Atlas of Emotion*, 6.
3. On the whole, the father is an authoritarian figure for Hopkins.
4. O'Connell, *Soundings in Augustine's Imagination*, 72; emphasis original.
5. Augustine *Confessions* 9.8.37.
6. Hopkins' etymological musings from 1863 reinforce the connection between fertility and virginity, *virgo* and *virga*: 'growth, anything growing vigorously, blooming it may be, but yet producing fruit. Hence *mead* in the sense of meadow, or *meadow*, mean a field of fresh vegetation. *Mead* the drink and *meat*, (active forms from the same root,) are so called from *strengthening*, nourishing. For *maid* compare the parallel resemblance between *virgo* and *virga*' (*Journals*, 4; emphasis original).
7. In a later poem, Hopkins describes the falling leaves as their 'unleaving': 'Márgarét, áre you gríeving / Over Goldengrove unleaving?' ('Spring and Fall', lines 1–2). He contrasts the decay of leaves to Margaret's 'fresh thoughts' (line 4).
8. Littledale, *A Commentary on the Song of Songs*, 12.
9. Wheeler, *Death and the Future Life*, 25.
10. Munich, *Queen Victoria's Secrets*, 95.
11. Steedman, *Strange Dislocations*, x.
12. Winefred, who had vowed her virginity to Christ, was romantically pursued (unsuccessfully) and subsequently decapitated by Caradoc. According to legend, a spring miraculously surfaced from where her head rolled, a place hitherto called Dry Valley. St Bueno reattached her head to her body to give her new life (Hopkins, *The Poetical Works of Gerard Manley Hopkins*, 440).
13. Brown explores smell in relation to freshness and filth in *Hopkins' Idealism*, 305–8.
14. Classen, *The Color of Angels*, 51.
15. Classen, *The Color of Angels*, 51, 40.
16. From undated notes on 'De Nativitate'.
17. From undated notes on 'The Principle or Foundation'.
18. From undated notes on 'Meditation on Hell'.
19. For more on God's sweetness, see Posset, '*Christi Dulcedo*', 245–65, and 'Sensing God with the "Palate of the Heart"', 356–86.
20. From a letter dated 8 October 1879.
21. Bashford, *Purity and Pollution*, 5.
22. Bashford, *Purity and Pollution*, 5–6. See also Haley, *The Healthy Body and Victorian Culture*, 10, and Hamlin, 'Providence and Putrefaction', 92–123.
23. From a sermon dated 25 October 1880.
24. 'Like Babylon, London was the centre of a global commerce that was subjugating the rest of the world; it was the seat of an empire that was defining contemporary history. But Babylon was a paradoxical image for the nineteenth-century city. It not only represented the most magnificent imperial city of the ancient world, but also conjured up images of the mystical Babylon of the Apocalypse. It was a place that symbolised material wonder and tumultuous destruction; a city whose splendour was its downfall' (Nead, *Victorian Babylon*, 3).
25. From a letter dated 1 May 1888.
26. For a fine discussion of the relationship – to Hopkins' mind – between class, filth and racial degeneration, see Alderson, *Mansex Fine*, 139–46.

27 For more on the division between city and country, see Constantini, 'The city tires to death', 114–29, and Thesing, 'Gerard Manley Hopkins's Responses to the City', 132–55.
28 From a letter dated 2 April 1878.
29 From a letter dated 2 October 1886.
30 From a letter dated 30 September 1886.
31 From a letter dated 1 May 1888.
32 From a letter dated 2 March 1880.
33 From a letter dated 15 June 1881; emphasis original.
34 From a letter dated 30 April 1880.
35 Waters, *The Garden in Victorian Literature*, 42. Waters holds that one of the reasons why Victorian writers championed sweet-scented flowers is because 'they associated them with the cottage and old farmhouse gardens in which they continued to flourish – or so it was thought' (37).
36 From a letter dated 16 October 1866. Other examples of his devotion to the Five Wounds include '*Rosa Mystica*', where the speaker refers to the 'immaculate white' rose that 'ran in crimsonings' (lines 32, 34). In the refrain the speaker declares, '*I shall worship His wounds with thee, mother of mine*' (line 36; emphasis original).
37 From a sermon dated 26 June 1881.
38 Thomas, *Hopkins the Jesuit*, 215–23.
39 Languet, *The Life of the Venerable Mother Margaret Mary Alacoque*, 185–6.
40 For more on his knowledge of *The Life of the Venerable Mother Margaret Mary Alacoque*, see *Further Letters*, 348, and *Sermons*, 251.
41 2 Corinthians 5:19.
42 Psalm 105:18.
43 Psalm 55:22.
44 Hebrews 4:15.
45 1 Timothy 3:16.
46 Psalm 86:5. Bernard of Clairvaux, *On the Song of Songs*, vol. 3, 61.2.4.
47 Bernard of Clairvaux, *On the Song of Songs*, vol. 3, 61.3.7.
48 Bernard of Clairvaux, *On the Song of Songs*, vol. 3, 61.3.7.
49 Porterfield, *Healing in the History of Christianity*, 89.
50 Moran, 'Lovely manly mould', 81–2. Moran also argues, 'when Hopkins drew on the feminised body in some of his representations of bodily denial and violation he… enhanc[ed] the nobility of the body in its own right' (83).
51 From 'Dublin Meditation Notes', dated 22 February 1884 to 25 March 1885.
52 From a sermon dated 23 November 1879.
53 Porterfield, *Healing in the History of Christianity*, 30–31.
54 From a sermon dated 31 August 1879.
55 From a sermon dated 17 August 1879.
56 From a sermon dated 23 November 1879.
57 Augustine *Confessions* 1.1 1.
58 Augustine *Confessions* 4.12.18.
59 Languet, *The Life of the Venerable Mother Margaret Mary Alacoque*, 187.
60 Languet, *The Life of the Venerable Mother Margaret Mary Alacoque*, 187–8.
61 Augustine *Confessions* 13.9.10. Augustine quotes from Psalm 121:6.

BIBLIOGRAPHY

Adams, James Eli. *Dandies and Desert Saints: Styles of Victorian Masculinity*. Ithaca, NY: Cornell University Press, 1995.
Alderson, Richard. *Mansex Fine: Religion, Manliness and Imperialism in Nineteenth-Century British Culture*. Manchester: Manchester University Press, 1998.
Aristotle. *De Anima (On the Soul)*. Translated by Hugh Lawson-Tancred. London: Penguin Books, 1986.
———. *The Works of Aristotle*. Translated by R. P. Hardie and R. K. Gaye. Edited by W. D. Ross. 9 vols. Oxford: Clarendon, 1930.
Armstrong, Isobel. *Victorian Poetry: Poetry, Poetics and Politics*. New York: Routledge, 1993.
Arseneau, Mary. *Recovering Christina Rossetti: Female Community and Incarnational Poetics*. Houndmills: Palgrave, 2004.
Astell, Ann W. 'Kristeva and Bernard of Clairvaux'. *Christianity and Literature* 50 (2001): 125–48.
Augustine. *Concerning the City of God Against the Pagans*. Translated by Henry Bettenson. London: Penguin, 1972.
———. *Confessions*. Translated by Henry Chadwick. Oxford: Oxford University Press, 1998.
——— *The Trinity*. Translated by Edmund Hill. Edited by John E. Rotelle. Brooklyn: New City Press, 1991.
Badin, Donatella Abbate. 'Uttering and Wording: Hopkins's Uneasy Relationship with the Written Word'. In *Gerard Manley Hopkins: Tradition and Innovation*, edited by P. Bottalla, G. Marra and F. Marucci, 247–60. Ravenna: Longo Editore, 1991.
Barfoot, C. C. '"In This Strang Labourinth How Shall I Turne?": Erotic Symmetry in Four Female Sonnet Sequences'. In *'And Never Know the Joy': Sex and the Erotic in English Poetry*, edited by C. C. Barfoot, 223–46. Amsterdam: Rodopi, 2006.
Bashford, Alison. *Purity and Pollution: Gender, Embodiment and Victorian Medicine*. Houndmills: Macmillan Press, 1998.
Beer, Gillian. *Open Fields: Science in Cultural Encounter*. Oxford: Clarendon Press, 1996.
Bell, David N. 'A Bibliography of English Translations of Works By and Attributed to St. Bernard of Clairvaux'. *Caiteaux: Commentarii Cistercienses* 48 (1997): 83–129.
Belsey, Catherine. *Desire: Love Stories in Western Culture*. Oxford: Blackwell, 1994.
Bender, Todd K. 'Scope, Scape, and Word Formation'. In *The Fine Delight: Centenary Essays on the Poetry of Gerard Manley Hopkins*, edited by Francis L. Fennell, 115–25. Chicago: Loyola University Press, 1989.
Bernard of Clairvaux. *On the Song of Songs*. Translated by Kilian Walsh and Irene Edmonds. 4 vols. Kalamazoo: Cistercian Publications, 1980.

———. 'Sermon for the Feast of the Nativity of the Blessed Virgin Mary'. Translated by A Priest of Mount Melleray. In *St. Bernard's Sermons on the Blessed Virgin Mary*, 79–103. Devon: Augustine Publishing Company, 1984.
The Bible: Authorized King James Version with Apocrypha. Edited by Robert Carroll and Stephen Prickett. Oxford: Oxford University Press, 1998.
Bischoff, Anthony. 'Hopkins's Letters to his Brother'. *Times Literary Supplement*, 8 December 1972, 1511–12.
Blair, Kirstie. 'John Keble and the Rhythm of Faith'. *Essays in Criticism* 53 (2003): 129–50.
Bodleian Library, Oxford University. Gerard Manley Hopkins Papers. MS. Eng. poet. e.90; MS. Eng. poet. e.91.
Boyarin, Daniel. 'What Do We Talk About When We Talk About Platonic Love?' In *Toward a Theology of Eros: Transfiguring Passion at the Limits of Discipline*, edited by Virginia Burrus and Catherine Keller, 3–22. New York: Fordham University Press, 2006.
Bridges, Robert. 'Memoir'. In *The Poems of Digby Mackworth Dolben*, edited by Robert Bridges, vii–cxviii. London: Humphrey Milford, 1915.
Bristow, Joseph. '"Churlsgrace": Gerard Manley Hopkins and the Working-Class Male Body'. *English Literary History* 59 (1992): 693–711.
———. *Effeminate England: Homoerotic Writing After 1885*. New York: Columbia University Press, 1995.
Brown, Daniel. *Gerard Manley Hopkins*. Horndon: Northcote House Publishers Ltd, 2004.
———. *Hopkins' Idealism: Philosophy, Physics, Poetry*. Oxford: Clarendon Press, 1997.
Brown, Peter. *The Body and Society: Men, Women, and Sexual Renunciation in Early Christianity*. New York: Columbia University Press, 1988.
Bruno, Giuliana. *Atlas of Emotion: Journeys in Art, Architecture, and Film*. New York: Verso, 2002.
Bugge, John. *Virginitas: An Essay in the History of a Medieval Ideal*. The Hague: Matinus Nijhoff, 1975.
Campion Hall, Oxford University. Gerard Manley Hopkins Papers. F; GI.
Carr, David M. *The Erotic Word: Sexuality, Spirituality, and the Bible*. New York: Oxford University Press, 2003.
Carson, Anne. *Eros the Bittersweet*. Normal: Dalkey Archive Press, 1998.
Classen, Constance. *The Color of Angels: Cosmology, Gender and the Aesthetic Imagination*. London: Routledge, 1998.
Colligan, Colette and Margaret Linley. 'Introduction: The Nineteenth-Century Invention of Media'. In *Media, Technology, and Literature in the Nineteenth Century: Image, Sound, Touch*, edited by Colette Colligan and Margaret Linley, 1–19. Farnham: Ashgate, 2011.
Constantini, Mariaconcetta. '"The city tires to death": Images of Urbanization and Natural Corruption in Hopkins' Work'. *The Hopkins Quarterly* 28 (2001): 114–29.
Cotter, James Finn. 'Hopkins and Augustine'. *Victorian Poetry* 39 (2001): 69–82.
———. *Inscape: The Christology and Poetry of Gerard Manley Hopkins*. Pittsburgh: University of Pittsburgh Press, 1972.
———. 'Orion Behind the Lattices: Stanza 1 of "The Wreck of the Deutschland"'. *The Hopkins Quarterly* 26 (1999): 24–6.
———. 'The Song of Songs and "The Wreck of the Deutschland"'. In *Gerard Manley Hopkins and Critical Discourse*, edited by Eugene Hollahan, 57–64. New York: AMS Press, 1993.
———. 'Sounding Alpha and Omega in Dante, Milton, and Hopkins'. In *Gerard Manley Hopkins (1844–1889): New Essays on His Life, Writing, and Place in English Literature*, edited

by Michael E. Allsopp and Michael W. Sundermeier, 164–72. Lewiston: Edwin Mellon Press, 1989.
Craft, Christopher. *Another Kind of Love: Male Homosexual Desire in English Discourse, 1850–1920*. Berkeley: University of California Press, 1994.
da Sousa Correa, Delia. *George Eliot, Music and Victorian Culture*. Houndmills: Palgrave Macmillan, 2003.
Dacey, Philip. *Gerard Manley Hopkins Meets Walt Whitman in Heaven and Other Poems*. Great Barrington: Penmaen Press, 1982.
Dante Alighieri. *The Divine Comedy*. Translated by Henry F. Cary. New York: P. F. Collier and Son Corporation, 1969.
Dau, Duc. '"Beautiful Action": Hopkins and the Perfect Body'. *The Hopkins Quarterly* 35 (2008): 3–18.
Davis, Lloyd. 'The Virgin Body as Victorian Text: An Introduction'. In *Virginal Sexuality and Textuality in Victorian Literature*, edited by Lloyd Davis, 3–24. New York: State University of New York Press, 1993.
Day, Brian J. 'Hopkins' Spiritual Ecology in "Binsey Poplars"'. *Victorian Poetry* 42 (2004): 181–94.
de Vere, Aubrey. *Essays: Chiefly Literary and Ethical*. London: Macmillan and Co., 1889.
Dellamora, Richard. *Masculine Desire: The Sexual Politics of Victorian Aestheticism*. Chapel Hill: University of North Carolina Press, 1990.
Denisoff, Dennis. *Sexual Visuality from Literature to Film, 1850–1950*. Basingstoke: Palgrave, 2004.
Dolben, Digby Mackworth. *The Poems and Letters of Digby Mackworth Dolben 1848–1867*. Edited by Martin Cohen. n.p.: Aveury Publishing Company, 1981.
Donne, John. *John Donne*. Edited by John Carey. Oxford: Oxford University Press, 1990.
Dowling, Linda. *Hellenism and Homosexuality in Victorian Oxford*. Ithaca, NY: Cornell University Press, 1994.
Drury, John. *Painting the Word: Christian Pictures and Their Meanings*. New Haven: Yale University Press, 1999.
Eliot, George. *The Mill on the Floss*. Edited by Gordon S. Haight. Oxford: Oxford University Press, 1996.
Elvey, Anne. 'The Material Given: Bodies, Pregnant Bodies and Earth'. *Australian Feminist Studies* 18 (2003): 199–209.
The English Hymnal. London: Humphrey Milford, n.d.
Feeney, Joseph J. 'His Father's Son: Common Traits in the Writing of Manley Hopkins and Gerard Manley Hopkins'. In *Gerard Manley Hopkins and Critical Discourse*, edited by Eugene Hollahan, 277–92. New York: AMS Press, 1993.
Foltz, William and Todd K. Bender. *A Concordance to the Sermons of Gerard Manley Hopkins*. New York: Garland Publishing Inc., 1989.
Fontana, Ernest. 'Patmore, Pascal, and Astronomy'. *Victorian Poetry* 40 (2003): 277–86.
Foucault, Michel. *The Care of the Self. History of Sexuality: Volume Three*. Translated by Robert Hurley. London: Penguin Books, 1986.
Gallwey, Peter. *Convent Life and England in the 19th Century*. London: Burns, Oates and Co., n.d.
Grabes, Herbert. *The Mutable Glass: Mirror-Imagery in Titles and Texts of the Middle Ages and English Renaissance*. Translated by Gordon Collier. Cambridge: Cambridge University Press, 1982.
Haley, Bruce. *The Healthy Body and Victorian Culture*. Cambridge, MA: Harvard University Press, 1978.

Halperin, David M. 'Plato and Erotic Reciprocity'. *Classical Antiquity* 5 (1986): 61–80.

Hamlin, Christopher. 'Providence and Putrefaction'. In *Energy and Entropy: Science and Culture in Victorian Britain*, edited by Patrick Brantlinger, 92–123. Bloomington: Indiana University Press, 1989.

Herbert, George. *George Herbert: The Complete English Poems*. Edited by John Tobin. London: Penguin Group, 1991.

Herrington, Eldrid. 'Hopkins and Whitman'. *Essays in Criticism* 55 (2005): 39–57.

Higgins, Lesley. '"Bone House" and "Lovescape": Writing the Body in Hopkins's Canon'. In *Rereading Hopkins: Selected New Essays*, edited by Francis L. Fennell, 11–35. Victoria: University of Victoria, 1996.

———. 'Hopkins and "The Jowler"'. *Texas Studies in Literature and Language* 31 (1989): 143–67.

Hopkins, Gerard Manley. *The Correspondence of Gerard Manley Hopkins and Richard Watson Dixon*. Edited by Claude Colleer Abbott. 2nd ed. London: Oxford University Press, 1955.

———. *The Early Poetic Manuscripts and Note-books of Gerard Manley Hopkins in Facsimile*. Edited by Norman H. MacKenzie. New York: Garland Publishing Inc., 1989.

———. *Further Letters of Gerard Manley Hopkins Including his Correspondence with Coventry Patmore*. Edited by Claude Colleer Abbott. 2nd ed. London: Oxford University Press, 1956.

———. *The Journals and Papers of Gerard Manley Hopkins*. Edited by Humphrey House and Graham Storey. 2nd ed. London: Oxford University Press, 1959.

———. *The Letters of Gerard Manley Hopkins to Robert Bridges*. Edited by Claude Colleer Abbott. 2nd ed. London: Oxford University Press, 1955.

———. *Oxford Essays and Notes*. Edited by Lesley Higgins. Vol. 4, *The Collected Works of Gerard Manley Hopkins*. Oxford: Oxford University Press, 2006.

———. *The Poems of Gerard Manley Hopkins*. Edited by W. H. Gardner and N. H. MacKenzie. 4th ed. Oxford: Oxford University Press, 1970.

———. *The Poetical Works of Gerard Manley Hopkins*. Edited by Norman H. Mackenzie. Oxford: Clarendon Press, 1990.

———. *The Sermons and Devotional Writings of Gerard Manley Hopkins*. Edited by Christopher Devlin. London: Oxford University Press, 1959.

House, Madeleine. 'Books Belonging to Hopkins and his Family'. *Hopkins Research Bulletin* 5 (1974): 26–41.

Irigaray, Luce. 'Introduction: On Old and New Tablets'. Translated by Heidi Bostic. In *Religion in French Feminist Thought: Critical Perspectives*, edited by Morny Joy, Kathleen O'Grady and Judith L. Poxon, 1–9. London: Routledge, 2003.

———. *To Be Two*. Translated by Monique M. Rhodes and Marco F. Cocito-Monoc. London: The Athlone Press, 2000.

Jameson, Anna Brownell. *Legends of the Madonna as Represented in the Fine Arts*. 2nd ed. London: Unit Library, 1903.

John of the Cross. *Dark Night of the Soul*. Translated by E. Allison Peers. Edited by E. Allison Peers. New York: Doubleday, 1990.

Johnson, Galen A. 'Introduction: Alterity as a Reversibility'. In *Ontology and Alterity in Merleau-Ponty*, edited by Galen A. Johnson and Michael B. Smith, xvii–xxxiv. Evanston: Northwestern University Press, 1990.

Johnson, Margaret. *Gerard Manley Hopkins and Tractarian Poetry*. Aldershot: Ashgate, 1997.

Jonson, Ben. *The Complete Plays of Ben Jonson*. Edited by G. A. Wilkes. 4 vols. Oxford: Clarendon Press, 1982.

Joy, Morny, Kathleen O'Grady and Judith L. Poxon. 'Editors' Introduction'. In *Religion in French Feminist Thought: Critical Perspectives*, edited by Morny Joy, Kathleen O'Grady and Judith L. Poxon, xv–xxvii. London: Routledge, 2003.

Kaylor, Michael M. '"Beautiful dripping fragments": A Whitmanesque Reading of Hopkins' "Epithalamion"'. *Victorian Poetry* 40 (2002): 157–87.

Kitchen, Paddy. *Gerard Manley Hopkins*. London: Hamilton, 1978.

Kollar, René. 'The Oxford Movement and the Heritage of Benedictine Monasticism'. *The Downside Review* 101 (1983): 281–90.

Kooistra, Lorraine Janzen. '"The Proportion of the Mixture": Stress and Slack in the Perception and Poetics of Hopkins'. *The Hopkins Quarterly* 17 (1991): 113–25.

Krasner, James. '"In Memoriam" 7 and the Song of Solomon'. *Victorian Poetry* 29 (1991): 93–96.

Langer, Monika. 'Merleau-Ponty and Deep Ecology'. In *Ontology and Alterity in Merleau-Ponty*, edited by Galen A. Johnson and Michael B. Smith, 115–29. Evanston: Northwestern University Press, 1990.

Languet, Jean Joseph. *The Life of the Venerable Mother Margaret Mary Alacoque, Religious of the Order of the Visitation*. 2 vols. London: Thomas Richardson and Son, 1850.

Levin, David Michael. *The Listening Self: Personal Growth, Social Change and the Closure of Metaphysics*. London: Routledge, 1999.

Liddon, H. P. *Sermons Preached Before the University of Oxford: First Series, 1859–1868*. 7th ed. London: n.p., 1881.

Littledale, Richard Frederick. *A Commentary on the Song of Songs From Ancient and Medieval Sources*. London: Joseph Masters, 1869.

Loughlin, Gerard. *Alien Sex: The Body and Desire in Cinema and Theology*. Oxford: Blackwell, 2004.

Madison, Gary Brent. 'Flesh as Otherness'. In *Ontology and Alterity in Merleau-Ponty*, edited by Galen A. Johnson and Michael B. Smith, 27–34. Evanston: Northwestern University Press, 1990.

Malpas, J. E. *Place and Experience: A Philosophical Topography*. Cambridge: Cambridge University Press, 1999.

Mariani, Paul. *Gerard Manley Hopkins: A Life*. New York: Viking, 2008.

———. *God and the Imagination: On Poets, Poetry, and the Ineffable*. Athens, GA: University of Georgia Press, 2002.

Marlowe, Christopher. *The Complete Works of Christopher Marlowe*. Edited by Fredson Bowers. 2nd ed. 2 vols. Cambridge: Cambridge University Press, 1981.

Martin, Robert Bernard. *Gerard Manley Hopkins: A Very Private Life*. London: HarperCollins Publishers, 1991.

Matter, E. Ann. *The Voice of My Beloved: The Song of Songs in Western Medieval Christianity*. Philadelphia: Pennsylvania University Press, 1990.

Maynard, John. 'Like a Virgin: Coventry Patmore's Still Unknown Eros'. In *Virginal Sexuality and Textuality in Victorian Literature*, edited by Lloyd Davis, 129–40. New York: State University of New York Press, 1993.

———. *Victorian Discourses on Sexuality and Religion*. Cambridge: Cambridge University Press, 1993.

Members of the University of Oxford. *Tracts for the Times*. 6 vols. New York: AMS Press, 1969.

Merleau-Ponty, Maurice. *The Visible and the Invisible*. Translated by Alphonso Lingis. Edited by Claude Lefort. Evanston: Northwestern University Press, 1968.

Miller, J. Hillis. *The Disappearance of God: Five Nineteenth-Century Writers*. Cambridge, MA: The Belknap Press of Harvard University Press, 1975.

———. 'Naming and Doing: Speech Acts in Hopkins's Poems'. *Religion and Literature* 22 (1990): 173–91.

Moran, Maureen F. '"Lovely manly mould": Hopkins and the Christian Body'. *Journal of Victorian Culture* 6 (2001): 61–88.

Müller, Friedrich Max. *The Science of Language*. 2 vols. London: Longmans, 1899.

Muller, Jill. *Gerard Manley Hopkins and Victorian Catholicism: A Heart in Hiding*. New York: Routledge, 2003.

Munich, Adrienne. *Queen Victoria's Secrets*. New York: Columbia University Press, 1996.

Najarian, James. *Victorian Keats: Manliness, Sexuality, and Desire*. Basingstoke: Palgrave, 2002.

Nead, Lynda. *Victorian Babylon: People, Streets and Images in Nineteenth-Century London*. New Haven: Yale University Press, 2000.

Newman, John Henry. *Sermons Bearing on Subjects of the Day*. Edited by W. J. Copeland. London: n.p., 1869.

Newman, John Henry, *et al. Lyra Apostolica*. 9th ed. London: John and Charles Mozley, 1849.

Nixon, Jude V. *Gerard Manley Hopkins and his Contemporaries: Liddon, Newman, Darwin, and Pater*. New York: Garland Publishing, Inc., 1994.

———. 'Gerard Manley Hopkins and Henry Parry Liddon: An Unacknowledged Influence'. *Renascence* 42 (1989–1990): 87–110.

Nygren, Anders. *Agape and Eros*. Translated by Philip S. Watson. Philadelphia: Westminster Press, 1953.

O'Connell, Robert J. *Soundings in Augustine's Imagination*. New York: Fordham University Press, 1994.

Origen. *The Song of Songs: Commentary and Homilies*. Translated by R. P. Lawson. Edited by Johannes Quasten and Joseph C. Plumpe. Westminster: The Newman Press, 1957.

Osborne, Catherine. *Eros Unveiled: Plato and the God of Love*. Oxford: Clarendon Press, 1994.

Oulton, Carolyn. *Romantic Friendship in Victorian Literature*. Aldershot: Ashgate, 2007.

Overholser, Renée V. '"Looking with terrible temptation": Gerard Manley Hopkins and Beautiful Bodies'. *Victorian Literature and Culture* 19 (1991): 25–53.

Patmore, Coventry. *Poems*. London: G. Bell and Sons, Ltd., 1915.

———. *The Rod, The Root, and the Flower*. London: The Grey Walls Press, 1950.

Patmore, Derek. *The Life and Times of Coventry Patmore*. London: Constable and Company Ltd., 1949.

Perella, Nicholas James. *The Kiss Sacred and Profane: An Interpretive History of Kiss Symbolism and Related Religio-Erotic Themes*. Berkeley: University of California Press, 1969.

Picker, John M. *Victorian Soundscapes*. Oxford: Oxford University Press, 2003.

Plato. *The Dialogues of Plato: Translated into English with Analyses and Introductions*. Translated by Benjamin Jowett. Edited by Benjamin Jowett. 2nd; 3rd ed. 5 vols. Oxford: Clarendon Press, 1875; 1892.

Pope, Marvin H. *The Anchor Bible: Song of Songs*. Garden City: Doubleday and Company, Inc., 1977.

Porterfield, Amanda. *Healing in the History of Christianity*. Oxford: Oxford University Press, 2005.

Posset, Franz. 'Christi Dulcedo: The "Sweetness of Christ" in Western Christian Spirituality'. *Cistercian Studies Quarterly* 30 (1995): 245–65.

———. 'Sensing God with the "Palate of the Heart" According to Augustine and Other Spiritual Authors'. *The American Benedictine Review* 49 (1998): 356–86.

Prins, Yopie. *Victorian Sappho*. Princeton: Princeton University Press, 1999.
Reid, J. C. *The Mind and Art of Coventry Patmore*. London: Routledge and Kegan Paul, 1957.
Rilke, Rainer Maria. *Translations from the Poetry of Rainer Maria Rilke*. Translated by M. D. Hertner Norton. New York: W. W. Norton and Company, 1966.
Rist, John M. *Eros and Psyche: Studies in Plato, Plotinus, and Origen*. Toronto: University of Toronto Press, 1964.
Roden, Frederick S. *Same-Sex Desire in Victorian Religious Culture*. Basingstoke: Palgrave, 2003.
Roy, Marie-Andrée. 'Women and Spirituality in the Writings of Luce Irigaray'. Translated by Sharon Gubbay Helfer. In *Religion in French Feminist Thought: Critical Perspectives*, edited by Morny Joy, Kathleen O'Grady and Judith L. Poxon, 13–28. London: Routledge, 2003.
Rudy, Jason R. *Electric Meters: Victorian Physiological Poetics*. Athens, OH: Ohio University Press, 2009.
Saville, Julia F. *A Queer Chivalry: The Homoerotic Asceticism of Gerard Manley Hopkins*. Charlottesville: University Press of Virginia, 2000.
Shakespeare, William. *The Second Part of King Henry VI*. Edited by Michael Hattaway. Cambridge: Cambridge University Press, 1991.
———. *Twelfth Night, or, What You Will*. Edited by Roger Warren and Stanley Wells. Oxford: Clarendon Press, 1994.
Shimane, Kunio. *The Poetry of G. M. Hopkins: The Fusing Point of Sound and Sense*. Tokyo: The Hokuseido Press, 1983.
Sobolev, Dennis. 'Hopkins's "Bellbright Bodies": The Dialectics of Desire in His Writings'. *Texas Studies in Literature and Language* 45 (2003): 114–40.
Srivi, Sara. 'The Song of Songs: Eros and the Mystical Quest'. In *Jewish Explorations of Sexuality*, edited by Jonathan Magonet, 41–50. Providence: Berghahn Books, 1995.
Steedman, Carolyn. *Strange Dislocations: Childhood and the Idea of Human Interiority 1780–1930*. Cambridge, MA: Harvard University Press, 1995.
Stewart, Susan. *Poetry and the Fate of the Senses*. Chicago: University of Chicago Press, 2002.
Sulloway, Alison G. *Gerard Manley Hopkins and the Victorian Temper*. London: Routledge and Kegan Paul, 1972.
Tennyson, Alfred. *The Poems of Tennyson*. Edited by Christopher Ricks. 2nd ed. 3 vols. Harlow: Longman, 1987.
Tennyson, G. B. *Victorian Devotional Verse: The Tractarian Mode*. Cambridge, MA: Harvard University Press, 1981.
Teresa of Ávila. *The Life of Saint Teresa of Ávila: By Herself*. Translated by J. M. Cohen. Harmondsworth: Penguin Books, 1957.
Thesing, William B. 'Gerard Manley Hopkins's Responses to the City: The "Composition of the Crowd"'. In *Critical Essays on Gerard Manley Hopkins*, edited by Alison G. Sulloway, 132–55. Boston: G. K. Hall and Co., 1990.
Thomas à Kempis. *The Imitation of Christ*. Translated by Leo Sherley-Price. Harmondsworth: Penguin Books, 1965.
Thomas, Alfred. *Hopkins the Jesuit: The Years of Training*. London: Oxford University Press, 1969.
Virkar, Aakanksha J. 'Gerard Manley Hopkins and the Song of Songs'. *Victorian Poetry* 45 (2007): 195–207.
Ward, Bernadette Waterman. *World as Word: Philosophical Theology in Gerard Manley Hopkins*. Washington: The Catholic University of America Press, 2002.

Waters, Michael. *The Garden in Victorian Literature*. Aldershot: Scolar Press, 1988.
Wheeler, Michael. *Death and the Future Life in Victorian Literature and Theology*. Cambridge: Cambridge University Press, 1990.
White, Norman. *Hopkins: A Literary Biography*. Oxford: Oxford University Press, 1992.
Whitman, Walt. *Complete Poetry and Collected Prose*. Edited by Mark Van Doren. New York: Viking Press, 1982.
Wierzbicka, Anna. *Emotions Across Languages and Cultures: Diversity and Universals*. Cambridge: Cambridge University Press, 1999.
Wiggins, David. 'Flux, Fire and Material Persistence'. In *Language and Logos: Studies in Ancient Greek Philosophy Presented to G. E. L. Owen*, edited by Malcolm Schofield and Martha Craven Nussbaum, 1–32. Cambridge: Cambridge University Press, 1982.
Wills, Garry. *Saint Augustine*. New York: Viking Penguin, 1999.
Zaniello, Tom. *Hopkins in the Age of Darwin*. Iowa City: Iowa University Press, 1988.
Zonneveld, Sjaak. *The Random Grim Forge: A Study of Social Ideas in the Work of Gerard Manley Hopkins*. Assen: Van Gorcum, 1992.

INDEX

Abbott, Claude Colleer 37
Adam 28, 30, 47, 48, 67, 80, 83, 87, 95, 98, 122n61, 127n60; in 'Spring' (Hopkins) 104
Adams, James Eli 121n24
advertising 75
agape 5, 116n26; *see also caritas*, charity
Alderson, Richard 131n26
amor: see eros
Aristotle 21, 70, 118n25, 126n17, 126n19, 129n46
Armstrong, Isobel 115n1
Arseneau, Mary 129n49
aspiration 79; as answer to God's inspiration 73, 84; as caress 87; as counter stress 87; and death 87, 88; in dialogue 88; foreshadowed by 'The Queen's Crowning' (Hopkins) 96; as intimate exchange with God 73; and the kiss 96; offers hospitality 73; and poetry 87; as sigh 73, 84; and sprung rhythm 85; as touch 84; *see also* breath, conversation, inspiration, kiss
Augustine, St 4, 7–8, 12, 23–5, 28, 68, 74, 102, 112, 113, 116n19, 117n43, 119n33, 119n42

Badin, Donatella Abbate 75, 128n4
Balliol College 5, 6, 11, 43, 57, 121n35; *see also* Oxford
Beer, Gillian 115n1, 129n35
Bell, David N. 116n30
Belsey, Catherine 83
Bender, Todd K. 76, 116n20
Bernard of Clairvaux, St 5–6, 22, 36, 95, 96, 110–11, 116n36
Blair, Kirstie 125n129

Blake, William: 'London' 107–8
blood 61–2, 111; in 'Awe' (Newman) 41; of Christ 41, 49, 61, 62, 110, 112; in 'The Prodigal's Benediction' (Dolben) 61; in '*S. Thomae Aquinatis Rhythmus ad SS. Sacramentum*' (Hopkins) 112; *see also* heart, Sacred Heart
body 23, 50, 83, 119n33, 132n50; central role of 1; of Christ (*see* Christ); compared to a bell 78, 90; compared to a house 50–1, 123n76; and death 32, 33, 105; and its disclosure 61; of Dolben 58; in Gallwey 48; and healing 105–6; and hearing 90; in Hopkins studies 2–3, 4; in Hopkins' writings 2–3; and kissing 94–5; and Merleau-Ponty 17; paralysed in a nightmare 71; and Paul 44; pregnant 67, 68, 125n1; secret language of 76; and sound amplification 79; of the working classes 108; of the Virgin Mary (*see* Virgin Mary); and virginity (*see* virginity); *see also* blood, ear, hearing, heart, Sacred Heart, taste, touch, sight, smell
Boyarin, Daniel 116n38
breath 12, 14, 73, 74, 75, 79, 81, 82, 83, 84, 86, 94, 95, 96, 99, 126n21, 128n27; in '*Ad Matrem Virginem*' (Hopkins) 98, 99; in 'The Blessed Virgin compared to the Air we Breathe' (Hopkins) 71–2, 87; in '*Deliciæ Sapientiæ De Amore*' (Patmore) 91; in 'Duns Scotus's Oxford' (Hopkins) 86; in 'The Leaden Echo and the Golden Echo' (Hopkins) 87–8; in 'Ode to a Nightingale'

(Keats) 87; in 'Prayer' (Herbert) 87; in 'The Queen's Crowning' (Hopkins) 96, 97, 98; in 'The Wreck of the Deutschland' (Hopkins) 87; *see also* aspiration, conversation, inspiration, kiss, touch

Bridges, Robert: as editor of Dolben's first edition of poetry 60, 124n107; as editor of Hopkins' first edition of poetry 60; Hopkins' attraction to 2; as Hopkins' fellow Oxonian 58; introduces Hopkins to Dolben 58; opinion of Dolben's poetry 60; Patmore's letter to, after Hopkins' death 38; poetry of 60

Bristow, Joseph 3, 124n95

Brown, Daniel 77, 86, 93, 115n1, 127n30, 127n36, 129n35, 129n46, 131n13

Brown, Peter 43, 122n48

Bruno, Giuliana 101

caress: *see* Irigaray, touch

caritas 7, 8, 23; *see also agape*, charity

Carr, David M. 4

Carson, Anne 25, 64, 65

catching, metaphor of 27, 77–8, 79, 81

celibacy: 1, 4, 14, 40, 42, 43–4, 48–9, 58, 60; *see also* virginity, virgin marriage

charity 7, 8, 24, 38, 113; in 'At the Wedding March' (Hopkins) 39; God as 25; kiss of 96; *see also caritas, agape*

Christ 10, 71, 74, 120n87–8, 121n13, 122n47, 124n111; in '*Ad Matrem Virginem*' (Hopkins) 8, 67, 68, 74, 98–9, 109; in 'As kingfishers catch fire, dragonflies draw flame' (Hopkins) 27; In 'At the Wedding March' (Hopkins) 39–40; in 'Awe' (Newman) 41; beauty of 3, 27, 34, 57, 58; beloved disciple at the breast of 36; in 'The Blessed Virgin compared to the Air we Breathe' (Hopkins) 71–2, 77; body of 34, 49, 50, 57, 58, 61, 68, 72–3; in '*Brevi Tempore Magnum Perfecit Opus*' (Dolben) 62; as bridegroom 31, 37, 62, 111; as brother of believers 67; 'burl of being' in 73; in *City of God* (Augustine) 7; conception of 14 (*see also* heart, pregnancy, Virgin Mary); consummation with 4, 6, 62; in the Eucharist 4, 68; friendships in, at Oxford 57; in 'He Hath abolish'd the old drouth' (Hopkins) 45, 46, 63, 93; and the Holy of Holies 102; in '*Homo Factus Est*' (Dolben) 62–3; in 'Hope holds to Christ the mind's own mirror out' (Hopkins) 29–30, 31; Hopkins' relationship with 4, 14, 38, 42; humans putting on 28–9, 34; in 'Hurrahing in Harvest' (Hopkins) 58–9, 93–4; in 'I lay my sins on Jesus' (Bonar) 36; in 'I wake and feel the fell of dark, not day' (Hopkins) 13; in *The Imitation of Christ* (Thomas à Kempis) 5; in *In Memoriam* (Tennyson) 54; kiss of (*see* breath, kiss); 'A Letter' (Dolben) 62; in *The Life of St Teresa* (Teresa of Ávila) 31, 33; in *The Life of the Venerable Mother Margaret Mary Alacoque* (Languet) 110, 112–13; love of 12, 111, 112; as lover of believers 67; and magnetic attraction 91, 129n49, 130n54; in 'Margaret Clitheroe' (Hopkins) 127n56; marriage with (*see* marriage, virgin marriage); as 'mártyr máster' 111; miracles of 77; as object of love 4, 5, 6, 8, 27, 34, 56, 58, 63; in *On the Song of Songs* (Bernard of Clairvaux) 95, 96, 110–11; in '*Pro Castitate*' (Dolben) 62; in 'The Prodigal's Benediction' (Dolben) 61, 62; in 'The Queen's Crowning' (Hopkins) 97–8; and redemption 44, 112; in '*Rosa Mystica*' (Hopkins) 104, 107; in '*S. Thomae Aquinatis Rhythmus ad SS. Sacramentum*' (Hopkins) 107, 112; as Second Adam 67, 98; in 'The Soldier' (Hopkins) 94; as son of believers 67; in *The Song of Songs: Commentary and Homilies* (Origen) 7; suffering of 50, 111; reconciling humanity and divinity 27–8; in 'St. Thecla' (Hopkins) 42; to turn away from 31, 34; union with 11, 36; and vocation 88; in 'Vocation' Dolben

60–1; in 'The Windhover' (Hopkins) 77; as wounded healer 112; wounds of (*see* blood, Sacred Heart); in 'The Wreck of the Deutschland' (Hopkins) 13, 25, 30, 56–7, 63–4, 65, 80–1, 94, 111, 113; *see also* God, Holy Ghost, Trinity
clouds: Hopkins' observations of 18, 19; in 'Hurrahing in Harvest' (Hopkins) 58–9; in 'The earth and heaven, so little known' (Hopkins) 20–1
Colligan, Colette 12
conception: *see* catching, heart, Holy Ghost, pregnancy, Virgin Mary, virginity
Constantini, Mariaconcetta 132n27
consumerism, rise of 75
conversation: in '*Ad Matrem Virginem*' (Hopkins) 98, 130n71; as circulation of breath 84, 96; as emotional engagement with others 14, 83–4; in 'He hath abolish'd the old drouth' (Hopkins) 93; in 'The Queen's Crowning' (Hopkins) 96–7; wedding vow as initiation of 93; *see also* aspiration, breath, inspiration, kiss
conversion: in 'At the Wedding March' (Hopkins) 39; of Augustine 28–9; as experience of love 4, 13; as one of Hopkins' most romantic acts 5; of Paul 13; and reconciliation 25; in 'St. Thecla' (Hopkins) 42–3; and touch 13, 24; as 'turning' 13, 24; and vocation 88; in 'The Wreck of the Deutschland' (Hopkins) 13, 25; *see also* Hopkins
Cotter, James Finn 17–18, 49, 50, 64, 86, 128n20
Craft, Christopher 53, 54–6
Cupid: *see* Eros

da Sousa Correa, Delia 89, 129n34, 129n37
Dacey, Philip 3
Dante Alighieri 122n47
Davis, Lloyd 104, 122n55
Day, Brian J. 118n13
de Vere, Aubrey 35

death 30, 32–3, 50, 52–3, 55, 57, 58, 60, 62, 71–2, 79, 87–8, 92, 97, 101, 102, 103, 104–5, 111, 123n84; *see also* mourning, Tennyson
Dellamora, Richard 56, 57
Denisoff, Dennis 75
Dixon, Richard Watson 31, 39, 40, 49, 123n69
Dolben, Digby Mackworth: and attraction to men 124n107; friendship with Hopkins 58; Hopkins' attraction to 2, 58, 59–60; poetry of 22, 60–3
Donne, John: 'The Good Morrow' 26
Drury, John 123n76

ear 74–5, 76, 77, 81, 89; Christ conceived through 75; of God 81–2; in 'I hear a noise of waters drawn away' (Hopkins) 76; in 'Repeat that, repeat' (Hopkins) 76; in '*S. Thomae Equinatis Rhythmus ad SS. Sacramentum*' (Hopkins) 75; in 'St. Thecla' (Hopkins) 42; *see also* hearing
Eden 6, 14–15, 20, 102, 113; in '*Ad Mariam*' (Hopkins) 103, 104; in '*Rosa Mystica*' (Hopkins) 104; in 'Spring' (Hopkins) 104
Eliot, George 75; *The Mill on the Floss* 89–90, 129n34, 129n35, 129n44
Elvey, Anne 67, 125n1
Empedocles 19
eros 5–7, 26–7, 41, 59, 64, 111, 116n26, 116n38; as *amor* 5–8, 14, 15, 38, 39; and *amore* 98, 99; and *amores* 25
Eros, the god 7, 25, 113; arrow of 13; in 'Love Preparing to Fly' (Hopkins) 64; in *Phaedrus* (Plato) 64–5; and Psyche 36; in Sappho 64; in 'The Windhover' (Hopkins) 64; in 'The Wreck of the Deutschland' (Hopkins) 63–4, 65
Eve 28, 47, 47, 67; in 'Spring' (Hopkins) 104

Feeney, Joseph J. 130n54
flagellation, self- 13
Foltz, William 116n20
Fontana, Ernest 47

Foucault, Michel 14, 42
Francis of Assisi, St 47, 122n47
Francis Xavier, St 38

Gallwey, Peter 48–9, 122n59
God: as *Eros* 7; finger of 23, 24, 56, 78, 80, 87, 88–9, 92, 94; *see also* Christ, Holy Ghost, Trinity
Grabes, Herbert 33
'Great Stink, The' 107; *see also* London

Halperin, David M. 26–7, 119n56
hearing: in '*Ad Matrem Virginem*' (Hopkins) 74, 75; and 'close listening' 76; as conception of the Word 74; and Helmholtz 89; Hopkins' poetry written for 75; in 'I hear a noise of waters drawn away' (Hopkins) 76; in *In Memoriam* (Tennyson) 54, 55; as penetration by another 75, 89, 124n4; pleasure of 74; in '*S. Thomae Equinatis Rhythmus ad SS. Sacramentum*' (Hopkins) 75; and vocation 88; in 'The Wreck of the Deutschland' (Hopkins) 75, 80; *see also* ear
heart 1, 14, 43, 49, 50, 51, 55, 59, 61, 62, 65, 67 8, 72, 73, 74, 76, 81, 82, 84, 87, 110, 112–13, 125n129; in '*Ad Matrem Virginem*' (Hopkins) 67, 68; arrow of Eros in 13; in Augustine 112; beating of 64, 76, 105; Christ conceived in 14, 67–9; Christ reborn in 50; in 'The Elopement' (Hopkins) 64; in 'Felix Randal' (Hopkins) 9; of God 82; God's presence in 24, 74, 76; God searches 73; in 'Hurrahing in Harvest' (Hopkins) 59, 93; in 'I wake and feel the fell of dark, not day' (Hopkins) 12; inflamed 112–13; language of 41; melting 25; '*Nondum*' (Hopkins) 92; rests in God, 74, 112; in 'Ribblesdale' (Hopkins) 18–19; in Sappho's poetry 64; in the Song of Songs 52; in 'Spring and Fall' (Hopkins) 105; as symbol of love, 61, 110; in 'A Voice from the World' (Hopkins) 25; vulnerable to pain 50; warm 25; in 'The Windhover' (Hopkins) 64, 101; in 'The Wreck of the Deutschland' (Hopkins) 25, 63–4, 80, 81, 82; *see also* blood, Sacred Heart
Helmholtz, Hermann von 89, 129n35
Herbert, George: 128n27; 'Prayer' 87
Herrington, Eldrid 115n14
Higgins, Lesley 117n64
Holy Ghost 22–3, 44, 67, 71, 72–3, 80, 86, 96, 126n21, 126n25, 128n63; *see also* breath, Christ, God, Trinity, Virgin Mary
Holy Spirit: *see* breath, Christ, Holy Ghost, God, Trinity, Virgin Mary
Hopkins: and celibacy 1, 4; confessional notes of 2; conversion of, to Roman Catholicism 4–5, 40, 43–4, 45, 91 (*see also* conversion); education of (*see* Balliol College, Oxford); eroticism in the work of 1; fascination of, with male bodies 2–3; joins Society of Jesus 8; as nature lover 13, 18; and same-sex attractions 1–4 (*see also* Bridges, Dolben); as Tractarian 5
POETRY:
'*Ad Matrem Virginem*' 8, 67–8, 74, 75, 98, 125n2, 130n71
'Alchemist, The' 124n111
'As kingfishers catch fire, dragonflies draw flame' 27, 28, 77, 79, 123n76
'Ashboughs' 84
'At the Wedding March' 39, 45, 93
'Binsey Poplars' 78, 118n13
'Blessed Virgin compared to the Air we Breathe, The' 71–2, 77, 87
'Bugler's First Communion, The' 105
'Duns Scotus's Oxford' 86
'Elopement, The' 64
'Epithalamion' 124n110
'Escorial, The' 71
'Felix Randal' 9
'God's Grandeur' 86, 106, 107
'Habit of Perfection, The' 46–7
'Harry Ploughman' 3, 71, 76, 108, 124n111
'He hath abolish'd the old drouth' 45, 46, 63, 93

INDEX

'Hope holds to Christ the mind's own mirror out' 29–30, 31
'Hurrahing in Harvest' 58–9, 93–4, 96
'I hear a noise of waters drawn away' 76
'I wake and feel the fell of dark, not day' 12, 13, 92
'*Il Mystico*' 76, 119n47
'In the Valley of the Elwy' 69, 109, 117n49
'*Jesu Dulcis Memoria*' 116n31
'Kind Betrothal, The' 46–7
'Leaden Echo and the Golden Echo, The' 87–8, 92
'Loss of the Eurydice, The' 75
'Love Preparing to Fly' 64
'Margaret Clitheroe' 79, 111, 127n57
'*Nondum*' 30, 56, 92
'*O Deus, ego amo te*' 121n19
'On a Piece of Music' 106
'On St. Winefred' 106
'On the Portrait of Two Beautiful Young People' 104
'Pilate' 31, 79
'Queen's Crowning, The' 96–8
'Repeat that, repeat' 76, 89–90
'Ribblesdale' 17–18, 79
'*Rosa Mystica*' 102, 103–4, 107, 122n48, 132n36
'*S. Thomae Aquinatis Rhythmus ad SS. Sacramentum*' 31, 75, 107, 112
'Spring' 104, 105
'Spring and Fall' 105, 131n7
'St. Thecla' 42–3, 46, 47
'St. Winefred's Well' 105–6, 107
'That Nature is a Heraclitean Fire' 118n27
'The dark-out Lucifer detesting this' 32
'The earth and heaven, so little known' 21
'Thee, God, I come from, to thee go' 23, 24–5
'Thou art indeed just, Lord' 22
'To seem the stranger lies my lot' 102
'To what serves Mortal Beauty?' 27
'Trees by their yield' 22
'Voice from the World, A' 25, 123n70
'Windhover, The' 2, 64, 77, 101
'Wreck of the Deutschland, The' 12–13, 20, 23, 25, 30, 49, 50, 56–7, 63–4, 65, 75, 78–82, 83, 84–5, 87, 94, 102, 111, 113, 127n57
House, Madeleine 128n27

inscape: in 'Binsey Poplars' (Hopkins) 18–19; deep in things 18; destruction of 19, 118n2; as inner landscape 18; perception of 18; and reversibility 18; of speech 74, 127n36; unknown to 'simple people' 18
inspiration: as intimate exchange with God 73; as creative 87; foreshadowed by 'The Queen's Crowning' (Hopkins) 96; as God's breath 73, 79, 88; as source of human fullness 73; as touch 84; *see also* aspiration, breath, conversation, kiss
instress: all things upheld by 19; animates the soul 32; as binding principle in nature 19; and the 'burl of being' 127n30; excessive, and blindness 33; excessive, and pain 32; first used in 'Parmenides' notes 118n16; loss of 71; in 'The Wreck of the Deutschland' (Hopkins) 75; *see also* nature
Ireland 14, 102
Irigaray, Luce: on breath 99; religion in the work of 10; in *Religion in French Feminist Thought* 10–11; theory of the caress 9, 10, 15; *To be Two* 9, 10, 99

Jameson, Anna Brownell 130n72
John of the Cross, St 6, 25
Johnson, Galen A. 17
Johnson, Margaret 60, 116n1
Jonson, Ben: *Volpone* 94
Jowett, Benjamin 11, 117n64

Keats, John: 'Ode to a Nightingale' 87
Keble, John 62, 125n117, 125n129
Kingsley, Charles 40
kiss 1, 15, 26, 62, 83, 130n58; in '*Ad Matrem Virginem*' (Hopkins) 98–9, 130n71; as breath of life 95; as caress 96, 99; in *Doctor Faustus* (Marlowe) 94–5; in 'Fatima' (Tennyson) 95; in *Henry VI* (Shakespeare) 95; in 'Hurrahing in

Harvest' (Hopkins) 96; as intimate touch 94; as openness to the other 96; of peace 95–6; pneumatic 95–7; in 'The Queen's Crowning' (Hopkins) 96–8; in 'The Soldier' (Hopkins) 94; in Song of Songs 95, 130n67; of the Trinity 96; typological 97–8; in *Volpone* (Jonson) 94; *see also* breath, aspiration, conversation, inspiration
Kitchen, Paddy 1–2
Kooistra, Lorraine Janzen 126n24
Krasner, James 52

Langer, Monika. 118n13
Levin, David Michael 89
Lewes, George Henry 75, 89, 129n35
Liddon, Henry Parry 43–5, 112n37
Linley, Margaret 12
Littledale, Richard Frederick 91, 129n49
Logos 74, 75, 80, 81, 112
London 107–8, 131n24; *see also* 'Great Stink, The'
looking: *see* sight
love: *see agape, caritas, eros*, magnetic attraction, sympathetic vibration
Loughlin, Gerard 24

Madison, Gary Brent 24
magnetic attraction 1, 90–1, 129n45, 129n49; *see also* sympathetic vibration
Malpas, J. E. 122n43
Margaret Mary Alacoque, Venerable 110–11, 112–13
Mariani, Paul 115n3
marketing, rise of 75
Marlowe, Christopher: *Doctor Faustus* 94–5
marriage 6, 8, 14, 36, 37, 40, 43, 44, 46, 48, 50, 65; in 'At the Wedding March' (Hopkins) 39–40; of Francis of Assisi to Lady Poverty 122n47; in *In Memoriam* (Tennyson) 52, 55–6; in 'The Queen's Crowning' (Hopkins) 96–7; *see also* virgin marriage
Martin, Robert Bernard 1–2
martyrs 106, 111–12, 131n12
Mary Magdalene 41
Matter, E. Ann 130n67
Maynard, John 36, 47–8, 122n57

Merleau-Ponty, Maurice 9–10, 11, 15, 17, 18, 117n54, 118n2, 118n13; *see also* sight, reversibility
miasma 107; *see also* smell
microphone, invention of 76
Miller, J. Hillis 19, 86
mirror 14, 20, 33; eye as, reflecting the beloved 26–7; in 'Hope holds to Christ the mind's own mirror out' (Hopkins) 29–30, 31; ideal, faithfully reflecting God 29; representing the state of the soul 29, 33–4; *see also* sight
Moran, Maureen F. 111, 132n50
mourning: and Queen Victoria 105; *see also* Tennyson
Müller, Friedrich Max 83, 128n2
Muller, Jill 115n1
mystery 75

Najarian, James 124n111
nature 13, 17–20, 26; glorifies God 29; Hopkins' lifelong interest in 18; in *In Memoriam* (Tennyson) 57; as reflection of God's relationship with humans 26; unity in 19–20; *see also* waves, clouds, reversibility
Nead, Lynda 131n24
Newman, John Henry 40–2, 43, 60, 61, 121n23, 121n24
Nixon, Jude V. 115n1, 121n23, 121n35, 122n37
Nygren, Anders 5, 116n26

O'Connell, Robert J. 102
Origen 6–7
Oulton, Carolyn 123n84
Overholser, Renée V. 124n111
Oxford 26, 35, 40, 43, 57, 124n95
Oxford Movement: *see* Puseyites, Tractarianism

pain 32, 33, 50, 52, 65, 104–5, 111; of heart 50, 53; in *In Memoriam* (Tennyson) 52
Parmenides 19, 69
Passion, the 57, 110, 111–12
Patmore, Coventry 14, 35–8, 47–8, 91, 120–1n2

Patmore, Derek 38
Perella, Nicholas James 96
photography 75
Picker, John M. 76, 89, 129n34, 129n44
Pindar 25, 119n46
Plato 55, 124n95; *Phaedo* 119n52; *Phaedrus* 26–7, 64–5, 119n52, 119n56; *Republic* 119n52; *Symposium* (Plato) 7, 116n38, 119n52
Porterfield, Amanda 111, 112
Posset, Franz 131n19
pregnancy: as hospitality 67; *see also* catching, heart, virginity, Virgin Mary
Prins, Yopie 119n46
Pusey, Edward 40, 43
Puseyites 60, 40; *see also* Tractarianism

Queen Victoria: *see* mourning

Reid, J. C. 36
reversibility 9–10, 11, 15, 17, 18, 102, 117n54, 118n2; *see also* Merleau-Ponty, sight, touch
Rilke, Rainer Maria 84
Roden, Frederick S. 57
Rossetti, Christina 49, 123n70, 129n49
Rossetti, Dante Gabriel 49, 123n69
Rudy, Jason 13, 117n69, 129n46

Sacred Heart 76, 102, 109–11; linked to Song of Songs 50; wounded 50; *see also* blood, Christ, heart
Sappho 25, 64, 119n46
Saville, Julia F. 2, 6, 56, 57
Shakespeare, William 35, 53, 95, 101
Shimane, Kunio 78–9, 127n56, 127n57
sight: of beautiful male bodies 59, 124n111; in 'Binsey Poplars' (Hopkins) 18–19, 78; of the beloved 31; of Christ's body 57, 61, 124n111; and darkness 32–3; of dawn 55, 86; in 'Epithalamion' (Hopkins) 124n111; in 'Felix Randal' (Hopkins) 9; in the, of guardian angels 28; in 'Harry Ploughman' (Hopkins) 124n111; Hopkins wary of 75; in 'I wake and feel the fell of dark, not day' (Hopkins) 12; and Merleau-Ponty 17, 117n54; painful 32; pleasure of 74; in 'S. Thomae Aquinatis Rhythmus ad SS. Sacramentum' (Hopkins) 31, 75; and sexual temptation 124n111; in 'Spring and Fall' (Hopkins) 105; and touch 17, 59, 93; in 'The Wreck of the Deutschland' (Hopkins) 75; *see also* reversibility
smell: in *In Memoram* (Tennyson) 55; and malodour 106, 107, 108, 131n13 (*see also* miasma); in Song of Songs 52; and sweet odours 106, 107, 108–9
Sobolev, Dennis 2–3
Song of Songs 14, 22, 113, 116n31, 121n9, 123n75, 123n83, 130n67; allegorical interpretation of 6, 40; Bernard of Clairvaux's sermons on 5–6, 36, 95; and Bonar 36; and Dixon 49; and Dolben 62–3; and Eros and Psyche 36; and Hopkins 36, 49, 50, 63–4, 65; and *In Memoriam* (Tennyson) 50–6; and Jewish mysticism 6; and John of the Cross 6; and Littledale 91; and Origen 6–7; and Patmore 36, 37; and Rossetti, Christina 49; and Rossetti, Dante Gabriel 49; and Teresa of Ávila 31
speech: Christ as 74; as incarnation of breath and thought 74; pre-Babel 80; as 'pre-eminently significant sound' 83; *see also* conversation
sprung rhythm 84–6, 88, 116n21; *see also* aspiration, breath, inspiration
Srivi, Sara 6
Steedman, Carolyn 105
stethoscope, invention of 76
Stewart, Susan 12
stress: *see* sprung rhythm
sympathetic vibration 89–91, 129n35; *see also* magnetic attraction

taste 12, 106, 107; etymologically related to touch 106
tears: in '*Ad Mariam*' (Hopkins) 103, 104–5; in 'At the Wedding March' (Hopkins) 39; in 'Felix Randal' (Hopkins) 9; in *In Memoriam* (Tennyson) 53
Tennyson, Alfred 14; 'Break, Break, Break' 53; 'Enoch Arden' 86–7; 'Fatima' 95;

In Memoriam 50–6, 57, 105, 123n80, 123n83, 124n90
Teresa of Ávila, St 31, 32, 33–4, 106
Thales 19, 129n46
Thesing, William B. 132n27
Thomas, St 75
Thomas à Kempis 5
Thomas, Alfred 116n31, 117n43, 122n59
touch: 9–10, 11, 87, 119n33; and Augustine 12; in 'Awe' (Newman) 41; in 'Binsey Poplars' (Hopkins) 18–19; in 'Break, Break, Break' (Tennyson) 53; in '*Brevi Tempore Magnum Perfecit Opus*' (Dolben) 62; as caress 99 (*see also* Irigaray); central role of, in Hopkins' poetry 1; and conversion 13, 24; different modes of 13; etymologically related to taste 106; in 'Felix Randal' (Hopkins) 9; as figure of speech 13, 93; of God 13, 23–4 (*see also* God); and hands 23, 41, 53, 54, 56, 61; and the handshake 9, 54, 55, 56; healing, of Christ 112; in 'I wake and feel the fell of dark, not day' (Hopkins) 12; in '*Il Mystico*' (Hopkins) 119n47; in *In Memoriam* (Tennyson) 53, 54, 55, 56, 57; and Irigaray (*see* Irigaray); and Jowett 11; and the kiss (*see* kiss); as least regulated of the senses 12; linked to emotions 12; and love 11, 12, 14, 20, 101; in 'Lovesong' (Rilke) 84; and Merleau-Ponty (*see* Merleau-Ponty, reversibility); narcissistic 32; poetry's potential to 86–7; reciprocal 1, 14, 15, 20, 23, 24, 25, 26, 53, 59, 83, 84, 99, 102 (*see also* breath, conversation); in '*S. Thomae Equinatis Rhythmus ad SS. Sacramentum*' (Hopkins) 75; senses understood in relation to 12; and sight 17, 59, 93; in 'The Wreck of the Deutschland' (Hopkins) 23, 56–7, 78, 94
Tractarianism 5, 14, 40–6; *see also* Puseyites
Trinity 69, 79, 91, 96; *see also* God, Holy Ghost, Christ

unveiling 17, 60, 62; *see also* veil

veil 37, 41, 45–6, 61; *see also* unveiling
virgin marriage 40, 41, 43, 46; in '*Brevi Tempore Magnum Perfecit Opus*' (Dolben) 62; in 'The Habit of Perfection' (Hopkins) 46–7; in 'He hath abolish'd the old drouth' (Hopkins) 63; in '*Homo Factus Est*' (Dolben) 62–3; and the Jesuits 46, 48–9; in 'The Kind Betrothal' (Hopkins) 46–7; in 'The Prodigal's Benediction' (Dolben) 61–2; in 'St. Thecla' (Hopkins) 42–3; in *Unknown Eros* (Patmore) 47–8; in 'The Wreck of the Deutschland' (Hopkins) 63; *see also* celibacy, marriage
Virgin Mary 47, 67, 68, 71, 72, 74, 75, 77, 80, 81, 98–9, 102–4, 109, 122n48; as Second Eve 67
virginity 14, 40, 41–4, 46, 47–8, 80, 103, 104, 105, 106, 122n48, 131n6; represented by a lily 47; represented by a sealed fountain 62, 125n119; and 'revirginalisation' 14–15, 48, 104, 122n55; *see also* celibacy, virgin marriage
Virkar, Aakanksha J. 50
vision: *see* sight
visual culture 75

Wales 108, 109
Ward, Bernadette Waterman 115n1
Waters, Michael 109, 132n35
waves: off a sea-wall 20; representing harmony 26; *see also* Whitman
Wheeler, Michael 105
White, Norman 1–2, 128n2
Whitman, Walt: 'We Two, How Long We Were Fool'd' 25–6
Wierzbicka, Anna 93
Williams, Isaac 41
Williams, Robert 119n52
Wills, Garry 120n68
Wordsworth, William: 'London, 1802' 107–8

Zaniello, Tom 115n1
Zonneveld, Sjaak 115n1

www.ingramcontent.com/pod-product-compliance
Lightning Source LLC
Chambersburg PA
CBHW021832300426
44114CB00009BA/415